Romain Gary

CRITICAL AUTHORS & ISSUES

Josué Harari, Series Editor

A complete list of books in the series
is available from the publisher.

Romain Gary

The Man Who Sold His Shadow

Ralph Schoolcraft

PENN

University of Pennsylvania Press

PHILADELPHIA

10 9 8 7 6 5 4 3 2 1

Published by
University of Pennsylvania Press
Philadelphia, Pennsylvania 19104-4011

Library of Congress Cataloging-in-Publication Data
Schoolcraft, Ralph W.
 Romain Gary : the man who sold his shadow /
Ralph Schoolcraft.
  p. cm. — (Critical authors & issues)
  Includes bibliographical references and index.
  ISBN 0-8122-3646-7 (cloth : alk. paper)
  1. Gary, Romain.   2. Authors, French—20th century—
Biography.   3. Gary, Romain—Anonyms and pseudonyms.
I. Title.   II. Series.
PQ2613.A58 Z875   2001
843'.912—dc21
[B]   2001053011

Contents

Preface

Far as gold on earth transcends in estimation merit and virtue, so much higher than gold itself is the shadow valued; and as I had earlier sacrificed wealth to conscience, I had now thrown away the shadow for mere gold. What in the world could and would become of me?

Von Chamisso, The Wonderful History *12*

Adalbert von Chamisso's *Peter Schlemihl* (1813) tells a Faustian tale about what happens to a man who sells his shadow. Of humble means and origins, Schlemihl goes looking for work in a foreign country. A letter of introduction gains him entry into an elegant garden party, but the behavior of the guests shows that an outsider is worth little or nothing in their eyes. Late in the afternoon, however, a mysterious gentleman with magical gifts proposes an unusual deal: the gentleman will hand over an inexhaustible bag of riches in exchange for Schlemihl's shadow. Thinking his shadow an entity of little value or utility, Schlemihl lets himself be seduced by the promise of a life of money and ease. With boundless wealth at his disposal, he realizes that he could become anyone he desires. He willingly yields his shadow to the elderly man and embarks on what he imagines to be a limitless adventure of new existences.

Well-intentioned and even a bit unsettled by his sudden privilege, Schlemihl showers gifts upon a neighboring hamlet. The villagers celebrate him as a king, and soon he is engaged to a beautiful young woman of good heart and character. This idyll is shattered, however, when Schlemihl comes across a cluster of peasants in broad daylight. They react with horror and disgust upon noticing that he no longer has a shadow. Wounded by their scorn and insults, shunned by all, Schlemihl is forced to abandon his plans for marriage and takes up the solitary ways of a social outcast.

Why such humiliation over a missing shadow? What is a shadow in the final analysis? At first glance, it appears to be nothing but a vague and obscure surface, a projection that takes our form but not our consistency. But while it is not our double, it can be observed by those who meet us in public. It is that face of ourselves that we project in the light of public scrutiny, an intangible but perceptible image derived from our presence. Schlemihl comes to understand that he has been dispossessed of an essential part of himself, an aspect of his identity that is not so important in his intimate relationships but crucial to his position in society.

Through naiveté more than greed, through carelessness more than excessive self-interest, Schlemihl finds himself treated as a pariah. Now that he regrets his trade, however, he discovers that it is too late to negate the exchange. Worse, the only way for Schlemihl to get his shadow back is to enter into an even more diabolical pact: he must sign over his soul.

Seeing the devious stranger now for who he really is, Schlemihl is desperate and distraught but nonetheless much the wiser for the loss of his shadow. He recognizes that he is incomplete without it yet would incur even greater hardship were he to give up his soul. Schlemihl thus spites the devil by refusing the new offer. The two of them become locked in a strange battle of will and wits, Schlemihl desiring to take back his shadow and the devil lusting after Schlemihl's soul. In a fight with this powerful adversary, Schlemihl succeeds in stealing away a magic hat that gives him the gift of invisibility. Schlemihl is still shadowless, but at least now he can move about unbeknownst to others. His enjoyment of this brief triumph is short-lived, however, for outsmarting the devil has its price. Realizing the hopelessness of his situation but at peace with his new understanding of himself, Schlemihl ultimately chooses to abandon the society of humankind, leaving to others the responsibility of telling his story.

Von Chamisso's parable of a shadow imprudently surrendered and a soul artfully defended has its counterpart in the life of one of France's most popular novelists, Romain Gary. In the book that follows, we will examine the case of this impoverished émigré author who unwittingly sells his "shadow" for wealth and a new identity before he too discovers the difficulty of recovering it intact. Gary endures the curse of the schlemihl: in Yiddish, a person tracked by hard luck, an eternal underdog whose innocence and stubbornness are tested by many hardships. Like Schlemihl, Gary is not able to undo this pact and can only ease his sense of alienation by devising a trick that renders him invisible as well. Taking Von Chamisso literally when the nineteenth-century author advises that in seeking solutions one should not "overlook solid bodies,"[1] Gary invents a new person and shadow who circulate in his stead. In essence, as we will see, having failed to regain his old shadow, Gary creates a new one that borrows a body. Thus endowed with someone else's existence, he embarks on an adventure unparalleled by any other in French literature.

After the revelation in 1981 of the existence of Gary's elaborate pseudonymous alter egos, his return from literary exile was assured. Indeed, in the two decades since his death, twenty books on Romain Gary have appeared in French, German and Danish, spanning the gamut from popular biography to theoretical analysis. This book, the first in English dedicated to his complex literary career, provides an introduction to his work at the same time as it offers a test case of sorts for investigating the workings of public image and authorship in twentieth-century French letters.

For the several shadows we will be examining here, there is only one individual behind them. I will call him Romain Gary, since this became his legal name in 1951. My intention is not to reestablish Gary's biography (though of necessity I refer to it frequently and I provide brief summaries at the beginning of each chapter). Due to a variety of factors (Gary's moves from country to country, the chaos wrought by the Russian Revolution and World War II, the discretionary nature of the posts he occupied, the scarcity of living contemporaries or family members, and his personal philosophy on such matters), a full, accurate account of several periods of his life is no longer possible.[2] Moreover, as we will see, the very notion goes counter to important facets of his literary project. Instead, I will trace out, as accurately as possible, the *invention* of Romain Gary and the successive *reinventions* of Romain Gary; that is, I will draw up Romain Gary's various *authorial* biographies. My objectives thus are twofold: on the one hand, to examine the different strategies Gary employs in the construction of his authorial identities, relating them to his conception of the novel; and, on the other, to look at how these pseudonymous authors' images are constructed in the press and to what ends. In sum, this study will provide a history of Gary's literary production and reception, an account of the press's readings (and misreadings), and Gary's responses to the latter.

The Introduction provides background relevant for such a study: an overview of Gary's literary aesthetic and the dynamics of public image in modern French literary institutions. In chapters 1 and 2, I trace the stages contributing to the invention and consecration of Romain Gary. Thus, Chapter 1 returns to Gary's first steps as a writer, steps that he would excise from his past so effectively that the critical and biographical works currently available fail to appreciate what they represent in his development. Particular attention is paid here to the ideological evolution of his works and the press's readings of them. Chapter 2 focuses on the interaction between Gary's writing aesthetic and his public behavior. This chapter is broken into two parts. First, I outline Gary's rise to fame, looking specifically at how the postwar fascination with heroes of the Resistance and Gary's ease with the media provided an ideal opportunity for him to rescript his past. In the second part, I try to make sense of a curious pattern in his publications: his three most popular works (*A European*

Education, The Roots of Heaven, and *Promise at Dawn*) were each followed by satires (*Tulipe, L'homme à la colombe,* and *Johnnie Cœur*) ridiculing the type of hero presented by those popular works. I argue that Gary was seeking to moderate the success of his image by reminding the public of its artificiality. The failure of this gesture would push Gary to his most experimental period as "Romain Gary," which spanned the sixties and early seventies and is the subject of Chapter 3. During this period, he would develop what I term "strategies of mobile identity." I have broken these down into three principal elements: Gary's use of autofiction, his renewal of the picaresque tradition, and an examination of themes of clandestine identity. The combination of these elements would lead him to renew his experiments with pseudonymous publication. Chapters 4 and 5 therefore address primarily the Émile Ajar episode, with Chapter 4 recounting the period prior to Paul Pavlowitch's arrival on the scene and Chapter 5 tackling the period after. In both chapters, with a particular focus on those works not yet available in English, I juggle textual analysis with a study of the institutional construction of Ajar as an authorial persona, showing their constant interrelation. Chapters 4 and 5 thus mirror the first two as the invention and consecration of Émile Ajar. The Conclusion evaluates several features of Gary's career: the relationship between Romain Gary and Émile Ajar; the institutional pressures that would eventually defeat his theoretical approaches to transforming his image; and the consequences of his successful creation of Émile Ajar within the French literary scene. The Bibliography is the most extensive on Gary published in any language.

Abbreviations

Gary's bilingual writing creates certain difficulties for easy reference. Since this study focuses on Gary's public image in France, I have used French editions of his works for all citations, regardless of whether the texts were originally written in English or French. (The titles below in italics indicate the language in which the work was originally written.) Page number references therefore refer to the French editions. All citations, however, are translated; I bear full responsibility for their many imperfections. Within the text, I use English titles where English editions have been published of a work; if no English edition exists, I have maintained the original French title. For my references to critical books and works, I have used the author's name, for which the complete information can be found in the Bibliography. For the few instances where bibliographical information regarding newspaper articles is incomplete (owing to the overly eager scissors of Argus Press Service), the originals can be found in the archives at Éditions Gallimard.

In alphabetical order, these are the abbreviations and titles used throughout the text in reference to Gary's books:

BM = *La bonne moitié*
CD = *Les couleurs du jour* (The colors of the day)
CF = *Clair de femme*
CL = *Les clowns lyriques*
CM = *Le grand vestiaire* (The company of men)
CV = *Les cerfs-volants*
DFA = *Les têtes de Stéphanie* (Direct flight to Allah)
DGC = *La danse de Gengis Cohn* (The dance of Genghis Cohn)
EE = *Éducation européenne* (A European education)
Ench = *Les enchanteurs* (The enchanters)
Eur = *Europa* (Europa)
FA = Forest of Anger
Gasp = Charge d'âme (*The Gasp*)
GC = *Gros-Câlin*

GH = *La tête coupable* (The guilty head)

HC = *L'homme à la colombe*

HT = *Gloire à nos illustres pionniers*; also published as *Les oiseaux vont mourir au Pérou* (Hissing tales)

JC = *Johnnie Cœur*

KS = *L'angoisse du roi Salomon* (King Solomon)

LDEA = *Vie et mort d'Émile Ajar* ("Life and death of Emile Ajar")

LL = Lady L. (*Lady L.*)

MR = *La vie devant soi* (Madame Rosa)

NSC = *La nuit sera calme*

OH = *Ode à l'homme qui fut la France suivi de Malraux, conquérant de l'impossible*

P = *Pseudo*

PD = *La promesse de l'aube* (Promise at dawn)

PS = *Pour Sganarelle*

RH = *Les racines du ciel* (The roots of heaven)

SB = Adieu Gary Cooper (*Ski bum*)

T = *Tulipe*

TMR = *Les trésors de la mer Rouge*

TS = Les mangeurs d'étoiles (*Talent scout*)

WD = Chien Blanc (*White dog*)

YT = *Au-delà de cette limite votre ticket n'est plus valable* (Your ticket is no longer valid)

Introduction

Roman Kacew was born May 8, 1914, probably in Moscow but possibly in Kursk, in the shadows of the Russian Revolution. His mother, Nina Owczinski, was a Russian Jew from Kursk, in western Russia, just north of the Ukrainian border. She had broken ties with her family to become a stage actress working in a Muscovite troupe that performed French theater. The identity of Kacew's father is not known, though the patronymic Kacew is owed to Nina Owczinski's first or second husband, Lebja Kacew, from whom she separated shortly after her son's birth. (It is generally accepted that Roman never knew with any certainty who his father was.) With the fall of Nicholas II, Kacew's mother abandoned her stage career and took her son to Lithuanian Wilno, which soon returned to Polish control. The next move was to Warsaw around 1924 and finally to Nice in 1927. Kacew earned a French baccalaureate as a prelude to law studies in Aix-en-Provence in 1933 and then Paris the following year. He was naturalized as a French citizen in 1935 and pursued his literary ambitions in his adopted tongue.

Kacew vanished in 1943, however, leaving behind little more than an unpublished manuscript titled *Le vin des morts* (The wine of the dead) and two short stories that had appeared eight years earlier in the French journal *Gringoire*. In his place appeared "Romain Gary," whose first novel, *A European Education*, was an immediate success on both sides of the Channel. Gary quickly earned a prominent place among the new batch of writers who sought to tell the story of World War II.

This sparkling debut was unexpectedly followed by several literary failures. Despite his poor sales, the Gallimard publishing firm decided to give him a chance in 1948. In 1956, with Gary's prior renown forgotten by all but a few readers, Gallimard's patience paid off when *The Roots of Heaven* was nominated for a number of major prizes. Gary returned to the spotlight determined not to let his chance slip by again. With a keen sense of public relations, he courted prominent critics with interviews, radio appearances, and publicity materials in an effort to intervene more directly in the formation of his public image. He produced a fanciful new biography that added numerous episodes to his legend while dismissing his Jewish and Russian heritage. The result was a highly marketable public persona, a sort of Polish André Malraux: Romain Gary, acclaimed author and war hero. This persona was translated into literary form with the publication in 1960 of a well-received fictional autobiography, *Promise at Dawn*.

It is important to recall the extent to which Gary's strategies were rewarded in commercial terms. For the period of 1966 to 1992, Gary ranked twenty-eighth in France for the number of weeks spent on the best-seller lists of *L'Express*, placing ahead of perennial mass market successes such as Guy des Cars, Mary Higgins Clark, and San Antonio.[1] Thus, after *The Roots of Heaven* and *Promise at Dawn*, Gary's celebrity finally became durable. By the same token, it was ambiguous. In addition to his strong sales, he was an innovator in selling the movie rights to his works. As a result, Gary discovered financial security for the first time, but at the expense of being branded for life as a commercial author. With each new publication, he reaffirmed his popularity with an older reading public but was dismissed by the critical press. His widely discussed marriage to American actress Jean Seberg in 1963 ingratiated him with *Paris-Match* but further undermined his credibility in the eyes of journals like the *Nouvelle Revue française*. When Gary tried to explore new ground in his writing, critics were unreceptive to the change in direction. The publication in the sixties of a polemical literary manifesto (*Pour Sganarelle*) and several challenging experimental novels (*The Dance of Genghis Cohn, The Guilty Head, Europa*) failed to nuance his best-seller image. The wide diffusion of his name and the repetition of banal assessments of his work held him prisoner.

Moreover, as the sixties grew in political contestation, the student movement clamored for a changing of the guard. The political class born of the Resistance found itself under siege, with de Gaulle's government being the primary target during the riots of May 1968. Too closely associated with the General to survive the latter's fall from grace, Gary felt the sting of this shift. His image was dating badly and his newspaper articles in unapologetic homage to the former president only exacerbated his rift with certain sectors of the press and public. The Bohemian aspects of his Fidel Castro beard and Mexican poncho were hardly sufficient to offset the damage owed to his personal allegiances. At the same time, Gary's personal life was plagued by scandal and tragedy, culminating in the mysterious and sordid death of his ex-wife Jean Seberg.

Under a cloud of negative press generated in no small part from these extraliterary concerns, it was impossible for Gary to evolve as a writer in the public's eye. The press filtered each new novel through what it believed it knew of him, thereby confining his production to its previous categorizations. Gary would later write: "As a writer, I was considered a

known quantity, pigeon-holed and categorized, which dispensed professional critics from the chore of truly examining my works and coming to
know them" (*LDEA* 17). Bernard Pivot confirms that Gary could in fact
predict for each new publication which critics would champion or excori-
ate the book, and indicate the general terms of their reactions.[2] Undeterred by these objections, Gary's harshest critics often mocked him in
demeaning, personal terms, dismissing him as an impotent writer per-
sisting vainly after his time had passed. Gary slipped into a sort of purga-
tory, one reserved for aging Resistance veterans whose green jacket and
armchair awaited them in the French Academy.

Given this change of fortunes, when Gary was mentioned at all in literary reviews, it was in the role of a convenient foil for unflattering comparisons with a new generation of rising talent. In the late sixties and
seventies, he became overshadowed critically by younger writers such as
Philippe Sollers, J. M. G. Le Clézio, Patrick Grainville, Patrick Modiano,
and Émile Ajar.

Of these newcomers, Ajar was the first to break through to a broad
readership. His quirky, elliptical style was seen as a welcome departure
from the writings of a conservative literary establishment represented
by Gary. A shady outsider of Algerian descent reportedly exiled to Brazil, the reclusive Ajar seduced and confounded journalists for a number
of years. He was heralded by influential critics as the alternative hope
of French fiction, though only his publisher and a couple of journalists
had ever met him. In 1974 and 1975, critical support was strong enough
to make him a favorite for several major literary prizes, including the
Goncourt. His second novel, *Madame Rosa*, managed the difficult exploit
of becoming a bestseller endorsed by literary critics, and this in spite of
Ajar's refusal to grant interviews or make publicity appearances.

Seven months after Gary's death, in July 1981, the news broke that
Ajar's books were in truth written by Romain Gary. For the public and the
press, the mystery surrounding Ajar was now resolved. For those critical
of Gary, it was a mere commercial scheme generated by an author avid
for financial success. In the eyes of those more familiar with Gary's work,
there was a more complex and tragic scenario. Gary, having lost control
of his authorial persona by marketing himself too effectively, had realized that he was a prisoner of the very legend he had sold to the public. As
a last-ditch effort, he had concocted a highly risky strategy for redemp-
tion. Because the works no longer sufficed to communicate his particular
vision of literature, because prefaces and interviews no longer sufficed to
contextualize new novels in relation to prior publications, he had been
forced to expand the sphere of his activity. With great skill and cunning,
he used tactics that he had spelled out in his novels. First, he produced
not just a new literary style but a new author as well. Second, he height-

ened the mystery surrounding this new talent in order to draw journalists into his trap. Finally, emboldened by his critical success, he pushed the experiment a step further by recruiting a distant cousin to stand in as Ajar. From that point onward, it was the articles written by journalists that shored up the plausibility of Ajar's existence. Ajar, every bit as fictive as the novels appearing under his name, had now left the pages of Gary's books and was circulating in Paris, just like the hero of Raymond Queneau's *The Flight of Icarus*.[3]

Taking the battle to recover the public shadow of himself to extraordinary lengths, Gary gambled his own prior achievements for a final chance at winning the literary recognition he felt he deserved. With Ajar's critical and popular acclaim, Gary, moving invisibly behind the mask of Ajar, had momentarily reversed the situation, but had still failed to establish this prestige under his own name.

But the dynamics of this game were such that even in winning, he was losing. Typical of the critical disfavor that dogged him, once the press learned that the mysterious Ajar and his works were Gary's invention, they reacted with as much resentment as admiration. Gary's exploit was classified by many as a prank, an abusive publicity stunt directed at the dignity of French literary and journalistic institutions. With the revelation of his origins, Ajar acquired a new but damning fame: he and Gary were relegated to the files of literary oddities, to be ranked as the most consequent fraud since Scotsman James Macpherson provided romanticism with one of its founding icons, the apocryphal Celtic bard Ossian.[4]

This redefinition of Ajar amounted to his dismissal. Despite the near unanimous support that initially greeted these novels, their attribution to Gary now undermined their status as *literary* works. It was as if the texts themselves had suddenly changed: as the products of an over-the-hill commercial writer rather than a talented, original newcomer, they were no longer deemed to require exegesis and seemed to have lost their exotic, provocative charm. As Jean-Marie Catonné notes, "[The Ajar episode] was proof that Gary was and could be recognized as a great writer and master of language, *but not under his own name!*" (*Romain Gary* 107).

There are two sides to this tale, that of the person who writes and that of the professional readers who wish to deduce something about that writer. The author's image is constructed in the interstices of these two perspectives, a sort of shadow in the public arena thrown by two projectors. This shadow finds its origin with the writer, yet is but a dim outline not to be confused with that individual. With respect to this authorial figure, the two sides of the equation thus exist in a reciprocal but not symmetrical relationship. The writer and the critic operate according to different modalities because they seek different ends, the writer generally desiring transformation and the critic searching for resemblance, continuity. As a result, the writer's attempts at self-definition, often an essential step in the development of literary voice and themes, can quite naturally come into conflict with the labels bestowed by the press. This tends to be the reality facing any newly successful writer in France, but Romain Gary's career is undeniably one of its most dramatic illustrations. It has been evident that this conflict was one of the principal motors driving the evolution of his writing after 1960, but his correspondence shows that this was true even during his early years with French publisher Calmann-Lévy.

Scholarly criticism often takes for granted the roles of publishers and the daily press, assuming that they constitute more or less inconsequential links connecting reader and writer. But in France there is an intense activity surrounding the literary world the likes of which is not found in other national literatures.[5] One must recognize its institutions for what they are: bodies and practices that influence in a very real way which authors succeed, how they succeed, and even which genres or literary aesthetics succeed. An account of the changes that come about in modern authorial strategies or even in literary self-representation therefore depends in part upon an understanding of the institutional developments that contribute to producing and supporting them.[6]

To study the functioning of Gary's authorial inventions, in other words, one cannot limit one's analysis to the texts themselves. Indeed, it is ultimately the press that transformed Ajar's murky past into a successful narrative for the public. Without the determining influence of literary institutions in their role as intermediary between writer and reader, Émile Ajar could not have taken on the proportions that he did. Moreover, in reexamining the stages of Gary's career, we will see that Romain Gary is just as much as a work of fiction as Émile Ajar.

Slighting the role of literary institutions also causes substantial problems for critical readings of these novels. Conscious of the ways in which his authorial reputation interfered with the reception of his work, Gary wrote with an eye toward orchestrating his image. He anticipated how the press would read him and developed strategies designed to generate certain readings at the same time that he laid traps to expose critical preconceptions. The result is that his texts are often structured by hidden narratives, narratives whose operative meaning lies in Gary's struggles with the media. In order to understand the construction of his texts, then, one must understand which aspects of the literary milieu he took to task.

An analysis of Gary's career thus necessarily includes taking into consideration the practices prevalent in the institutions surrounding the production of literature, namely publishing, the critical press, and the literary prize system. Hence, I shall highlight certain traits regarding the contemporary context of the French literary world before discussing Gary's works and authorial strategies.

Publishing, Publicity, and Prizes

Generally speaking, twentieth-century French publishing can be broken into two periods separated by World War II. The first stage consists of the development of advertising and literary journalism, while the second consists of the development of marketing and distribution structures.

After World War I, the number of novels published and sold escalated beyond anything previously seen. To fuel this growth, new forums for publishing and publicity were needed. One of the means of diversification was the establishment of a variety of literary newspapers and reviews to provide authors with greater exposure. The founder of Éditions Gallimard, Gaston Gallimard, was a prime force behind this move. *La Nouvelle Revue française* was Gallimard's most distinguished annex operation at the time, but the publishing giant also funded the creation of a weekly literary paper in 1922, *Les Nouvelles littéraires,* and made forays into popular markets (*Voilà* for cinema and *Détective* for crime fiction) as well as specialized ones (*La Revue juive,* directed by Albert Cohen, and *La Revue musicale*). To offset the successes of right-wing opinion papers like *Candide, Gringoire,* and *Je Suis Partout*—also owned by literary publishers and established in 1924, 1928, and 1930, respectively—the usually apolitical Gallimard responded with the liberal leaning *Marianne* in 1932 as an alternative venue for his writers (Boschetti 530–31). The arrival of these competitors compelled newspapers to join in the expansion, and they extended regular literary sections or added weekly supplements.

The application of advertising strategies to the literary industry became much more prevalent during this period as well. Previously, publishers used publicity quite sparingly, almost apologetically, since it was considered incompatible with the high calling of literature (Raimond 106ff.). Critics of this generation vilified such tactics because they intervened in the assessment of authors and thus threatened their role as arbiters of taste (see Divoire 130–31; Albalat 19–26). In the end, however, the financial benefits of advertising revenue allowed for an increase in the number of working literary journalists and these opportunities sufficed to temper critics' complaints. But the nature of their activity was transformed accordingly, for where previously they were evaluating ideas for art, they were now ranking books for buyers.

Bernard Grasset was one of the first to invest heavily in advertising, taking the stance that a book should be sold like any other product. Operating on the hunch that authors sell books much better than explanations of literary merit, he developed a strategy of presenting his authors in anecdotal modes similar to those used for their fictional characters. A prime example is the publicity campaign he devised to promote Raymond Radiguet prior to the publication of his first novel in March 1923. Since Radiguet's *The Devil in the Flesh* tells the story of a cynical schoolboy who has an affair with a woman while her fiancé is away fighting at the Front, Grasset played up Radiguet's youth, claiming that Radiguet wrote the novel when he was just seventeen. Once the review copies were sent out (to forty-one critics), many of the journalists assumed that the work was autobiographical. Grasset then arranged for movie reels to record Radiguet signing the first check for 100,000 francs ever presented to an author of his age. The combination of scandal and fabricated celebrity helped move forty thousand copies in the first month.[7]

Authors increasingly took an interest in the promotional process of their own accord. Radiguet commented (with what measure of sincerity is anyone's guess), "More than anywhere else, it is in publicity that I see the future of the sublime, so threatened in modern poetry" (qtd. in Steegmuller 305). Some writers even acted independently of their publishers. With greater seriousness than Radiguet, Blaise Cendrars openly embraced advertising, both for its possibilities as a modernist poetic technique and in the orchestration of his image. His 1927 text, "Publicity = Poetry," is clear enough in this respect. In the same year, Georges Simenon took a more theatrical approach to self-promotion. For 100,000 francs, he agreed to write a novel while locked in a glass cage on a platform perched outside the Moulin Rouge, writing day and night for seventy-two hours consecutively. The scheme was designed to encourage the public to participate, insofar as the main characters were to be elected from a list of twelve provided by Simenon.[8] The nature of this spectacle is worth considering. Traditionally, publicity stunts played on the subject matter of novels: a prepublication party for another Simenon novel consisted of a nightclub converted into a jail with the invitations sent out as arrest warrants (Assouline, *Simenon* 96–99). In the Moulin Rouge scheme, however, it was the *writer's activity* that was turned into a public performance and his persona sensationalized as a celebrity. This is an entirely different field of activity from nineteenth-century attempts at advertising, where one finds Guy de Maupassant sending up a rented hot air balloon with *The Horla* painted on the side (Bonnefis 202).

As we can see from these examples, developments from outside of literature proper trigger changes within the literary scene. France differs significantly from most other countries in that the visibility given authors borrows from the forms used to promote celebrities from popular culture. In particular, the rise of the movie star marks a shift toward highly concentrated, univocal images and is naturally anchored in performative traits (role-playing, interviews, high visibility).[9] A quick glance at the prominent literary names of the period reveals that Radiguet and

Simenon are just two among many who fit well into the mode of author-performer. This is not to take anything away from the literary talent of this generation, but its extraliterary activities undeniably served as trampolines for success. Some had a knack for notoriety (André Breton, Colette, Jean Cocteau, Louis-Ferdinand Céline, André Gide, the American expatriates Henry Miller and Anaïs Nin), while others would seem to have led lives as interesting as their fiction (Cendrars, Paul Morand, Henry de Montherlant). A variation on this model is presented by adventurous writers who benefited from the vogue of *reportages* in high-circulation dailies like *France-Soir, Le Matin,* and *Le Petit Parisien.* Adding the label of "man of action" to the author's aura, Albert Londres, Joseph Kessel, Antoine de Saint-Exupéry, and Henry de Monfreid produced exotic, sensational columns cast in journalistic media but often only loosely based in fact. It is probably not by chance, then, that these different groups of writers also developed literary forms whose appeal lies at least partially in an ambiguous relation between the fictions and the authors' experience.

As this style of writing evolved toward the early stages of committed literature, publishing concerns and literary trends became intertwined in uncomfortable ways, since the use of journalism to enhance the reputations of these writers blurred the distinction between fictional and social persona. In particular, the known activities of writers—such as the presence of Malraux and Bernanos in Spain during its civil war—often suggested a verifiable factual relation between author and text that could be misapplied to their particular works. Along similar lines, the enormous prestige enjoyed by French writers in the middle of the twentieth century is owed in part to their achievements in other domains. Just to name those occupying important governmental functions, Paul Claudel, Jean Giraudoux, Benjamin Crémieux, Saint-John Perse, Morand, and later Malraux led double lives that made them highly visible symbols of French culture and society. Their second public career played an important role in contributing to their legend, for their image could be legitimized and amplified by their official state duties. A pseudonymous author like Perse (Alexis Léger, head of Foreign Affairs in 1940), who prohibited the publication of his poetry during his tenure at Quay d'Orsay for reasons of professional discretion, was an exception. For the others, the process was circular: the ticket into a ministry could be paid with literary laurels, and the acquired stature as political authority in turn reenforced literary cachet.

Thus, not long after Proust argued in *Against Sainte-Beuve* for the separation of the writing self from the social being, the trend in publishing was to confuse this demarcation by building authors' reputations through the assimilation of their personal identity to their works. These two attitudes toward authorship entered directly into competition, even if through very different modes: where modernism would problematize notions of authorship and authorial persona, publishing operations would give new life to the most traditional models.

The Liberation would bring a new developmental stage to the French publishing business. During this period, the major publishers evolved from family operations into corporate structures, thus marking a move from expansion to conglomeration. A major coup for Gallimard was a far-reaching deal with Hachette that gave Gallimard a cost-effective distribution circuit more extensive and efficient than any that previously existed in French letters (Assouline, *Gaston Gallimard* 340). Given their material resources, Gallimard was also able to buy up several smaller publishers in this period and pry away authors from those companies that could not be purchased. Néopublicité, Gallimard's advertising firm founded in 1927, cornered the market in the early postwar period, overseeing the publicity campaigns of 80 percent of all French publishers by 1957 (Parinet and Tesnière 142). This trend only grew stronger: by the late seventies, French publishers spent 70 million dollars per year on advertising, with up to 5 percent of a book's shelf price dedicated to covering those costs (Boncenne and Laille 90). The existence of large networks with specialized branches (diversified literary and popular collections, smaller satellite publishers), coupled with extensive distribution capabilities, paved the way for the next important innovation: the introduction around 1950 of market research and merchandising. Reflections of these changes can be found in the inauguration of the Frankfurt International Book Fair in 1949, the 1953 broadcast of the first television show devoted entirely to books (Pierre Dumayet's *Lectures pour tous*), and the controversial inception in the same year of what is now the cornerstone of French publishing, the "pocket book" (*livre de poche*).

What would mark the situation of the writer after 1945, then, is that nearly every facet of the book trade would undergo a swift and far-reaching metamorphosis dictated by commercial imperatives, from the connotations conveyed by the material book itself down to readerships and the means of reaching them.[10] This new merchandising spirit multiplied ceremonial contacts with the public, presenting the author as a conspicuous social celebrity, the "genius" behind the book. A numbing spectrum of activities now awaited the budding author, including book club promotions, university conferences, signature sessions in bookstores, dedicating copies for critics, radio appearances on stations like France-Culture, fan letters to answer, visits to high schools, photo requests, cocktail parties, public readings, translations to oversee, film adaptations, and so forth.

The publishing industry and media began increasingly to function together in ways that constrained authors to participate directly in the promotion and sale of their books. This went from the most blatant, signature sessions at the annual Salon du Livre, to the most difficult, appearances on live television programs. Bernard Pingaud writes: "On the one hand, the process consists of putting the *author* on display for the booksellers and potential readers so that he participates directly in the book's dissemination. On the other, the mass media is used to present the author as the official commentator and principal publicity agent of his work, the pinnacle of the operation being, of course, an appearance on *Apostrophes* combined with a literary prize."[11] One should not underestimate the importance of the fact that these rituals oblige authors to lend their physical person—appearance, demeanor, and voice—to their authorial image. The strong association of the two reifies the author's image and in turn contributes to the reader's construction of the "paper" author. Henri Beyle, who liked to imagine himself as tall, blond, and handsome in the image of his Germanic pseudonym Stendhal, would today be continually confronted with his pudgy, balding self (Stendhal 96). These elements are anecdotal, but they nonetheless significantly impact writers' careers in contemporary France. Despite the theoretical arguments of modernism and postmodernism, today's writers are not purely products of their own pen, for their identities are staged and rehearsed in media outside their own: "No longer dead, the author has now become the very condition of the book's reality" (Heath 1055).

The consequence of this state of affairs is that authorial image is increasingly produced by the press and marketing firms and not by literary specialists or even the writers themselves. In other words, a modern writer's image is to a great extent determined by institutions that do not even read the writer, much less possess the training or intention to read one critically.

As Pingaud suggests above, no feature of France's literary industry displays these elements more noisily than the tradition of the Goncourt Prize. It is the most powerful promotional vehicle for the novel in France today, with even the most conservative estimates valuing it at three hundred thousand in extra sales (Robichon 305). With ritual pomp and circumstance, the Goncourt marks the one occasion during the year when books break out of the literary supplement and onto the front page. The general public is briefly shown the trappings of an essentially closed milieu, with its own institutions, hierarchies, and distribution of roles.[12] It is an exercise divided between modern influences—its format turns authors into celebrities and creates an event in a domain usually devoid of them—and the centuries-old tradition of the essay contest, whose mission is (at least in part) to reaffirm literature as a cultural value and codify (implicitly or explicitly) the valorized criteria for its performance.

The evolution of the Goncourt mirrors and in turn accentuates that of modern French publishing. Though the prize originated in 1903, it was only after World War I that it fully established itself as a coveted guarantee for strong sales. From the twenties onward, the Goncourt has been the object of extensive intrigue, with publishers maneuvering to control the composition of the jury and to court its members with offers of publication or places on editorial committees.[13] After the Liberation, the continued success of the Goncourt invited the extension of this model to all different categories of writing and writer. By 1965, one authoritative source lists 1,472 annual prizes, from the Grand Prize of the French Academy to the Literary Award of the French Federation of Football.[14] Though only a handful of them carry financially significant purses, even the smaller awards can imply institutional consecration and generate name recognition.

Grouped in early winter, the major prizes soon entrenched publishing in a yearly cycle. Henceforth, there had to be new stars every year, regardless of the actual literary crop. As Julien Gracq writes, "In 1949, the birth of a *great writer* corresponds not to an award bestowed for services rendered (usually posthumously) but rather to the need to fill in gaps when there is a shortage of *headliners*" (Gracq 67). Young writers reach celebrity based as much on their perceived promise as on actual achievements. Albin Michel's trend-setting campaign for Pierre Benoit's *Atlantide* is one of the most flagrant examples: counting down until the novel's release, ads promised that "In 15 days [etc.], this writer will be famous" (Assouline, *Gaston Gallimard* 124). Marcel Arland's early assessment of Malraux is equally indicative of the changing tone: "I cannot speak of André Malraux without emotion. At an age when most writers burn up their energy in idle words and gestures, or seek minuscule scandals for cheap publicity, André Malraux goes to Cambodia to play out an adventure whose stakes . . . seem rather negligible to him. [At twenty-three years old, he] has lived, thought and suffered more than most of our official greybeards."[15] This review dates from 1924, when Malraux's publications amounted to *Paper Moons* and a couple of pieces bearing titles like "Domesticated Hedgehogs" and "Pneumatic Rabbits in a French Garden." In this context, the creation of reputations obeys the rhythm established by publishers and the press, not that of literary production.

The result is a transformation in the trajectory of authors' careers. Previously only established authors tended to produce significant sales in literature, such as Gide or Valéry after decades on the literary scene. And even here their other professional activities contributed: Valéry spent twenty-two years as personal secretary to one of the directors of Havas, France's biggest publicity firm, while Gide helped establish the *Nouvelle Revue française* and Gallimard's Pléiade collection of classic works. After World War I, consecration would increasingly come at the beginning of one's career, not in its twilight.

The system would change the status of prizewinners, too. While in the running for honors, they are expected to set themselves off from others, but having won it they are called upon to remain true to the formula that brought them recognition. Their celebrity guarantees them continued visibility, but they are hard-pressed to evolve beyond their Goncourt image. Moreover, they are henceforth out of the running for any prize they have already won. In order not to interfere with the publishers' annual prime picks, their new works are generally released shortly before summer for beach reading or in winter after the prize season. Gary's career was no exception to this rule of thumb. *Le Matin de Paris*, for instance, published an interview in which Henri Quiquéré describes Gary as having fallen into the category of "February authors": "[Gary] is the writer who comes in from the cold! The one who puts out his books during publishing's dead season, and who does not need the fanfare of literary prizes to guarantee his publisher sufficient sales."[16] Goncourt authors in effect fall into a new category, one of living out the sales promise acquired with the prize rather than challenging the literary forms of their day.

Taking these peripheral activities into consideration reminds us of the extent to which the writer is caught up in a constant juggling of pressures, expectations, and problematics of identity. For young writers who win the Goncourt, the conditions under which they work are thereafter dramatically altered. The dividing line between promotion of a published work and intrusions into writers' creative routines is constantly crossed. Their private life becomes fair game for public speculation, and advertising strategy often takes their self-definition out of their hands and places it in the publisher's. Michel Deguy, the philosopher turned poet whose highly theoretical works have integrated post-structuralist thought into contemporary French verse, recalls his bewilderment at learning from the dust jacket of his first collection that his poems "bore the influence of Saint-John Perse" (Deguy 101n).[17] Writers become like fictional characters, caught up in an episodic narrative that they only partially direct.

The media attention is the most destabilizing. After 1930, there were as many as 30 Parisian dailies and nearly 175 more in the provinces. This type of market produces a frenzy of reiteration, for each newspaper seeks to include what its competitors are covering: Céline's 1932 Renaudot Prize for *Journey to the End of the Night* is estimated to have generated nearly twenty-five hundred articles in a few weeks.[18] After World War II, the repetition became aggravated by the fact that the papers were now working with the same wire sources (e.g., Agence France-Presse), publishers' circulars, and bibliographical services. The result was a faster and more intense circulation of names and information, producing a reductive portrait that would obey the prerogatives of the mass media: "Set upon by this disfiguring fixity, contaminated in its essence by the intervention of this crowd phenomenon, closely woven into the continuum of *daily marvels* that newspapers and radio shows blare out in sound-bites, the modern writer is now a *current events figure*" (Gracq 69). In following the day-to-day trace of a writer's name in the press, one is especially impressed by these aspects of paraphrase and repetition, with very few pieces of original, analytical criticism ever appearing. The majority merely relays and thus extends the hold of the conventional wisdom concerning an author.

Ruth Amossy studies the perverse effects of media saturation in her book *Les idées reçues* (Received notions). The hyperbolic repetition slips writers into the confines of a stereotype even as it occasionally elevates them to the status of quasi-mythical figures. The stereotyped image then casts its shadow over interpretations of the author's publications or life insofar as it essentially redefines a given author in its own terms: "The text is refashioned according to the imperatives of a prefabricated model existing outside the narrative in question. Deciphering the text privileges those elements of the description that correspond to the slots in the pre-existing schema . . . Any nuances that are not immediately pertinent are erased while any variations are reduced and forced back into the initial mold" (Amossy, *Idées reçues* 22–23).

Thus, even a diversity of features or opinions does not necessarily break the interpretive mold. Noting the remarkable capacity of stereotypes to recuperate widely varied bits of information, Amossy writes: "Myths manage to undergo all variety of mutation and interpretation without ever losing their powerful unity. They do not break down in the process of being rearticulated, nor do they dissolve in the innumerable variations that offer new readings of the myths. The plurality of meanings does not diminish the magnified image, which in the end always recomposes itself. In short, myths accommodate textual reworking according to their own modalities: they at once lend themselves to it and yet elude it as well" (*Idées reçues* 107). Authors subjected to such highly economic dynamics are destined to be the victims of their own success: "[This] constant 'textualization' is proof of consecration: the more ink a legendary figure draws from journalists, the more his stature is reenforced" (*Idées reçues* 106). Even when an author's moment of glory has passed, the constraints of the stereotype remain, maintaining an image that most writers are powerless to alter.

The evolution of Gary's image as an author obeyed that of figures who become cultural icons once the mass media or other popular forms ensure wider exposure. Wrested from Gary's hands, his biography underwent a type of rewriting in the press that carried out the work of simplification or distillation for the public. It resulted in a vulgarization that retained only what is most obvious in his personality. This is the price a writer like Gary pays for being transformed into a national hero as Resistance fighter-cum-author-cum-diplomat: "An author loses control over his character. For it to make its mark in the public's imagination, it must first have undergone the extreme schematization that transforms it into a stereotype. The polyvalence and richness of the text have been erased, leaving in their place a simplistic frozen image. In a sense, the disappearance of the work turns out to be the price of glory" (*Idées reçues* 100). By the very extension of his name beyond its literary context, Gary's successful promotion of his persona ended up burying his own works.

Some writers are less prepared to handle these circumstances than others. Jean-Louis Bory was twenty-six years old when his *French Village* received the 1945 Goncourt Prize. At one point, Bory remarked that it took him ten years to get over it, referring to his "GP" as "General Paralysis."[19] In another interview, the number grew to fifteen years, while still elsewhere he confided that it took him twenty (qtd. in Ezine 166–67; Carrière, *Le prix d'un goncourt* 131). His suicide in 1979 led some to wonder if he ever got over it. André Schwarz-Bart (the 1959 Goncourt Prize winner for *The Last of the Just*) turned his back on his career altogether and skipped off to the Antilles with his wife, Simone, who would take over as the prominent author in the household.[20] Another young author derailed by this sudden success was Jean Carrière. He won the Goncourt in 1972 for *L'épervier de Maheux* and can be taken as emblematic of more minor writers whose place in the spotlight is at times out of proportion with their talent, and certainly out of tune with their personalities.

In his cleverly titled *Le prix d'un Goncourt* (*prix* is both "prize" and "price" in French), Carrière gives us one of the rare detailed accounts of this experience. As a novelist with a quiet reputation for regionalist fiction, he was originally writing with the expectation of 1,500 readers; the Goncourt would bring him 805,000 (Caffier 100). The radical shift in sales would mean an equal shift in audience, which would completely disrupt his internal dialogue with an imagined reader: "After having believed that one was writing for a couple hundred or thousand readers, one finds oneself in front of an arena packed with spectators who gasp every time they spot a sign of failure—or the renewal of the artist's exploit. It is enough to paralyze your pen and call into doubt the slightest word traced by your hand" (Carrière, *Prix d'un Goncourt* 29).

The Goncourt imposes an *étiquette*, in the double sense of a label (author of authentic regionalist fiction) and a certain type of behavior (he now has to perform as a great writer to justify his Goncourt): "The Goncourt Academy even haunted my dreams, calling on me to prove with a major work that I was in fact the writer they had crowned . . . What had been a passion became an obligation" (*Prix d'un Goncourt* 130). In the commotion of public exposure, Carrière feels dispossessed of his identity, as if his name no longer belongs to him: "[I could feel] my identity getting away from me, to the point that my own name sounded odd to me, as if, having become a public entity, it no longer belonged to me and a puppet was bearing it in my place. Ever since that twenty-first of November [the date of the Goncourt award], names strike me as fraudulent" (14).

His feeling of estrangement becomes an obsession, seeping down into the deepest levels of his imagination. It amounts to an alienation from his own signature—the very guarantee of one's claim to originality and proprietorship. He finds himself spending hours filling up notebooks in the attempt to reinvent it, as if this would allow him to regain control of his writing voice: "This obsession poisoned my life for so long and sterilized all of my obstinate efforts that it went beyond a mere personality tic. I spent time trying to modify the shape of my letters, in order to create a new graphological identity for myself. It is in a case like this that we are confronted with the bizarre ties that exist between the depths of the heart and the hand which reveals those secrets without meaning to. One cannot do anything about it, short of acquiring the virtuosity of a counterfeiter" (*Prix d'un Goncourt* 132–33).

To free himself of the weight of critical preconceptions, Carrière concludes that he would have to change names: "I guess I would have to take on a pseudonym—I've considered it: a writer is never forgiven for abandoning the role that word-of-mouth has attributed him" (*Prix d'un Goncourt* 19). Carrière's own experience and reactions explicitly point the way to Gary's picaresque antics.

Gary's Literary Practice

Born Roman Kacew, Gary would spend his career writing under a series of pseudonyms. The one that has drawn attention, of course, is Ajar, and this has strongly colored how critics have understood the role of pseudonymous authorship in Gary's writing. Since the episode seemed in large part directed at them, critics have focused on Gary's personal motivations for the undertaking, with the result that the creation of Ajar has been assessed primarily in legal, ethical and moral terms. In other words, his detractors have employed the terms "mystification," "hoax" and "fraud" to define (and thus limit) the event because for them Gary's anger over his critical reception fully explains his act. While it is true that the desire for revenge is a common motivation for such pseudonymous mystifications,[21] the unfortunate result here has been that discussions were oriented away from any creative features involved in Ajar's successful invention. Posed in terms of charlatanism, Ajar's relation to literary practice and esthetics has gone unexplored. Granted, much of the viciousness in the attacks upon Gary's work is doubtless better explained by his Gaullist ties than by the imperfections of his work; and, to concede a point to these hostile critics, many of his novels suffer from repetition and heavy-handed symbolism. One can decide for oneself what ratio of blame to mete out between these polarized camps—but to stop here would be to miss the larger and more interesting issues.

Why, for instance, if Gary's work was only a pastiche by a washed-up hack, did critics promote *Madame Rosa* for the Goncourt Prize and the public buy 1.2 million copies? Or, seen from Gary's point of view, the Ajar episode is much more than a public revenge exacted on Parisian critics, since the first thirty-five years of Gary's writing moves gropingly toward this adventure. The staging of Ajar and the creation of works in his image are the logical culmination of a career-long investigation into the formation of public images and the dynamics of authorial identity. Ajar, after all, is not Gary's only metamorphosis. In 1958, an unknown political satirist named Fosco Sinibaldi ridiculed the hypocrisy of the United Nations and the gullibility of the American public. Sixteen years later (but only months before Ajar), Shatan Bogat appeared, identified as a spy novelist of Turkish-American origins and staunch opponent of black-market arms traders. One must remember too, that Romain Gary did not exist either until he adopted the name during the French Resistance. And there are at least several others. I have uncovered the example of Jack Ribbons (see Chapter 4), previously uncited by journalists and biographers. After Gary's death, one critic wondered, "Who knows what a full bibliography of his writings would look like?" (Bondy, "On the Death of a Friend" 33).

Among the critics following the Ajar affair, a few did seek interpretive approaches to Gary's gesture. Prominent writers and reviewers like Max-Pol Fouchet, Jean-Marie Rouart, Michel Tournier, and François Nourissier defended the idea that this pseudonymous excursion involved more than a well-tuned marketing strategy. Writes Rouart, "It's a philosophical tale in which creator and hero are one and the same. Gary also could have said: 'I am forming an undertaking which has no precedent, and the execution of which will have no imitator.'"[22] While Rouart is perfectly correct in underlining the dramatic equivalence of author and protagonist in Gary's project, certainly no one would say that Gary set out to show his peers "a man in all the truth of nature." Gary's aims, of course, were the exact inversion of Rousseau's. For his part, Tournier rejects outright the label of hoax, citing the quality of Ajar's writing as proof of the experiment's literary significance (Tournier 340). Nourissier also brushes aside the idea that Gary's deceptions trivialize the Ajar novels, arguing that Gary showed the pseudonym to be a means of creating literature, not defrauding it:

Not only do I understand this temptation [taking a pseudonym] but I believe it to be beneficial. One can write very well behind a mask, sometimes even better than without it. Obstacles fall away, and one's reserve dissipates. In becoming Ajar, Romain Gary succeeded beyond his expectations, because he used it to perform a metamorphosis, whereas often writers only resort to a pseudonym for writing minor texts: erotica, detective stories, etc. One should dare to try to *best oneself*... Writing under a pseudonym does not have to be limited to practical jokes. It can also be an attempt to escape oneself: then it's a serious matter.[23]

Nourissier recognizes that pseudonymous authorship is not solely an institutional device but is also a literary one capable of producing a creative transformation. The exact nature of this metamorphosis is complex, however, and Nourissier's comments are too cursory to offer many leads. Clearly though, he points the way to larger stakes when he identifies this act as a potentially effective solution to a *writing* problem. For Gary, this was indisputably the case: in the five years following the invention of Ajar and Bogat (1974 to 1979), he published twelve works under four different names. Such a creative burst at more than sixty years of age, after forty years of writing, bears witness to the doors opened by these transformations. Just as importantly, when we turn to Gary's early years, we see that the metamorphosis of Roman Kacew into Romain Gary could well be understood along essentially the same lines as the later ones: a new name was selected, a largely fictional biography elaborated, and works produced in its image. This process is in fact a fundamental feature of Gary's approach to writing and not merely a tactic adopted for an anecdotal settling of scores or for self-promotion in the twilight years of his career.

What is most striking in the Ajar episode is not simply literary—or, rather, it is literary at every step of the way, but *the fictions are no longer confined to the practice of writing*. "Ajar" is not just a matter of changing topics; *"Ajar" is an attempt to project a literary creation into social reality*. In an enthralling history of apocryphal writers like Ossian, Bilitis (Pierre Louÿs), and Émile Ajar, Jean-François Jeandillou comments on this extension of fictional production: "The supposititious author is an even more complete mode of literary creation because textuality wins out over reality. Quite similar to the work in this respect (a linguistic construction), the author and sometimes the reader discover that they have been transformed into the strange state of beings made of words" (Jeandillou, *Les supercheries littéraires* 494).[24] Where Gary-Ajar breaks significantly with his predecessors is in the extension of his fabrication to the real world. Ajar is intended to exist as a living fiction of sorts, a fiction seemingly turned real when the public is treated to a large newspaper photograph of this mysterious author punching an overly persistent journalist.

In this initial survey of the issues, we get to the heart of what is most puzzling about the critical reactions to Gary's stunt: the theatrical dimension of the Ajar legend is the episode's most notorious feature, yet it is the least analyzed. This shortsightedness in itself almost justifies Gary's ire. In rereading Gary's work, one discovers extensive mirroring between the literary aesthetics promoted in his fiction and the theatricalization of Ajar. In this light, the unwieldy and often garbled literary essay from 1965, *Pour Sganarelle*, takes on different dimensions, for it is now much more apparent what brand of fiction Gary was calling for as an alternative to the New Novel. Characterizing most literary movements as trying to incorporate some new element of the real into literature, Gary was striving for just the opposite. In his vision of a total novel (*roman total*) whose author is created by the same means as the protagonist, literature succeeds in infiltrating reality. It also becomes apparent that novels published in the seventies under Gary's name mean something else altogether. An example of a text structured by hidden narratives, *Your Ticket Is No Longer Valid* presents Rainier—one of Gary's alter egos in prior novels—as an aging businessman who maintains his sexual virility only by visualizing a "thuggish immigrant" in his place. What Gary does in this novel is serve up the press's own image of him, both in the portrait of a waning Rainier and in the choice of a phallocentric topic. Critics are led into a trap where their harsh judgment of the work will in truth be more a measure of their own stereotyping of Gary than an accurate reading of the work. He thus accomplishes two things at once: he mocks the "sterile" image (in the sense of no longer productive of fictions) that the press presents of him and works out (secretly) on paper the narrative of his creative renewal in the guise of Émile Ajar, another reputedly "thuggish immigrant."

Over the course of his career, Gary illustrates his vision of authorship and identity with references to past "literary" legends, real and imagined. Almost all of these figures are masters of disguise of one sort or another. Gary's archetype is taken from the eighteenth century, where mystification flourishes in the shadows of the Enlightenment. He sees the alchemists, medicine men, and adventurers—figures such as Count Saint-Germain, Cagliostro, and Casanova—as having succeeded in keeping reality and rationality at bay through the force of their imagination. Of these, Saint-Germain is the most frequently cited in Gary's novels (see *Lady L.*, *Europa*, and *The Enchanters*). A seductive mix of aristocrat and rascal, he is the perfect embodiment of Gary's protagonists. Protected by Louis XV and Mme de Pompadour, he would nurse his reputation at the Royal Court into mythical proportions. No one knows when or where the "count" was born, nor even his real name. He would travel freely throughout Europe under a variety of identities and pass for possessing the secret of eternal youth. Some of his contemporaries even believed that he had met Christ and the Apostles. An encyclopedia entry further illustrates his mystique:

[Count Saint-Germain's] profligate spending, without anyone ever being able to ascertain the source of his fortune, made some suspect him of espionage and gave strong credit to the rumor that he could make gold and diamonds . . . Wherever he went, Count Saint-Germain provoked the same admiring and credulous interest. He had a knack for never slipping up and thereby permanently whetted people's curiosity. He succeeded in preserving for the entirety of his life the mystery that surrounded him . . . Having later won the affection of landgrave Charles of Hesse, a man greatly intrigued by sciences of the occult, the Count joined his court where he eventually died. Saint-Germain's protector burned his papers and refused to give the slightest bit of information concerning his mysterious guest. ("Saint-Germain, le comte de," *La grande encyclopédie*, vol. 29, 1886 ed.; emphasis added)

Gary was fascinated by this perfectly managed coexistence of fiction and truth, in which Saint-Germain determined the rules for his identity and left historians few means of reestablishing the empire of fact.

This fiction is, in a sense, Saint-Germain's "truth," and the move to see authenticity within imposture is one of Gary's most characteristic literary traits. In *Talent Scout*, for instance, a Swedish journalist (Leif Bergstrom) tracks a Latin American dictator by posing as a Nazi war criminal (Otto Radetzky) in order to infiltrate the leader's inner circle and get his story. When the dictator is toppled, the would-be Radetzky risks being executed because of his perceived loyalty to the dictator. Faced with a choice between betraying his real identity (to save his life) or being true to his lie, Bergstrom is tempted by the latter: "[Bergstrom] could even claim that, in a certain sense, he had managed to go farther than all the other artists whose performances he had witnessed . . . He could have saved his hide, instead of . . . remaining faithful to his role . . . He had almost succeeded in going beyond acting to attain a sort of authenticity. After all, in the final analysis . . . there was no other authenticity available to man than that of acting out one's role to the very end and remaining faithful unto death to the theater and character one had chosen" (*TS* 386). For Gary, the feat of taking one's secret to the grave is synonymous with a victory over reality.

The anarchists of late nineteenth-century Europe are identified in *Lady L.* as the direct descendants of the Count Saint-Germain (*LL* 79).[25] The novel's protagonists treat their lives as their primary artistic creation. An apocryphal essay on art presents Gary's thesis: "The human soul's need for beauty had to extend sooner or later *beyond the limits of art and take aim at life itself.* We thus encounter inspired creators who are pursuing *lived masterpieces* and who have taken to *treating life and society as a plastic material*" (*LL* 106–7; emphasis added).

In the case of one of the novel's main characters, (fictional) anarchist Armand Denis, the narrator explains repeatedly how Denis's acts of cultural terrorism—such as kidnaping a famous composer in mid-concert, transporting him to a whorehouse, and seating him at the bordello's piano as a critique of bourgeois culture—orchestrate a spectacular legend in order to capture the public's attention:

This sort of exploit was common in Armand Denis's career . . . His predilection for the striking and dramatic bore witness to a talent for propaganda that was new to his day, but whose secret the twentieth century would uncover. Ideas alone did not suffice to carry off mass hypnosis—which the coming age would see as its unique aim in all domains. Staging, a knack for theatrics, and a demagogy capable of pulling on all of one's heartstrings, mixed in with imagination and thought, were the indispensable arms for the great projects of seduction looming on the horizon . . . The tragedy of Armand Denis's life was to have been a pioneer before his time. (*LL* 75–76)

Though Gary's pervasive irony obscures his exact attitude toward these issues, *Lady L.* nonetheless presents the nineteenth and twentieth centuries as periods in which the mediatization of social space evolved rapidly in the struggle for symbolic capital and the control of popular opinion. These characters can thus be considered anarchist insofar as they aim to wreak havoc with the dominant class's ability to determine and control social representations. To this end, the crimes committed by Armand Denis and Lady L. consist largely of falsifying the means by which identities are conferred and verified.

Gary locates the perfect milieu for a twentieth-century model in the world of film and the relations that exist between movie stars and the media. In *The Colors of the Day*, Willie Bauché is a Hollywood filmmaker who writes his own scenarios, directs, and plays all the parts as well. The same approach applies to his life, about which he proudly claims, "I am a work of art of my own creation" (*CD* 141). Constantly switching roles with complete cynicism, Bauché alone knows that his image is all there is of him. It is impossible to establish fundamental features of his identity, such as his true name, nationality, or race (*CD* 34). Even his "private" life is slyly conceived in anticipation of how the press will interpret it.

Under the watchful eye of the Hollywood press, however, Bauché realizes that continued flexibility or transformation becomes increasingly difficult the more exposure one receives. He must up the stakes if he wants his persona to escape paralyzing definition. Once more, the approach used by Bauché is based not on treating life's questions through art but on transferring the techniques of one's art into life. It is the attempt to live out one's fictions: "Art no longer sufficed. [Willie] had to raise the dose. Otherwise, reality would regain the upper hand. He needed to be creating at every moment, constantly active. He couldn't settle for mere art which, at best, was but an intermission in the reign of the real. He had decided to go to work on reality and life itself; [he] had resolved to elevate his life to the status of a serial novel" (*CD* 36). The difficulty with this "serial novel" (*roman-feuilleton*) is that each successful fiction commits Bauché to playing a new role that in turn he will have to devise a means to shed in the near future. Bauché gradually loses his grip on reality as the struggle to counter all media representations of him escalates beyond his capacity to control them. In the end, he slips into a psychotic state and falls to his death from a cliff.

Gary's analysis of the mechanics of celebrity is at times acidic, at others joyously playful. On still other occasions, he shows himself to be politically committed. There are many parallels here to Gary's own handling of authorship and his future dilemmas in the public eye. The hitch, of course, is that as long as plans of producing fictions to compete with reality are made *within* novels, the project remains a fiction's fantasy, without impact upon reality. It is one thing to map out a revolt in writing, it is another to make it happen. In the attempt to act upon one's image, it does not suffice to try to correct the content of an unsatisfactory representation. One must instead turn one's attention to the modes by which representations are produced and circulated. This is what could lead Gary to abandon his more or less direct representations of these themes and to widen the frame in which we normally consider the construction of an authorial persona. Gary would solve his dilemma by taking a central *topos* of modernism—the staging of the figure of the artist—and translating it into a bold and unpredictable performative art. For if one takes seriously Gary's Malrucian stance that art's role is to compete with reality, the only means truly to do this is to take one's fictions off the page and introduce them into the real world.

Chapter 1

The Invention of Romain Gary, 1935–1952

Little is known of Kacew's activities in 1936–37, though one can probably discount his claims of having fought in the Spanish Civil War, completed a Slavic languages degree in Warsaw, or traveled in Ethiopia. In 1938, he enlisted in the French Air Force but the following year suffered the affront of being the only one in his officers' training class to be refused promotion (putatively because of his recent citizenship). Despite this snub, Kacew's service to France turned out to be exemplary. At the armistice, he escaped France in an Air Force plane and flew to North Africa, where he was admitted to the Lorraine, *"the oldest and most glorious bomber squadron in the Free French forces" (Kessel 42). Serving as spotter, navigator, and bombardier, Kacew fought with his unit against Rommel's forces (among others) throughout Africa for two years before being recalled to England. Assigned to the Hartford Bridge Air Base,* Lorraine *now included future French prime minister Pierre Mendès-France and Pierre Louis-Dreyfus (uncle of Adidas and Olympique de Marseille soccer team owner Robert Louis-Dreyfus, great-uncle of American actress Julia Louis-Dreyfus, and Kacew's reluctant bunkmate). It is at this time that Kacew began using* Gari *(soon anglicized to* Gary*) as a nom de guerre. Over a seven-month period in 1943– 44, he flew many perilous missions over northern France, Belgium, and Holland. Having already survived typhoid in Syria and a crash near Lagos that killed the other passengers, Gary was one of the few from his squadron to reach the Liberation alive. In 1944–45, he was decorated with high honors. He received the French equivalent of the Purple Heart* (la Croix de guerre) *and the Legion of Honor and was named by de Gaulle as one of the general's 798 surviving Companions of the Liberation (Larat 49). Gary married English author Lesley Blanch upon his return to Paris and was named embassy secretary, second class. His first diplomatic assignment, beginning in December 1945, was to the French embassy of Sofia, Bulgaria. Sympathetic to the cause of the Bulgarian liberals, Gary would watch powerless as Georgi Dimitrov gradually brought down the monarchy and installed a Communist regime. Gary was then named to a position in Moscow, but the nomination was never carried out—doubtless his former associations in Bulgaria would have compromised him in the eyes of Soviet authorities (Larat 75). In February 1948, Gary returned to Paris, where he worked on a team monitoring reconstruction in central Europe, under the orders of Paul Claudel's son-in-law, Jacques-Camille Paris. After one-and-a-half years at the Ministry of Foreign Affairs, Gary was sent to Berne,*

Switzerland, where he took on the post of first secretary in the French embassy. The ambassador was Henri Hoppenot, formerly assigned to Washington, D.C., during the war and friend of Claudel and Saint-John Perse.

Romain Kacew (1935)

Having adopted a French spelling of his first name, "Romain Kacew" signed his first publications in 1935: two short stories, "L'orage" and "Une petite femme," appeared in the French paper *Gringoire*. Neither has been reprinted, an anomaly for a writer who in the course of his career would often publish the same piece in two or three venues or recycle entire novels for republication decades later under different forms and titles.

In "L'orage," a sullen stranger's arrival on a remote colonial island disrupts the lives of a French doctor and his wife, Hélène. Kacew's description of the couple's failed marriage — "the tropical sun had killed the man in him and the love in her" — paves the way for a dramatic triangle, which is not long in materializing. The mysterious visitor (Pêche) has come to see the doctor, but stumbles first across Hélène and is immediately seduced by her beauty and vulnerability. Unfortunately, Pêche is no Paris; rather, he is a bearded brute more in the image of Zola's Jacques Lantier. A mute animal rage invades him, and he is on the point of raping Hélène when suddenly he releases her and turns away in despair. Later, after Pêche has met briefly with the doctor (a consultation from which the reader and Hélène are excluded), Pêche heads back to his raft under stormy skies that would surely mean his death were he to set to sea. Despite the violence to which she has just been subjected, Hélène wants to prevent him from leaving under such dangerous conditions. It is now she who forces herself upon him, and they make love despite Pêche's reticence. This fails, however, to dissuade Pêche from his suicidal departure, and only upon Hélène's return to the bungalow do we learn from her husband the reason for Pêche's visit and the fate that now threatens Hélène: Pêche wanted confirmation from the doctor that Pêche had in fact contracted leprosy.

Kacew's second story, "Une petite femme," takes place in Indochina, where a French railroad crew is laying down tracks in the sodden jungle. Here, it is an engineer's wife (Simone Lacombe) whose arrival from France sets the tale in motion. The story initially appears to call into question the authoritarian attitude of its narrator, camp foreman Fabiani, who disapproves of the charming but capricious woman. Though Fabiani's discipline over the crew is undermined by her presence, Madame Lacombe's record player, dancing, and impetuous good humor improve the spirits of the bored and lonely workers. But when Fabiani is unable to prevent her from accompanying the crew on a visit to the potentially hostile neighbors (a tribe identified as the Moï), Madame Lacombe inadvertently brings about disaster. Having strolled off on her own, she witnesses a gravely ill woman, the wife of the tribal chief, languishing in a hut. Wanting to ease the woman's suffering, Madame Lacombe administers her a sedative. The elderly woman dies immediately thereafter, and the tribe is convinced that Madame Lacombe has poisoned her. They attack the French crew, taking several workers hostage, Mr. Lacombe among them. The Moï chief, whose men are notorious for torture (says Fabiani), will release his captives only in exchange for the woman who "killed" his wife. At story's end, Madame Lacombe evades the foreman and his assistants and turns herself over to the Moï in order to secure the freedom of the prisoners. The tale ends with captives being allowed to rejoin their camp, and we are left to assume that Madame Lacombe's fate was an unkind one.

Both tales are cut from the same exotic cloth, obey a similar plot pattern, and differ markedly from anything that would appear under Romain Gary's name after 1944. Despite Kacew's mere twenty-one years, these short pieces are surprisingly mature in their mastery of suspense and structure; arguably, they even compare favorably with many of his later works in these respects. The writing style is terse, sober and without symbolic adornment.

The most noteworthy aspect of Kacew's literary beginnings is the venue of publication, however. Founded in 1928 by Horace de Carbuccia, *Gringoire* cannot be deemed fascist in the strictest sense, but its relentless attacks on the "anti-fascists" (the French Communists and Socialists in particular) place it in that neighborhood. A strong dose of anti-Semitism boils on the surface as well, as shown by the tenor of the paper's haranguing of Popular Front leader and French president Léon Blum (see Soucy 42–43). By 1935, *Gringoire* was fully engaged on the path that would lead it to become one of the most notorious papers in twentieth-century France. In the two issues containing Kacew's work, for instance, one finds tributes to Abel Bonnard and Benito Mussolini, as well as articles by Philippe Henriot and Drieu La Rochelle. For figures such as these, Nazi Germany's eventual defeat would in essence be a death sentence.[1]

Reconsidering this stage of Gary's career raises some awkward questions about a writer best known to the public as a Resistance hero, Gaullist diplomat, and liberal humanist. How do we reconcile these literary submissions with the fact that just three years later Kacew would begin his officers' training in Salon-de-Provence and in 1940 would reject without hesitation Pétain's pact with Hitler?

In later years, from 1956 to 1960, Gary sidestepped the issue on several occasions, downplaying the contributions as youthful ignorance.

In his brief comments, he gave conflicting accounts of how he and his mother perceived *Gringoire*.[2] Given that in 1935 the foreign-born Kacew was freshly arrived in Paris from the provinces, it is *possible*—though unlikely—that the budding lawyer and writer was not fully aware of the paper's politics. In *Gringoire*'s favor, from a young writer's point of view, was its audience of nearly a million readers during this period (Soucy 42–43). Kacew could have been swayed, too, by the prior participation of famous authors like Kessel, François Mauriac, Somerset Maugham, Roland Dorgelès, Bernanos, and André Maurois. Be that as it may, however, the content of Kacew's stories inclines us to consider the issue more carefully.

First of all, while Kacew's oft-announced debt to Malraux is undeniable in both stories, Kacew has borrowed only the colonial settings, the emphasis on virility, and the unflinching violence, without the metaphysical or revolutionary dimensions that were the innovative elements in Malraux's first novels. Far from questioning the colonial status quo (which Malraux had done to some extent in his 1920s newspapers *Indochine* and *Indochine enchaînée*), Kacew's tales unreflectingly reproduce the most abusive aspects of it. In "Une petite femme," for instance, the narrator guns down his native interpreter for no better reason than a fit of frustration. The death is dismissed as inconsequent, with neither the crew nor the Moï making any note of it. Moreover, Kacew's use of the term "Moï" to identify the indigenous population is telling, for in the prewar period it was a pejorative label applied by the Vietnamese to various mountain tribes in the Annam region. "L'orage" portrays the French *colons* as debauched beings, a characterization in line with the editorial cartoons drawn by Pavis for *Gringoire*, where criticism of colonial lifestyles took issue only with the decadence of French mores.[3] Like Pavis, Kacew makes no objections to the economic and physical enslavement depicted within his works. And in both of Kacew's stories the pidgin French of the servants is accompanied by a blissful, unthinking docility. With respect to the sexes, the tragic fates that befall the women characters are seen as stemming from their own "inherent" weaknesses.

While these stories constitute a meager output and are clearly derivative, one cannot easily dismiss the portrait they suggest of "Romain Kacew, French author in 1935." Kacew certainly never embraces, nor even for that matter discusses, the fascist and neofascist ideas already sprinkled throughout *Gringoire*'s columns at the time. To be more precise, these stories steer clear of any deliberate moral lesson or explicit political philosophy. But their narrative implications and character development depend upon a vision of life in the French colonies not inconsistent with the content of *Gringoire* in 1935. The authorial persona one deduces from these stories would have to be placed well out on the Right.

Romain Gary (1940–45)

"Romain Gary" is another writer altogether. Unlike Kacew's economical short stories, the plot in Gary's texts is nearly always secondary to a morality tale. Gary's tireless championing of humanist values is one of the most characteristic features of his work, his occasional overreliance on allegories or symbolism one of the most disappointing. Though still situated right of center, Gary from the outset would break definitively with a world-view that allowed Kacew to publish in the same pages as fascists and virulent anti-Semites. Indeed, in the postwar period, some of Gary's fiercest critics would come not from the Left but from a new generation of right-wing journalists much in the tradition of *Gringoire* (to some degree Kléber Haedens of *Paris-Presse* but especially the pseudonymous editorialists of *Rivarol* and *Minute*).

At what point did Gary make this move from the company of the future villains of Vichy to the opposing ranks of liberal humanism (philosophically) and Gaullism (politically)? The question is more difficult than one might suppose. The biography circulated from 1946 to 1948 by Gary's French publisher states, "On June 19, 1940 [Gary] answered General de Gaule's [*sic*] call and set out for England with his plane."[4] Based also on Gary's articles in conservative venues like *Le Figaro* and *France-Soir*, his book of conversations with François Bondy (*La nuit sera calme*), and the definitive edition of *A European Education*, the commonly held belief is that Gary fully and permanently espoused Gaullist humanism from the moment he committed to the French Resistance. In large part because of his reputation, Gary would bear the mantle of being one of de Gaulle's most unflagging, long-term supporters in the world of letters.[5]

There is no question that Gary's refusal of the armistice was immediate and complete. Gary repeatedly risked his life to join up with French forces in North Africa and England. He continued to fly right up to the Liberation, even though it would have been far more prudent for him to retire from active duty owing to the gravity of his accumulated war injuries. What is dubious, however, is the claim that Gary's *Gaullist* allegiance—one of the founding blocks not just of his political beliefs and public persona but of his literary project as well—dates from de Gaulle's famous June 18 call to resist the German Occupation.

To begin with, Gary did not leave France on June 19, 1940, as the Calmann-Lévy press release asserts. Gary flew out of Bordeaux's Mérignac Airport on either June 15 or 16 and therefore cast his lot with armed resistance before Churchill granted de Gaulle access to BBC radio.[6]

The evidence provided by Gary's writing itself is even more important for deducing his opinions at this juncture, for it suggests that his adoption of specifically Gaullist politics did not occur until several years after the Liberation. In looking more closely at Gary's literary production from this period, we discover that he managed a remarkable sleight-of-hand in revising his first novel for subsequent editions. Begun in 1940 aboard a steamer bound for Libya and completed in the fall of 1943 in his barracks in Surrey, England, *A European Education* was written during Gary's combat duty. It was first published before the war's end in an English translation as *Forest of Anger* (1944), and then in its original version in France with Calmann-Lévy in 1945 (under the title *Éducation européenne*). After Gary switched publishers in 1948, Gallimard eventually purchased the rights to *A European Education*. It was not until 1956 that the first Gallimard edition of *A European Education* appeared, however, the one that is currently considered the definitive text. Gallimard editions bear no mention of any changes from the original publication, and at first glance the new text seems essentially the same (one short chapter has been added and two others have traded places). A closer comparison of the 1945 and 1956 editions, however, reveals that important alterations were made that fundamentally transform the meaning of the novel. While Gary's best-known works are undeniably Gaullist (e.g., *The Roots of Heaven, Promise at Dawn* and the 1956 edition of *A European Education*), it turns out that the *original* version of *A European Education* is not in the least.

A European Education is the tale of a young boy's encounter with a Polish Resistance unit that has taken refuge in the forest outside of Wilno. The episodes are quite bleak as the partisans perish one by one, succumbing to starvation, frostbite, and the German forces. No adventure is found in the harrowing experience of combat, which is shown here as empty of any real glory. In keeping with the tone of European romanticism, which characterizes the novel, temporary relief from the partisans' desperate circumstances comes primarily through occasional contact with the masterpieces of the creative spirit—music, poetry, and novels.

Ultimately, however, in the 1956 edition, those partisans that survive are sustained by an unusual hero: "Nearly all of our leaders had been struck down or arrested by the Germans. To give us back our courage and confuse the enemy, we invented Partisan Nadejda . . . We were inventing a myth, the way one sings to oneself to brave a dark night" (*EE* 1956: 263). Nadejda's "absence" (since he is imaginary), rather than being a handicap, is in fact an enabling sort of omnipresence: "Their hero was elusive, invincible, protected by an entire population. No power or material force in the world could keep him from persevering and triumphing" (105). The wave of hope built up around Nadejda eventually misleads the Germans into trying to capture this nonexistent leader: "It became obvious to the psychological warfare bureau in Berlin that it was essential to do away with the man whose name had ended up creating, in a conquered country, a veritable myth of invincibility" (104–5).

Gary's vision of the partisans' struggle thus takes the form of an extended morality tale, a fable of sorts where belief in this mythical leader and the ideals he represents prove more vital than any military feat on the fields of battle. But this stance should not be mistaken for the abstractions of romantic idealism. Here, the figure of Partisan Nadejda corresponds to a specific understanding of de Gaulle's role in the French Resistance, one promoted by de Gaulle himself in his *War Memoirs* and adopted by Gary in a series of articles written for U.S. and French magazines.[7] In the following passage from a piece published in *Life* magazine in 1958, for instance, we can see the parallel with Nadejda take shape more clearly, for Gary presents de Gaulle as having played on the effects of absence to create a larger-than-life image of himself, thus turning exile into a weapon:

This future leader [reasoned de Gaulle] must keep his distance, avoid familiarity, remain something of a mystery . . . [De Gaulle] followed his own rules of aloofness in order to remain a symbol of national resurgence . . . When he arrived in London in 1940 to lead the resistance, his name meant nothing to the French masses. Then, during the four years that followed, news of de Gaulle's lonely stand kept reaching occupied France as if from another planet. He was invisible, far, far away, and yet present in the hearts of the French people, a legend growing bigger and bigger. ("The Man Who Stayed Lonely," 6)

Through the terminology and strategy evoked, Gary echoes the device used in *A European Education*. Other facets of Nadejda's portrait extend this fictional transposition of de Gaulle as focal point and savior of the French. As with the French Resistance, the Polish partisans fight for a little-known leader whom they never see, binding their efforts and faith to a single name. Just like de Gaulle speaking from London, Nadejda's voice reaches the partisan underground by radio: "All of Poland is in his voice" (*EE* 1956: 107). Elsewhere, a rumor about the Polish leader—and thus by extension de Gaulle—places him on equal footing with the heads of state of the major Allied powers: "[Nadejda] has met with Roosevelt and Churchill and laid out his terms. Stalin has finally found someone with whom he can work" (215). Consistent with de Gaulle's own historical argument concerning his contributions to World War II, Nadejda's role is that of a unifying principle that oversees and symbolizes the Resistance effort, provides cohesion to its scattered ranks, orients and gives meaning to its actions.

The 1956 edition of *A European Education* bears many other hallmarks of the Gaullist vision of the French Resistance. The Gallimard edition of Gary's novel acknowledges a position of near military helplessness for the partisans in order to highlight the inspirational role of a solitary leader. It obliquely downplays the contributions of the Anglo-Saxon armed forces as well as those of domestic resistance (and thus, by extension, the French underground, which was dominated by the Communists). Finally, in Gary's later treatment, the fable of Partisan Nadejda (understood as de Gaulle) elevates the French war effort to the status of a model of resistance for all other European nations. Thus, in the 1956 edition of *A European Education*, the Polish partisans pass their time in the frozen Wilno forest reading "The Declaration of the Rights of Man— the French Revolution of 1789" or breaking into renditions of "La Marseillaise" (*EE* 1956: 89, 73). The Polish Resistance, in other words, is subsumed within the French Resistance, becoming a mere imitation of the Gaullist legend, whereas, historically speaking, a reversal of role models in this instance is possibly more appropriate.[8]

In the 1945 edition of *A European Education*, the story unfolds quite differently. Gary does denounce fascism in favor of humanist idealism throughout the novel, thus marking an unequivocal break with his *Gringoire* associates.[9] The ideological underpinnings of his brand of humanism in 1945, however, were not at all those grounding the Gaullist argument of 1956. First of all, *the character "Partisan Nadejda" simply does not exist in the 1944 and 1945 editions of the novel.* In fact, even though Gary was active with the Free French forces throughout the entire composition of the original manuscript, there is not a single reference in it to de Gaulle. On the contrary, where one might expect to see the June 18 radio address mentioned to inspire the beleaguered Polish partisans, Gary instead cites at some length Churchill's famous "Blood, Toil, Tears, and Sweat" speech of May 13, 1940 (*EE* 1945: 41). An interesting switch also occurred from one edition to the next. In the 1945 edition, the Resistance journal run by students from Wilno University is titled *Nasza Walka* (Our combat), a phrase that distinctly evokes the French Communist clandestine networks. In the 1956 republication, the underground paper is changed to *Liberté*, a closer echo of de Gaulle's "La France Libre," or Free French forces (cf. *EE* 1945: 34 and *EE* 1956: 59). An attentive comparison of the two French editions of *A European Education* makes it apparent that *the entire Gaullist fable was grafted onto the novel retrospectively for its republication in 1956.*

The difference between these two texts thus cuts to the heart of the Gaullist legend. Without Nadejda, there is no "Resistance" in *A European Education*, Resistance (with a capital R) being understood here as a network of underground groups organized under a central military command and united in the defense of national sovereignty and other ideals. Instead, one has only isolated, makeshift clusters of individuals banished into the forest, cut off from each other and the towns they would defend. In the 1945 edition, then, the sacrifices of the Polish partisans prove their tremendous courage but do not weigh on the result of the historical conflict, since they represent no significant military or even symbolic entity.

In the absence of the Nadejda character, the decisive focal point of the novel shifts entirely. For example, the title originally proposed by Gary for the 1945 edition was *Les environs de Stalingrad* (The outskirts of Stalingrad).[10] In this version, the outcome of the war hinges on the Russian army's stand in the Battle of Stalingrad: "This Winter, the heart of humanity beats on the outskirts of Stalingrad just as in 1940 it beat in the suburbs of London [for the Battle of Britain] . . . This Winter, the outskirts of Stalingrad no longer concern Russia alone: the whole world is suffering and struggling for its deliverance" (*EE* 1945: 43). Poland's geographical location does not suffice to explain the prevalence of the Russian argument in this novel; Chapter 15 shows Parisians in the French Resistance pinning their hopes on Stalingrad as well.

It is hardly surprising that Gary would see salvation as coming from the East rather than the West, given that the work was written between 1940 and 1943.[11] But with the eastern front placed as the key to the war's outcome, the historical claims later made by the Gaullist ranks are severely curtailed here. The French Resistance is no longer construed ideologically or militarily as the center of the effort to free Europe. On the contrary, in the 1945 version, each of the European national resistance movements is essentially defenseless, hanging on for their very survival and hoping for a Russian victory. The heroic French Liberation celebrated by de Gaulle on the Champs-Élysées is indirectly deflated.

In keeping with this view, Russia supplants France in the 1945 edition as the world capital of romantic tradition. In one passage, for example, a German soldier near death characterizes Russia in the following admiring manner: "It's . . . a country where only dreams count and nourish you in life. Great men are measured by the scope of their thoughts and reality is but a vile thing without importance" (*EE* 1945: 128). In fact, rather than constituting a fable about France's pivotal role as the defender of humanist values in Europe, *A European Education* in its original form even offers some harsh critiques of the French population's attitudes. Commenting on a colleague's fable about France, a Polish partisan leader offers this assessment: "I would bet a bundle that Mr. Honoré [from your tale] has now taken a job with the Vichy government and I'm afraid that your Mr. Brugnon is probably calmly selling off his cheeses to the Germans at cut rates" (62). Anticipating the themes that would make Jean Dutourd's *The Best Butter* famous in 1952, Gary contradicts the Gaullist account of the German Occupation of France in several important aspects: in this specific instance, de Gaulle's tendency to disregard the extent of popular collaboration with the invaders. Gary's initially skeptical view of France's behavior during World War II is muted in—when it is not absent from—the revised edition of 1956.

Instead of serving to articulate a particular ideological vision of the

French war effort, the 1945 edition of *A European Education* develops a catalogue of references specific to Polish concerns. In the years preceding Gary's youth in Poland, Wilno had been passed back and forth among Germany, Russia, Lithuania, and Poland. The issue of Polish nationalism thus looms large as one of the primary stakes for these partisans. This manifests itself in the 1944 English edition when the resistants sing the Polish national anthem and, at novel's end, after the war, the protagonist is shown as an adult serving in the Polish army.[12] The specter of the Holocaust, an element generally elided from Gaullist discussions of World War II, also surfaces in this first version of *A European Education*. With allusions to pogroms an ominous echo resonating throughout the work, one recalls that Gary was personally familiar with the Jewish communities of Warsaw and Wilno, having lived within a few blocks of them.

Thus, the image of Gary that we derive from the 1945 edition differs substantially from that of 1956. In its original form, without any references to Gary's French nationality or to his role in de Gaulle's Free French forces, the novel heralds an "atmosphere of cultural pluralism," as suggested by the eight different languages that appear in it (Larat 25). More specifically, however, it constitutes a return to and a celebration of Gary's own roots, a return to the world of Roman Kacew's childhood. All varieties of regional cultural expression are named in these pages, a sort of testament to the peoples whose very societies were threatened with annihilation: from Polish street songs and tangos to Chopin's masterpieces, from Poland's poets and polemicists (Jan Kochanowski, Juliusz Slowacki, Adam Mickiewicz) to the kosher butcher's prayers in Hebrew, from marching and cabaret songs, Cossack lullabies, and insults to the works of great Russian authors like Gogol and Pushkin. The richness and diversity of these selections suggest a genuine passion on Gary's part for his two homelands: the tenor, tenets, and texture of this debut novel portray him as a Russian and Polish émigré more than as a proud French national.

Quay Conti or Quay d'Orsay? (1945)

Having established facets of the authorial persona projected by Gary's first novel, let us now look at how he broke into the world of letters and how his image took shape on the literary scene.

While in England, Gary was stationed outside of London. Once the tide of the world conflict began to turn in favor of the Allied forces, Gary had in the back of his mind his eventual return to civilian life. In the years prior to the war he had known real poverty as a student in Paris, and he was anxious about his future. Using his days of leave, he headed into London, where he established contacts among soldiers, writers, and political figures. He had the pleasure of spending time with his famous predecessor from Nice, Joseph Kessel, and met other influential people at London's Petit Club Français (Bona 93). Of these, perhaps none would prove more crucial in Gary's professional debuts than Raymond Aron.

Himself of Jewish extraction, Aron in 1945 was not yet the famous sociologist and philosopher that he would become in the decades after the war. Nonetheless, he was a graduate of the prestigious École Normale Supérieure, a professor, and had made a name for himself in London editing *La France Libre* from November 1940 to September 1945. The voice of French intellectual prestige in England during these years, *La France Libre* made Aron a central figure in the community of writers and publishers in exile.

Having been impressed by the manuscript of Gary's work-in-progress, Aron introduced him to Pierre Calmann-Lévy, who agreed to take on *A European Education* for eventual French publication (Bona 93–94). Aron also published three short pieces by Gary in *La France Libre* during this period. It is probably Aron as well who directly (or indirectly) introduced Gary to the Baroness "Moura" Budberg, a German aristocrat from Estonia who would find an English publisher for Gary's novel.[13]

But Gary also had a strong interest in the French foreign services, an ambition made possible by a decree granting a number of foreign-born French citizens eligibility for the normally closed ranks of the Quay d'Orsay (Blanch 46).[14] Here again Aron would play a role, though not entirely as Gary had hoped. According to Gary, it was Georges Bidault, minister of foreign affairs in de Gaulle's provisional government, who asked Gary to join the diplomatic corps (*NSC* 115). Gary hoped for a position in London, in part because of his plans to marry British author Lesley Blanch. André Malraux, who had been de Gaulle's "Technical Adviser on Culture" before becoming minister of information, promised Gary a similar cultural post in the French embassy in London and asked Aron, head of Malraux's ministry cabinet, to see to the logistics of the assignment. Malraux had apparently overstepped his bounds, however, as Aron ran up against stiff opposition from Gaston Palewski, one of de Gaulle's top aides and closest associates among the Free French representatives. Palewski would not budge on Gary's nomination, giving as his reason the opinion that Gary was too young and undisciplined for such a prestigious position (Aron 148–49). Aron had to content himself with facilitating Gary's entry into the diplomatic corps at a less advantageous post.

It is worth noting that this entry into elite circles was as much due to Gary's usefulness as a Slavic polyglot and his talent as a writer than to any Gaullist loyalties. In fact, at this juncture, his "protector" Aron was already at odds with influential Gaullist aides because of his moderate enthusiasm for their political ventures (Colquhoun 217). In this respect, the name of Aron's journal, *La France Libre*, is misleading. Founded by André Labarthe (who recruited Aron to direct it), the journal was never directly related to de Gaulle's Free French forces. It was started with Polish money, continued with British subventions, and published by Hamish Hamilton for the entirety of its run (Colquhoun 220–22). Despite the positive press it received, de Gaulle reportedly disliked it (Lacouture 331). Labarthe would ultimately turn overtly anti-Gaullist and Aron maintain his intellectual independence. In response, the inner circle of the Free French forces established an official publication, *La Marseillaise*, under Palewski's supervision and ideological directives (Crémieux-Brilhac 191–92, 380). Thus, Palewski's suspicion of Gary may have had as much to do with the former's quarrels with Aron than with Gary himself (who probably was not well known to a powerful figure like Palewski). Whatever the case in London may have been, Gary was not—and never would be, for that matter—welcomed into the inner circles of Gaullism's political wing.

Though faced with this small setback to his diplomatic ambitions, Gary was buoyed by the immediate success of his novel. By the end of summer 1945, it had attracted the attention of some of France's most influential writers. Raymond Queneau, whom Gary would encounter on his path at several key crossroads, wrote that "this novel is certainly one of the best that has been written on [World War II]," noting an echo of American literary techniques that gave it "such a particular and original tone."[15] Jean-Paul Sartre suggested that *A European Education* could well be the best novel on the Resistance and, according to Gary, requested Gary's next novel for serial publication in *Les Temps Modernes*.[16] Similarly, according to Dominique Bona, Albert Camus sent a letter of praise encouraging Gary to submit a manuscript for Camus' Gallimard collection "Espoir" (Bona 110). Of all this high praise, though, perhaps Joseph Kessel's remarks, with their comparison to the author of *Man's Fate*, caused Gary the greatest satisfaction: "In the last ten years, ever since we first heard the names of Malraux and Saint-Exupéry, there has not been a novel in French fed by a talent as deep, new, and brilliant as this one" (Kessel 43).

In the first months after the war, however, paper was scarce. The Calmann-Lévy firm, run by brothers Pierre and Robert Calmann-Lévy, was particularly strapped for printing supplies because it had been closed down during the Occupation under Vichy's anti-Semitic legislation.[17] The few newspapers that were not under postwar sanctions for collaboration offenses were also unable to meet their needs (the daily *Figaro* was reduced to a single page, front and back). As a result, media coverage and publicity were limited as well. Under these conditions, the literary prize season took on added significance for a writer hoping to break into the scene. The primary target as always was the Goncourt, but more so than ever in 1945: in addition to the recognition it would bring, it temporarily included an extra allotment of paper for printing needs. Given the early postwar context—the Goncourt Academy was under a shadow of disgrace, having named laureates during the Occupation while other juries desisted—it was considered a foregone conclusion that the Goncourt would go to a novel on the Resistance, the only question being which one.[18]

Initially, things looked to be going Gary's way. Pierre Descaves, son of the academy's president, served with his father on the jury. He contacted Gary's publishers to tell them of his admiration for *A European Education* and asked that copies of the novel be sent to fellow voters Dorgelès, André Billy, Léo Larguier, and the elder Descaves.[19] After word leaked out that Gary was the Goncourt favorite, however, a pseudonymous note in the *Figaro* soon dampened Calmann-Lévy's hopes: "Some electors [of the Goncourt Academy] have read *A European Education* and, like all readers of Romain Gary's book, were struck by it. We nevertheless note that it would be problematic to name, on the heels of Madame Elsa Triolet, a second laureate 'born in Moscow.'"[20] In the divisive climate of the postwar purge and struggle for political hegemony, one of the stakes of the Goncourt prize was likely to be the institutional promotion of a specific account of the Resistance. In the eyes of some, the note insinuates, before Gary could receive consecration as an important new "French" writer, the issue of his national loyalties and political convictions had to be addressed. Was Gary, the *Figaro* asked its readers, a Communist sympathizer born in Russia like Louis Aragon's wife?

Whether the culprits giving rise to this note believed Gary to be from the Communist ranks of the Resistance or were simply playing on conservative sentiment to help another Goncourt candidate's cause is impossible to tell. Aside from *A European Education,* one of the few other alleged clues to Gary's loyalties might have been found in his brief story "Citoyen pigeon" (Citizen pigeon) published in 1945. A sort of miniature and burlesque precursor to Lederer and Burdick's *The Ugly American,* it mocks two wealthy U.S. businessmen touring Moscow. This text, however, was known only to a handful of people and could hardly have weighed on his public image. Whatever the case, Pierre Calmann-Lévy was no doubt familiar enough with Gary's political sympathies from their days in London to know that the implied ties to Triolet's comrades were unfounded.

The question of Gary's birthplace was another matter altogether. In a letter informing Gary of the remarks printed in the *Figaro,* Pierre Calmann-Lévy made it apparent that he believed the label "born in Moscow" to be a falsehood.[21] If this is so, where did the publishers, and the reading public for that matter, believe Gary to have been born?

From 1935 onward, Gary's identification papers would list him as being born in Wilno (Bona 41). As we have seen earlier in this chapter, the original edition of *A European Education*, with its tribute to the Polish Resistance and wealth of local cultural detail, would certainly lend credence to this in the eyes of readers. One of Gary's letters of reply to his publisher reveals a surprising twist, however. Gary writes, "How could we discreetly let it be known to the Goncourt jury members that *I'm not from Russia but from Nice*? For my part, I refuse absolutely to refute [the *Figaro*]. Do you have any ideas?"[22] Others close to Gary would endorse this version of the "facts." Gary's wife, for instance, also stated that Gary was born in Nice.[23]

Digging further, we discover the matter is even more complicated. Among the biographical information that dates from Gary's London years, we come across an editor's note that identifies Gary as "born in Russia thirty-one years ago, raised in Poland and in France" ("Romain Gary," *Cadran* 18: 31). Most confounding of all, the press release circulated by the Calmann-Lévy firm itself also lists him as being "born in the countryside near Kursk, of a Russian father and French mother"![24] These latter documents would seem to confirm the *Figaro*'s claims.

Ultimately, however, Gary's maneuvers for the Goncourt were for naught. As October progressed, rumors would name him as the probable winner of the Prix des Critiques, which was scheduled to meet in the days prior to the Goncourt Academy's deliberations. With Maurice Blanchot, Jean Paulhan, Gabriel Marcel, Émile Henriot, and Malraux admirers Marcel Arland and Jean Grenier among the eleven members of the jury, its award was arguably a greater honor than the Goncourt in literary terms. Its laureate, however, would not be the beneficiary of extra paper allotments, and thus over a two-week period Gary and Calmann-Lévy would scramble to dissuade the Critiques from selecting *A European Education*.[25] In the end, though, lacking any assurances from the Goncourt voters, they would reverse course and withdraw opposition to the Prix des Critiques, which was indeed awarded to Gary on November 7, 1945.

But what was Gary up to with this chaotic dissimulation of his past? Why the fluctuations between Russia, Poland, and France? Doubtless, it was a combination of a number of factors. On the one hand, the displacements could aim to enhance his possibilities for a literary career as a "French" author. It is true that the Russian émigré-authors from Gary's generation and immediately prior—Kessel, Henri Troyat [Lev Tarassov], Claude Aveline [Evgen Avtsine], Georges Govy, Roger Ikor, Zoé Oldenbourg, Nathalie Sarraute—generally tended toward French assimilation, as shown by their use of pseudonyms and western European novelistic themes. Gary might also have believed that his background could jeopardize his standing with the Quay d'Orsay, given the ominous signs of the coming Soviet "menace." Other factors, such as lingering fears of the racial persecution that had already pursued him throughout Europe or a desire to distance himself from a disappointing father, à la pseudonymous authors Stendhal and Nerval, could also weigh in the balance.[26] Finally, he could even be concerned about his naturalization and diplomatic status if it were discovered that his identification papers were false.

One can only speculate as to the proportion played by each. As a first step, however, we can delineate three stages, covering the years leading up to the war, Gary's spell in London with the French air force, and his beginnings as a novelist and diplomat after the Liberation.

As alluded to above, in the course of his 1935 naturalization proceedings, Gary took advantage of his missing birth certificate to change his place of birth from Russia to Poland. Either origin, it is true, could have made him the target of discrimination against immigrants and Jews. Nevertheless, in the 1930s, there was much greater animosity toward Russia in the conservative ranks of law and the military. Moreover, once Léon Blum and his Popular Front government gave up on attempts to create alliances with the French Communist Party (PCF), the latter finds itself having alienated portions of the Left as well. The PCF's political fortunes reached a low on August 23, 1939, when the German-Soviet Non-Aggression Pact was signed. A few days later *L'Humanité* was banned and the PCF took on a semiclandestine status. All of these factors could have encouraged Gary to distance himself from his past. In addition, Gary himself could well have felt ambivalent about his background, since both the Bolsheviks and the "White Russians" in exile had histories of hostility toward Russian Jews.

The one period during which Gary would proclaim his Russian birth corresponds to his years in London, when the Soviet Union became a Western ally and even its savior. Although the majority of Gaullists were anti-Communist, they tempered these attitudes once the eastern front opened. Along these lines, Gary's public acknowledgment of his Russian birth appears to have been subsequent to 1943, the year during which the PCF announced its support for de Gaulle. The zenith, of course, was the Soviet victory at the Battle of Stalingrad, an occasion when Gary could openly celebrate his heritage.

Immediately after the war, though, we see Gary do an about-face. Given the Gaullists' tense relations with the PCF concerning the makeup of the new French government, Gary's Muscovite origins could have been troublesome for those promoting his diplomatic career. After all, by December 1945 Gary was in Sofia, reporting back to France about the gradual Communist takeover of Bulgaria. And what little ambivalence there may have been on his part before, the events he witnessed in Sofia—especially the execution of his friend Nikolai Petkov—clearly turned him against the USSR in its postwar incarnation. Poland, in contrast, was aligned with France as a victim of Nazi aggression.

Gary's refusal to deny the *Figaro* report is probably easier to explain.

By the fall of 1945, Gary would be a representative of the French government and no longer in a position to lie about his past. Thus, he carefully toed the line, encouraging his publishers to spread the idea that he was born in Nice, yet abstaining from making the claim himself in print. In short, vigorously avoiding his Russian birth after 1945, he appears to have viewed his origins as a political liability to be quietly swept under the carpet, preferring to be thought of as Polish or, in certain circumstances, French.

As this complex evolution shows, Gary's demeanor with respect to his past was in flux during these decades and was demonstrably different from that shown in other periods of his life. There appears to have been no comprehensive strategy behind the changes in his *authorial* identity at this point. His haphazard self-representations in various publications from London and Paris were more those of a self-protective young émigré adapting in the interest of his material circumstances, with finances and professional security taking priority over image. For instance, in one letter immediately following the war, having already urged the Calmann-Lévy brothers to use "the most tact possible" in their negotiations with literary jury members, Gary again advises, "Be especially careful not to maneuver too much"—before adding without transition, "When will you send the dough?"[27] Along the same lines, an earlier letter has Gary fretting over delays in publication, which he needs "as soon as possible to help [him] acquire certain potential posts that [he] would like in civilian life."[28] While typical of many writers' relations with their editors, these concerns suggest that Gary's liberties with the truth at this time were in fact directed toward protecting his livelihood rather than fabricating an authorial persona. In the preceding quotation, the publication of his novels is presented *as the means to another career*, that of the diplomatic corps. Thus, the colorful, reckless mythologization during the Resistance, such as the report that Gary was a veteran of the Spanish Civil War and was imprisoned under Franco ("Romain Gary," *Cadran* 18: 31), initially gave way after the war to much more discreet alterations that seem to have had a single design: to safeguard his future.

It is apparent, however, that Gary considered his past a malleable resource to be deployed according to his needs or desires. And while on certain issues we must satisfy ourselves with hypothetical answers, we nonetheless have uncovered important stages in Gary's evolution, previously obscured by his legend as a "first-hour" Gaullist. After his literary debut in the company of the Right-wing extremists at *Gringoire*, he made two of the determining decisions of his life: from a political and military point of view, he chose combat over collaboration, and, from an ideological standpoint, he embraced humanism in its battle against fascism. The tabula rasa of the Liberation allowed him to return from the war with a new identity, that of Romain Gary, Resistance hero, prize-winning author, and young diplomat. At this juncture, however, the Resistance for Gary was "European" before it was "French." *A European Education*, with its passionate tribute to "his" people and "his" culture, suggests that Gary's identifications and loyalties lay with his youth spent in Poland. Too young to remember his infancy during the last days of the czar and hesitant to avow his Russian birth for political (and perhaps personal) reasons, one would have to characterize the Gary of the war years as nostalgic for Poland and not yet fully assimilated to a French identity. At the Liberation, though, when the hallowed halls of Quay d'Orsay and Quay Conti beckoned, France offered him a self-image that had not previously been in the cards for the fatherless and impoverished immigrant.

Cynic Without an Audience (1946–1952)

Gary's second work, *Tulipe*, was ready to go to press early in the spring of 1946. It is a work so different from *A European Education* that one would scarcely believe it to be from the same author. Where *A European Education* is a dignified, romanticist tribute to the spirit of European Resistance and the Polish people, *Tulipe* is a no-holds-barred satire about a Buchenwald survivor who exploits a Gandhi-like social movement out of sheer disgust with postwar mentalities. We pass from a prose Mickiewicz to an embittered Voltaire.[29]

Calmann-Lévy's misgivings about the book—they advertised it in only four newspapers, despite the success of Gary's first novel—were matched by the public's lack of enthusiasm. While *A European Education* reached sixty thousand in sales in its first year alone, barely two hundred copies of *Tulipe* would leave the shelves over a ten-year stretch (Calmann-Lévy Publishers' Archives). The poor response was exacerbated by the fact that the deteriorating situation in Bulgaria intensified Gary's obligations in Sofia, eliminating any possibility of his participation in promotional activities for his publisher.

In critical circles, the work confounded and disappointed many of the reviewers who had been impressed by Gary's first effort. One senses that Gary was spared harsher criticism because of the respect that *A European Education* had earned him. Two of the more perceptive critics of the period, for instance, are fairly restrained in their rhetoric. Maurice Nadeau faults Gary with having missed his audience as a result of "having tried to play it too smart," while Robert Kemp observes that "the parody suffocates the ideas which, though not insignificant, lack a bit of originality."[30]

The commercial and critical failure of this work hit Gary hard, and his initial response in his correspondence was to fault his publisher for delays in printing and inadequate publicity. With his next novel nearing completion, Gary was concerned about Calmann-Lévy's reluctance to invest in promoting him. Thus, when Gaston Gallimard dangled a large advance in an attempt to lure Gary away, Gary's decision was a rather easy one.[31] He signed a contract with Gallimard, marking the beginning of a thirty-two-year relationship with the French publishing giant.

Gallimard's greater resources notwithstanding, however, the next novel, *The Company of Men*, fared just as poorly in bookstores as *Tulipe*. Again cast in an acerbic, satirical vein, it centers on the misadventures of black marketeers and former collaborationists during the postwar settling of scores in France. Though Gary stops short of fully rehabilitating the principal collaborationist in this tale, his account shows compassion for the character (Gustave Vanderputte) and condemns as a witch hunt the public's thirst for revenge. In 1948, the climate was not yet ripe for such pleas for clemency and reflection. Moreover, Gary combines this weighty, controversial topic with a second plot line, a lighthearted farce about kid gangsters on a rampage in Paris, a somewhat curious decision from both formal and thematic standpoints. An analogous device was well handled in *A European Education*—Gary shows us the cruelty of World War II through the eyes of two children, Janek and Zozia—but in *The Company of Men* it mostly trivializes the difficult issues of the postwar penury and purge (not to mention the Occupation). Even Émile Henriot, a venerable critic who was supportive of Gary, found himself unable to endorse the work: "Romain Gary's talent is not in question, but everything in this book is poorly constructed."[32]

On the heels of these disappointing works, Gary was forced to take a hiatus from writing when the Ministry of Foreign Affairs recalled him from Bulgaria to a time-consuming position in Paris. The following assignment to Switzerland allowed him to resume his creative activities, and in 1952 his fourth novel, *The Colors of the Day*, appeared with Éditions Gallimard. Typical of its reception is the review by *La Revue de Paris* editor Marcel Thiébaut, who grants it but a single paragraph in his roundup of recent books.[33] This latest novel disappeared with scarcely an echo in France.

Just seven years after his rush into the limelight, Gary's literary career had fizzled. While one can attribute much of this fate to unfortunate formal choices and execution, it does not suffice entirely to account for his curious fall from grace. Judging from a brief mention of *The Company of Men*, Claudel was impressed by the novel, while Nobel laureate Roger Martin du Gard admired *The Colors of the Day*.[34] Moreover, written in a narrative mode similar to Gary's later successes, *The Colors of the Day* sold well in the United States (*NSC* 19). Despite its flaws, it is mature in its thinking, a powerful study of human psychology, and a savvy analysis of the workings of public image. Prophetic to an astonishing degree of the Ajar adventure still twenty years distant, it remains one of the fullest statements of Gary's novelistic vision.

In this moving letter recording his parting of ways with Calmann-Lévy, Gary acknowledges his struggle to rediscover the paths and themes that led to the success of *A European Education*:

I know full well that the public has forgotten me . . . I will have passed like a dream. It's horrible. Sometimes, when I look back and see my brilliant beginning and what I am today, a knot forms in my throat. Success went to my head and alcohol only made things worse; we can see the result. You were right to avoid any expensive publicity for that poor *Tulipe* . . . Ah, vanity, dust and the pursuit of nothingness. If only I could write a big, beautiful novel again . . . Oh well, let's put aside those unthinkable dreams. It's a shame—our time together will have been brief but beautiful.[35]

Though the content of *The Colors of the Day* marked a step in the right direction, Gary's quest to write another "big, beautiful novel" would continue to escape his grasp for more than a decade.

Chapter 2

The Consecration of Romain Gary, 1952–1961

When Gary's superior in Switzerland (Hoppenot) was once again named French ambassador to the United States, Gary followed him in 1952 to become embassy secretary for the French delegation at the United Nations in New York City. Gary's role was soon expanded in recognition of his excellent handling of the media, and he found himself saddled with the delicate task of being spokesperson for France during its war in Indochina. A number of other controversial issues stretched Gary to his limits, and his firsthand experience at the UN profoundly disillusioned him as well. In the fall of 1954, he cracked under the accumulated pressure. After a period of difficult negotiations and a brief passage through London, he was appointed French consul in Los Angeles in January 1956. Aside from a three-month assignment to La Paz, Bolivia, in late 1956, Gary enjoyed a profitable sojourn in California, which lasted until the summer of 1960. His contacts with de Gaulle progressed during these years and Gary met with the general at the latter's private residence in 1957 and at the Élysée mansion in 1960. Gary also traveled intermittently, visiting Mexico, Guatemala, Tahiti, Thailand, Hong Kong, Nepal, and India. In December 1959, he met American film star Jean Seberg, who divorced her husband nine months later. Through his time spent in Seberg's company, Gary learned about the movie industry and filmmaking. His blossoming relationship with the actress was unacceptable in the eyes of the Quay d'Orsay, however, since Gary was still officially married to Lesley Blanch. Prominent Gaullist and minister of foreign affairs Maurice Couve de Murville blocked any new promotions for Gary. Finally, Gary was reassigned to Paris, where he worked on an interim basis until March 1961. That same year, Gary's affair with Seberg became public knowledge when photographers in Italy caught them together several times. Gary's request for a ten-year disposition from the diplomatic corps was granted.

The Committed Writer (1956)

In 1956, Gary finally provided Gallimard with the "big, beautiful novel" he was struggling to produce: *The Roots of Heaven*, a 443-page epic adventure set in France's West African colonies. One of the first conservationist novels in Europe, it recounts a loner's quest to educate the public and media concerning endangered species (in this case, elephants). With its condemnation of the ivory trade and safari hunts presented as a symbolic blueprint for 1950s activism, the hero's mission is set against a larger backdrop of characters struggling to reconstruct a meaningful, humane universe in the wake of the Holocaust. Where *Tulipe, The Company of Men,* and *The Colors of the Day* could only reply with derision and despair, *The Roots of Heaven* affirms a strong faith in humankind's willingness to defend what Gary considers to be certain essential universal values. With its hero dubbed an *"esperado"* (*sic*), *The Roots of Heaven* thus reconnects with *A European Education* in the responses it urges to moral, psychological, and philosophical dilemmas.

Gallimard knew it had a winner and first released the revised edition of *A European Education* to refresh critics' memory of Gary's past promise. One week later, in early October, just two months before the Goncourt Academy was to make its annual selection, *The Roots of Heaven* arrived in bookstores. Of the nearly three hundred novels Gallimard was publishing per year and of the twenty-two that appeared in September 1956,[1] *The Roots of Heaven* was the focus of their efforts to capture France's most important literary prize.

Gary's second try at the Goncourt strongly resembled the first. On the positive side, his decision to abandon pessimistic satire manifestly paid off. Henriot resumed his enthusiastic support, while, among the Goncourt jury members expressing opinions, glowing reviews from Billy and moralist Gérard Bauër more than offset Alexandre Arnoux's noncommittal evaluation.[2] Citing Céline several times as a counterexample (the controversial writer had been added to the Gallimard roster following his amnesty in 1951), reviewers welcomed Gary's tribute to a French tradition of literary humanism. Resistance hero Édouard Corniglion-Molinier writes, "[I have] the impression that *The Roots of Heaven* is a sign that the French novel is finally crawling out of the rut of defeatism in which it was wallowing."[3] Billy echoes these sentiments: "[This novel] can be described as a fascinating tale of adventures in which the most urgent topics of today's world are reflected in the light of classical humanism" (Billy 15). Elsewhere, similar appreciations were expressed but were cast as a response to a different dilemma. Gary's novel exemplifies what the genre "should be," writes Henri-François Berchet, who sees *The Roots of Heaven* as a timely alternative to some of the more experimental works in the running for the Goncourt: "Romain Gary does not content himself with psychological novels a few pages long in which action gives way to soul-searching . . . He likes broad, colorful works, full of life and passion, in the true tradition of the novel. His breath and pace, which set him off from the generation of young writers, allow him to vanquish all the

obstacles that he has strewn across his own path."[4] Whether the disapproving diagnoses took issue with the recent past (Céline and company)
or the near future (psychological sketches or the growing brood of New
Novelists), Gary's novel was hailed by many as a remedy for all that ailed
French letters. The elements praised—the focus on wildlife conservation
as a social cause and his reworking of the humanist epic—share the values
that were appreciated in his vision of the Resistance for *A European Education*: "[In Gary's latest novel] the reader will recognize the author of
A European Education which was so well-received in 1945," states Clermont-
Ferrandian and literary historian Henri Clouard.[5] For his part, Henri
Amouroux lauds Gary for "his devotion to a great cause," though clearly
Amouroux, a popular historian of the Resistance, has the war effort in
mind as well.[6] Similarly, conservative Catholic André Rousseaux turns a
deaf ear to Gary's unorthodox Christian views borrowed from Teilhard de
Chardin but, as a prominent Resistance figure who evolved from Pétainist sympathies in 1940 to embrace de Gaulle by war's end, Rousseaux responds favorably to the Free French forces as a model for defending traditional humanist values.[7] Gary's success, in other words, is largely in having
rediscovered the conception of man and of the novel that conforms to
that of the critical consensus of classical humanists.

On the negative side, the two threats to Gary's candidacy for the 1945
Goncourt Prize also reappeared, in strangely similar forms. The jury of
the Fémina Prize was among those impressed by *The Roots of Heaven*, and
it announced its intention to change the date of its meeting in order to
preempt the academy's pick. The tactic was part of an ongoing battle with
the Goncourt for institutional influence and provoked an aggressive reply from Bauër and Dorgelès.[8] At the same time, a late strike from the
right wing sought once more to sink Gary's hopes under a new wave of
anti-immigrant innuendo. The chief culprit here was Kléber Haedens. As
a young journalist during the Occupation, Haedens made his reputation
baiting Gaullists and Communists alike with his inflammatory articles in
collaboration newspapers (see Sapiro, 548). Increasingly influential in
postwar years in spite of (and because of) his abrasive style, Haedens became one of the stalwarts of the "Hussard" group, built loosely around
authors Roger Nimier, Antoine Blondin, and Jacques Laurent and characterized by hostility toward the Fourth Republic and denigration of the
Resistance. Haedens mocked *The Roots of Heaven*, asserting that Gary did
not know the French language well enough to be able to write his own
novels.[9] Another critic from the Hussard clan, Stephen Hecquet, granted
the novel some qualities, but he too poked fun at what he saw as Gary's
tendency "to cheat on [verb] conjugations."[10] With the tone thus established, a number of other critics on the Right were delighted to amplify
these accusations in the days prior to the Goncourt decision.

If the press was divided along much clearer ideological lines than before, it was doubtless because Gary's own positions were finally explicitly delineated. In his earlier satires, the embittered sarcasm and iconoclastic humor made it hard to detect Gary's allegiances. If we take *Tulipe* as an example, what are we to make of a novelist who dedicates to Radical Socialist Léon Blum a book that reverses the historical roles of Hitler and de Gaulle and whose title refers to a carefree soldier from the days of France's absolute monarchy (Öostman 160)? But as I showed in my reading of the revised edition of *A European Education*, Gary now clearly announced Gaullist sympathies. *The Roots of Heaven* adds an occasional touch of anti-Communist sentiment as well (see *RH* 28–29, 64–65). Thus, while the most hostile reactions would still come from the far Right, the Communist papers—*L'Humanité, Ce Soir, Les Lettres françaises*, and, to an extent, *Combat* and *Le Franc-Tireur*—would now join in against him. One of the bluntest attacks came from PCF ideologue and polemicist André Wurmser, the daily editorialist for *L'Humanité* and part-time literary critic in the columns of *Les Lettres françaises*. Making light of Gary's "saccharin humanism" and professions of fidelity to de Gaulle, Wurmser accuses Gary of political opportunism: "Of course, there's a degree of baseness . . . in making a big show of one's anti-Communism at such an opportune moment . . . Like it or not, the Goncourt has acquired such far-reaching importance that the prize necessarily finds itself caught up in the pressures that weigh upon public opinion. The Goncourt is a *political* event, like everything that has repercussions (however fleeting) on people's minds. Romain Gary would not have won the prize in 1945, nor Elsa Triolet in 1956."[11]

One cannot really contest Wurmser's remarks on their general contextualization. Triolet's Communist ties certainly would have played to her advantage in 1945. The PCF was at the height of its influence, owing largely to its important role in the French domestic resistance and its control of the National Committee of Writers (Comité National des Écrivains, or CNE) overseeing the postwar cleanup of French letters. As a result, *L'Humanité* was at its peak circulation, and *Ce Soir* was right behind it as the fourth highest selling daily paper. Both outdistanced the *Figaro* and the fledgling *Monde*, ranked fifth and twelfth at the time (Bellanger 453). The mid-fifties, as Wurmser states, would see the political winds shift and the fortunes of the PCF slip considerably. In 1954, Prime Minister Mendès-France could allow himself to spurn Communist support for his governmental coalition (Mortimer 363), and de Gaulle's return to public life was gaining momentum with the publication of the first volume of his memoirs. Again, trends in the press reflected these changes. *Ce Soir* closed its doors in 1953, *Franc-Tireur* (which in 1948 had chased out journalists from the Right and veered toward the Communists) was in its dying throes, and *L'Humanité* had lost nearly half its sales (Bellanger 421–22; Albert 123). Benefiting from this realignment in public sentiment were the *Monde* and *France-Soir,* which under Lazareff's direction would become France's most prominent populist newspaper. This advantage for Gary is clear, since *France-Soir* had close ties with Gallimard and embraced Gaullism in the course of those years (Albert 123). Most importantly, however, as Wurmser insinuates, Gary's novel came out the very same week that the Soviet Union invaded Budapest. A telegram sent to Gaullist deputy and friend Jean de Lipkowski reveals Gary's sentiments on this issue: "We have to save the Hungarian elephants" (qtd. in Catonné, *Romain Gary* 29). In the wake of this public relations disaster for the PCF (among other consequences), Gary's stature as Companion of the Liberation could have well played in his favor.

Wurmser's partisan but astute assessment would prove correct. On December 3, 1956, with a good portion of the literary establishment solidly behind him, Gary won the Goncourt Prize he had so narrowly missed eleven years before. The jury elected Gary by a wide margin, with only one dissenting vote apiece going to Michel Butor's *L'emploi du temps* (Passing time) and Angelina Bardin's *Angelina, fille des champs* (Bona 172). Propelled by the award, half a million books would be sold in two years, dwarfing the meager three- and four-digit sales of Gary's three preceding works (Huston, *Tombeau de Romain Gary* 55). All things considered, Gary's victory is a logical one. Henriot had served on the Prix des Critiques jury that chose Gary in 1945, and Gary had the backing of France's two most respected newspapers, *Le Figaro* and *Le Monde.* In addition, the academy was weighted with septuagenarians (Arnoux, Billy, Dorgelès, Pierre Mac Orlan, and Francis Carco) who were perhaps less inclined to be enthusiastic about unconventional works like Butor's *Passing Time.*

But a closer look reveals the extent to which institutional decisions in the surprisingly small world of Parisian letters are inevitably tinged by various other personal motivations.

Henriot began corresponding with Gary as early as 1945 (see Calmann-Lévy Publishers' Archives), and the two had every reason to see eye-to-eye. Henriot is described by his biographer as a figure whose contribution to French letters is to "maintain [its] indispensable humanism" (Dulière, *Émile Henriot* 159). Henriot took his seat in the French Academy very seriously, became president of the Alliance Française in 1948, and compiled a copious series of volumes dedicated to French literary history (his *Courriers littéraires*). He thus shared with Gary a particular humanist notion of French culture as a collective heritage to be preserved, promulgated, and actualized. Moreover, he had the same penchant for literary romanticism (Stendhal in particular) and was on personal terms with de Gaulle (Dulière, *Amitié littéraire* 151). With respect to the Goncourt, he was in a good position to help Gary's cause, having spent part of the Occupation years in the company of Billy, Arnoux, and Carco (*Émile Henriot* 24).

A more unusual name to find in the literary columns is that of Corniglion-Molinier, destined to become minister of justice the following year. Here we see the old Free French connections at work. Corniglion-Molinier initially headed Gary's *Lorraine* squadron in Africa before becoming his commander in chief in the French air force in England. Corniglion-Molinier also had excellent ties with Malraux, having piloted the plane in 1934 that took Malraux on his Yemen expedition in search of the Queen of Sheba's lost realm; he also produced Malraux's award-winning film, *Sierra de Teruel*, in 1939. And looking further back, the television program *Un siècle d'écrivains* has since reported a considerably more personal note: Corniglion-Molinier had grown up in Nice, where it was rumored that he was the illegitimate half-brother of—Romain Gary!

Just as many of the endorsements have their own history, the attacks can be predictable, too. Leaving aside the straightforward ideological differences opposing Gary to the Hussards, I will limit my example to that of Wurmser's article. That Wurmser's objections are grounded in ideological and personal contentions is equally evident, given that the comparison between Gary and Triolet occurs in *Les Lettres françaises*, run by none other than Triolet's husband, Louis Aragon.

But the divide separating Wurmser and Gary runs deeper than this. The incident drawing them into indirect conflict in 1956—the Communist takeover of Hungary—is a more overt version of another incident that marked their past, the installation of Dimitrov's Communist regime in Bulgaria following World War II (King Boris III had sided with Germany, and thus Bulgaria was occupied by Soviet troops at war's end). During Gary's spell in Sofia, he befriended many of the Bulgarians fighting against Soviet domination. One of his closest acquaintances was Nikolai Petkov, Sorbonne-educated head of the Agrarian Union Party and editor in chief of a national newspaper that published *A European Education* in serial form, translated into Bulgarian. In reports to the Quay d'Orsay, Gary presents Petkov as "a man of great integrity . . . whose optimism is often little more than a form of courage" (qtd. in Bona 116). Petkov's anti-Communist activities led to his arrest, his conviction "on spurious charges of conspiring in an armed plot against the [Bulgarian] government," and, despite protests from Western governments, his death by hanging (Karel Bartošek, "Central and Southeastern Europe," in Courtois 401).

The PCF would present a very different account at the time. In a book prefaced by Wurmser, *L'Internationale des traîtres*, Renaud de Jouvenel argues that the Central European nations are being destroyed by a series of reactionary figures who have been bought out by foreign capitalist governments to turn against their own people. An entire chapter is dedicated to Petkov, denounced as a spy rightfully condemned by the tribunal (Jouvenel 63ff.). Wurmser fully supports de Jouvenel's inflammatory thesis, which in particular singles out members of the privileged class in these Eastern nations who are now living in the West and are actively or passively anti-Communist (Jouvenel 32–36). From Wurmser's point of view, Gary would fit this description perfectly: a Russian émigré returning to an Eastern bloc nation as a representative of the French government and thus of the ruling class. Gary would also be a natural target for Wurmser, given that Gary's two principal heroes, de Gaulle and Malraux, were the primary figures in the anti-Communist fervor that gripped the Rassemblement du Peuple Français (RPF) in its occasionally bloody campaign battles with the PCF in the late forties and early fifties (Lacouture 349–50).[12] The issues placing Gary and Wurmser in opposition thus are fundamental to both men but are only distantly reflected in *The Roots of Heaven*.

Once Gary was awarded the Goncourt, a second publicity campaign began. His literary career having suddenly come back to life, he was granted a brief leave of absence from his interim post in Bolivia for the extensive rounds of interviews and public appearances that accompany the prize. In the ten years since his last success, he had faded from public memory, and thus this second passage from anonymity to notoriety required that journalists renew the public's awareness of his general biography. Moreover, with *The Roots of Heaven* already crowned, the newspaper pieces that appeared from mid-December onward were of a different nature. Whereas reviews prior to the Goncourt decision evaluated the book's content for a more literary audience, many of the later articles concentrated on presenting the laureate to the public at large.

Having seen fame slip through his hands the first time, Gary was determined to make the best of this new opportunity. He was already a seasoned veteran at handling the media, since his extraliterary functions focused on assessing public perception and shaping opinion. In particular, his stint as press secretary for the French UN delegation allowed him to study the functioning of the mass media, a phenomenon largely foreign to France at the time with its state-run structures. Surrounded by the 579 journalists working the hallways of the UN Building, Gary made forty-seven live radio and television appearances and spoke at more than 250 press conferences in the 1952–54 period (Bona 149–51). Now that he found himself on a literary stage, he would negotiate its rituals with assurance and panache, and his willingness to play to the press would clearly accelerate the growth of his reputation: "His legend as a charmer is not overblown," writes Roger Grenier. "He is one of those people that it suffices to meet—and you cannot help but like him."[13] This ease with the media was complemented by a dandyish appearance that confirmed the image his books projected: "A healthy tan, impassive mustache, pale eyes a shade ironic, shiny eyebrows and Slavic charm . . . This writer-adventurer-hero-diplomat and man-of-the-world bears a profile appropriate for his persona."[14] Moreover, the fact that diplomatic duties kept him far from France in the early years of his career added the touch of mystique so propitious to nascent legends: "[Gary] is probably the most mysterious French writer of today. He is almost never seen in Paris."[15]

In the flurry of articles churned out by newspapers and magazines of all varieties, Gary's biography quickly became scrambled. Journalists confused him with Oklahoma governor *Raymond* Gary and identified his British wife as American.[16] A regional paper granted him a post in San Francisco, while even Henriot mistakenly presented him as a diplomat in West Africa (the setting of *The Roots of Heaven*).[17] Furthest off the mark was *Le Parisien libéré*, for whom Romain *Cary* [*sic*] was born in 1940![18]

While the errors cited here were doubtless due to shoddy journalism, Gary himself was the source of many other inaccuracies. The Goncourt brought him his first significant exposure on the public stage *as a writer*. Thus, parallel to his analysis of the creation of fictional legends, Gary was now himself an actor under the spotlight with the opportunity to orchestrate his own persona. His diplomatic career was firmly established, and he no longer seems to have felt a need to negotiate timidly with his past. As one might imagine, his conception of the constructed nature of public figures (the Gaullist fable in the revised version of *A European Education* and Morel's strategic legend in *The Roots of Heaven*, as well as Gary's articles on de Gaulle) would become central to his handling of celebrity. And not all of his fictions are gratuitous improvisation, for one can distinguish a few general directions taken by his fables.

The first area of concentration completed a project begun decades before. As we saw in Chapter 1, at roughly the same time as his literary career began, Gary was already at work muddying the trace of his origins. His name underwent a series of mutations, as did his nationality. Initially, this was relatively private, moving through administrative processes to distance himself by increments from the Russian Jew Kacew. By 1951, the primary elements of Gary's legal identity—place of birth, national origin, name, parentage, date of birth—had all become fabrications entangled in his literary persona.[19]

Recognizing that his literary success provided an opportunity to build a more definitive and striking identity to replace that of Roman Kacew, Gary resumed his tale spinning with a more elaborate turn. Thus, the pseudonym Romain Gary was now not a nom de guerre adopted during the Resistance but a name given to him by his mother to make him sound more French.[20] For her part, Nina Owczinski had become French in most articles, with Gary's foreign birth due only to her theatrical engagements in Moscow: "She wanted to give birth in France, but she arrived too late," *Combat* quotes Gary as saying.[21] On another occasion, the tale becomes even more elaborate, with Gary's birth again shifted to Poland: "From what I've been told, we were going from Moscow to Paris for my mother to give birth . . . and I was born in a small clinic next door to the Polish theater of Wilno. My mother said she wasn't feeling well, so we had to stop in Wilno, but I wonder if this wasn't just her way of apologizing for not having had me in France" (qtd. in Huston, *Tombeau de Romain Gary* 17). Presenting himself as being born in proximity of a theater is entirely appropriate for this writer-cum-performer. As for Gary's father, he was announced alternately as a Russian-born French national employed at the French embassy in Saint Petersburg, a Russian diplomat, or an organizer of traveling theater troupes.[22] In falling back on this mysterious "from what I've been told"—the voice of legends, tall tales, and rumors—Gary was making little attempt to hide his fables, but each of these anecdotes was passed along as news by the press. Curiously, journalists never objected to any of these contradictions.

While this first area of concern settled scores with his humble beginnings, the second tried to influence his categorization within the literary field. Gary identified Malraux on numerous occasions as his mentor, claiming, for instance, that Malraux was the first to have encouraged him to pursue a literary career back in 1935.[23] Gary further nursed this association by drawing on the tactics Malraux perfected: as mentioned earlier, Gary claimed on occasion to have participated in the Spanish Civil War. Paul Chadourne, extrapolating from the *Cadran* biography, writes, "Journalist during the Spanish Civil War, [Gary] experienced first-hand the rigors of Spanish jails, having been arrested for his anti-fascist activities."[24] Much like the irony of Malraux passing himself off as an archaeologist in Indochina when he was in fact pilfering their national treasures, Gary was publishing in *Gringoire* at roughly the time he claims to have been fighting for the Republican cause in Spain. Again, these discrepancies never surfaced, and it did not take long for accounts to put Gary in Malraux's aviation unit, *España* (see Elgey 2). Now on the verge of fame, Gary again linked their names during an acceptance speech for the Goncourt Prize: "There is one thing that would give me as much joy as having received the Goncourt: seeing the Nobel Prize [for Literature] awarded to André Malraux."[25] Such a pronouncement was a tribute to an admired icon, but also a way to try to ride on his coattails or place himself within the same field of reference (Gaullist, humanist, adventure novelist, man of action). When a critic as influential as Pierre de Boisdeffre compared Gary to Camus and Malraux—even if Gary came out on the short end of it—Gary's goal had been attained.[26]

The allusions to Malraux are not without justification. In literary terms, *The Roots of Heaven* is, along with *The Colors of the Day* right before it, the most recognizably Malrucian of Gary's novels. In addition to its thematic and formal debts, it functions similarly to *The Royal Way* or *The Conquerors* in its manipulation of authorial image. By returning to the regions Gary frequented during the Resistance, by presenting characters who are described as being ex-members of Gary's air force squadron or who wear the Cross of Lorraine (the medal distributed by de Gaulle to veterans of the Free French forces), by having Morel resist the degradation of humanist values, *The Roots of Heaven* leads the reader to identify the protagonist with the author. Add to this certain presumed personal resemblances — both author and hero have a markedly anachronistic, elusive, and solitary demeanor that makes them something of a mystery to the press — and one can be led to presume autobiographical inspiration. Pierre Rocher even speaks of *The Roots of Heaven* as a "novelized documentary," while the usually more circumspect Hubert Juin goes so far as to class it among nonfiction works: "This is an excellent job of reporting. Romain Gary brings to mind Kessel's most spectacular pieces."[27]

Whereas it was generally understood that *A European Education* was a work of pure imagination, we see here that *The Roots of Heaven* was assimilated in some cases to nonfiction genres. With his reputation of Resistance hero fresh in everyone's mind, in addition to the ecological argument and firsthand knowledge of the terrain, Gary moved into the category of committed writer (*écrivain engagé*). René Lalou writes, "By everything that it implies, as by everything that it so vigorously portrays, [Gary's] work is certainly one of those that do honor to the literature of commitment."[28] Further proof that this trait of Gary's public image became clearly established can be found in the fact that even his detractors agreed on the label; they simply gave it a different valorization. In a lengthy article belittling *The Roots of Heaven*, a journalist from the Communist paper *Franc-Tireur* ironizes that Gary has assimilated Malraux's "man-of-action writing techniques," concluding, "No one will reproach [Gary] with being too Ivory Tower; this is a man of 'commitment.'"[29]

At the same time, nearly every article about Gary played on the popular appeal of his dual career as diplomat and writer. The succession of posts in a variety of exotic locales, plus the connotations of distinguished urbanity, added another seductive trait to the image of this emerging celebrity whose appearance more resembled that of a Slavic Errol Flynn than a bureaucrat. Gary was no longer just a writer but a statesman, called upon to defend humanist beliefs in an official capacity. His declaration from La Paz acknowledging his Goncourt Prize shows to what extent he enjoyed mixing his roles of author, diplomat, and war hero:

I'm torn between the joy of winning the Goncourt Prize and the sadness of realizing that the ideals of liberty and human dignity that I defend in my book have never been so threatened.

The appeal that I am making to all writers worthy of the name throughout the world—that the Rights of Man be respected—receives only rounds from automatic weapons in response. I will continue to defend, both in my life and in my books, what I have ceaselessly defended, gun-in-hand, since 1936.[30]

This echoes earlier remarks, such as his answer to the question of where he would prefer to be assigned as a diplomat: "It does not matter where, as long as I can continue to fight the good fight and write" ("Romain Gary," *Cadran* 18: 31). On the one side, then, he falls into the group of hardened adventurers and unconventional reporters, sleeves rolled up, short on philosophy but long on courage. And on the other side, there is the elite fraternity of statesmen-writers, urbane and cosmopolitan. Gary was in the position of being able to occupy most all of the points along the way between the two extremes, due to the variety of related stereotypes that he could claim in his past—vagabond and émigré, Resistance hero, man of action, committed writer, reporter, French diplomat, intellectual, and man of letters. This third area of elaborating his authorial identity thus consists of capitalizing on a number of the roles he would play in public life to consolidate his social persona and authorial persona.

With this catalog of figures at his disposal, he merely needed to produce a succession of episodes confirming these personae, the *gesta* of his legend. The apparently true story from World War II of a miraculous landing after his reconnaissance plane was hit by enemy fire resurfaced during promotion of the rerelease of *A European Education*: on November 25, 1943, with the pilot blinded and Gary's abdomen lacerated, Gary, the navigator, guides them back to the base, where the sightless pilot manages on his third attempt to land the plane with no further damage.[31] Playing off of such accounts, Gary spun new tales to add to his already impressive biography. One of the most outlandish examples is his story of a bet made with a friend that Gary could seduce Clark Gable's date in a London bar. Taking advantage of the 15 to 1 odds his friend offers him, Gary wins over the ravishing redheaded Irish girl, invites her back to his room, but then is forced to exit the building via a fireman's ladder when a bomb rips the facade off the hotel.[32]

The public at large had no way of differentiating between the truthful and the fanciful in these stories, and thus even when these anecdotes did not find their way into Gary's novels, they contributed to the contours of his authorial persona. Most of these instances of fabrication are difficult to document, for legends tend to circulate without their sources. Nonetheless, it is worth untangling some of these tales because it is here that Gary's public fabulation enters into a more complex relation with his writing.

In his interviews, he often fell into behaving like a character from one of his own novels. Asked about his commitment to protecting endangered species, for example, Gary assured his interviewer, in an article that was decisive in Gary's quest for the Goncourt, that a freak accident awakened him to the urgency of wildlife conservation (Bauër, *Journal d'Alger*). Gary went into greater detail on another occasion. As he told it, he was a passenger during World War II in a small spy plane skimming recklessly close to the surface of an African lake. Without warning, the plane struck an elephant, killing the pilot and the beast. Gary, badly shaken, extricated himself from the plane and was gathering his wits when an outdoorsman confronted him on the shore: "It was then that a man in shorts and a pith helmet suddenly materialized, carrying a rifle. He punched me right in the face. I thought it was to bring me back to my senses, but I realized I was mistaken when I heard him add: 'You have no right to treat animals that way.' "[33] Journalists passed this tale along as accurate, despite its improbability.[34] Here the techniques of public self-invention had become indistinguishable from those of the novelist constructing his narrative; Gary had become Morel, recounting adventures in West Africa. The activity simply changed venues, from the typewriter to the press conference. Moreover, whereas Gary's maneuvers at the publication of *A European Education* were aimed at stabilizing his material circumstances, the interviews now had become part and parcel of his literary production.

When Gary acted out his authorial persona in this manner, he fell into a circular process of invention. His life's activities were seen as the origin of his novel, which encouraged belief in its contents. But this allowed Gary to take on a profile drawn from the world of his fictional characters and use it to work up new episodes for his works in progress. In the example above, once Gary's tale about the death of the elephant became public knowledge, it underwent several variations in succeeding interviews before later being incorporated into a supposedly autobiographical work, *Promise at Dawn* (*PD* 356).

This practice of fabulation used within one novel to provide the history of another is disorienting for biographers and critics alike. When *Promise at Dawn* retroactively explains important features of *The Roots of Heaven*, features that could feasibly alter one's interpretation of the work, one wonders whether it is in a fictional or factual mode.[35] As a result of this technique, novels could be continually reinterpreted or extended in light of an ever-evolving authorial persona readjusted in succeeding works. Any distinction between Gary's literary and biographical persona becomes difficult to establish, since the fictions he has written encroach upon his own extraliterary behavior. As with the works of Malraux and

Cendrars, Gary's biography and novels benefit reciprocally: the weight of his life story lends authenticity to his heroes, and his protagonists' exploits seep into his own legend.

Consecration of the Legend (1960)

Gary's next major publication, *Promise at Dawn*, shifts the shaping of his legend into a new stage. In his previous works, even though they contain allusions to aspects of his past, Gary never appears nominally. The adventure novels only raise the possibility of a biographical connection between his life and characters, without ever specifying the nature of this relation. In *Promise at Dawn*, Gary uses for the first time his proper name, the first person, and by all formal appearances sets out to tell us the tale of how he became a writer.[36] An autobiographical work written midway through his career would represent a direct intervention into the composition of his public portrait, particularly given the existence of a large readership eager to learn more about the foreign-born author's mysterious past.

Though the narrator speaks to us from the present, his biographical account only takes us up to the end of World War II. *Promise at Dawn* thus purports to recount everything *prior* to Gary's entry into public life. In theory, then, it should more properly be considered the autobiography of Roman Kacew, a restoration of his occluded past. On the surface, the work seems to confirm this expectation. The self-deprecating, intimate anecdotes are disarming and speak of facets of Gary's past that he had previously taken care to hide (his Jewish ancestry, his birth in Russia, the uncertainty of his origins, etc.).

The novel's central theme is Gary's struggle to live up to the extravagant expectations placed upon him by his mother. A key image in this regard is the search for a pseudonym, *the* pseudonym, the one that would facilitate his passage from impoverished Russian immigrant to French diplomat and famous author: " 'We have to find you a pseudonym,' [my mother] said sternly. 'A great French writer cannot have a Russian name. If you were a virtuoso violinist, it would be great, but, for a titan of French literature, it just won't do' " (*PD* 24). Indeed, this gesture fits the classic scenario of socially motivated pseudonyms, but avowed here in an intimate and playful manner.

Curiously, though, for all its seeming demystification of Gary's identity, this account of his literary apprenticeship forefronts the notion that an appropriate authorial image takes precedence over all else, even the works themselves: "To start our dreams on the road to realization, all that remained for [my mother and me] to do was find a pseudonym worthy of the masterpieces the world was expecting from us. I spent entire days closed up in my room, blackening page after page with tremendous names . . . The idea that these hours of labor could have been put to better use by actually writing the masterpieces in question never crossed our minds" (*PD* 31–32). The quest for the right image, referred to by the narrator as his daily "rosary of pseudonyms," takes on the trappings of a religious ritual where the conjurative powers of each name are assessed by his mother and him.

What should we make of this account? The tenor of the prospective names places the episode under the sign of adolescent romanticism. There is a sprinkling of aristocratic patronyms (Roland de Chantecler, Romain de Mysore, Hubert de la Roche Rouge) and a predilection for pseudo-Spanish derivatives or other exotic inspirations (Alexandre Natal, Armand de La Torre, Roland Campeador, Artémis Kohinore). Romain Gary's generalized irony in these passages seems to imply that these are youthful excesses consigned to days long past. Yet, as we saw with his behavior in 1956, the issue of authorial self-invention would remain at the root of his practice of writing—and thus there would appear to be no rupture with this initial adolescent stage. To shift the question slightly, we can ask: Is *Promise at Dawn* really the autobiography of Roman Kacew or is it pure fabrication? Is it an attempt at accurate self-representation or does it use these supposedly biographical details as the springboard to a work of fiction? Catonné points out that it is precisely "the ambiguity of this confession that [has] contributed to its success" (*Romain Gary* 143). Gary deliberately casts his story in a register where it is up to us *to choose to believe* (or not) in the image of himself that he offers.

What appears to be a full confession is in truth another sleight-of-hand deftly executed by Gary. It promises essentially to recount the passage from Kacew to Gary. Yet, despite the fact that fully one-third of the novel is dedicated to his search for a pseudonym, the narrator never gets around to telling us something as fundamental as how he settled upon *Gary*. Gary in fact is not preoccupied with telling us how he became a talented novelist; the craft of writing is constantly put aside at the expense of self-invention. *Promise at Dawn* recounts not the metamorphosis from Kacew to Gary but the *legend of that metamorphosis.* In playing on the illusory promise of unveiling the story "outside" of his fictions (i.e., the origins of the writer), Gary in fact only buries it further.

The refusal of autobiography in favor of mythologization is built into the dynamic of the story. A good part of the dramatic intensity arises from Gary's attempt to bridge the gap between his humble beginnings and his mother's seemingly unrealizable expectations. With the reader already aware of Gary's professional achievements, however, the improbable yet necessary advancement of the novel's protagonist makes his success seem fated. Behind the moving tribute to his mother's determination is concealed a particularly effective claim: given the force of his mother's will and love, given his own sense of obligation to prove himself worthy of such devotion, it was *inevitable* that he become a famous author. In explaining a known event (Gary's accomplishments) with a fictional origin (the reinvention of his childhood), in giving this progression the air of destiny, Gary slips from the structure of autobiography to that of myth and legend.[37]

To some extent, Gary himself signals the nature of this project. The publisher's insert for *Promise at Dawn,* which Gary elected to write, owns up to the essential part fiction plays in this work's composition: "This book is based on my life, but it is not an autobiography. At every instant, artistic preoccupations slipped in between the event and its literary expression . . . In the end, be it by pen, paintbrush or chisel, all truths boil down to artistic truths."[38] Exceeding any possible verisimilitude (as in his account of eating a kilo of cherry pits and ten meters of cotton thread to impress a would-be girlfriend), Gary's inflated portraits pitch the tale on a plane other than the autobiographical and should in principle draw attention to the artifice employed.

Promise at Dawn pushes the logic of this process of self-invention to its extreme. In this passage from his years in Nice, Gary describes his reaction to a neighbor who tries to provoke him by calling him the "offspring of a circus act and an adventurer": "It was thus that my interesting origins were suddenly revealed to me, though [this discovery] did not bother me in the least. I gave no importance to what I could or could not have been at some temporary, transitional stage, since I knew that I was destined for dizzying heights" (*PD* 47). In basing his authorial identity on his legend rather than on his past, Gary operated according to the notion that the facts about Kacew are irrelevant since Kacew could and would become someone else, anyone else. Since there was to be no determinate relation between his past and present selves, the basic objectives of autobiography—explaining the passage from past to present—are futile.

In this aspect, Gary drew another lesson from one of his primary models, Malraux. In the course of his career, Malraux formulated a strategic model for self-invention, which functions first by the conception of an ideal image of oneself, followed by premeditating one's subsequent actions in the aim of embodying that persona.[39] One becomes in a sense the product of one's own imagination, and for Malraux this operation was an inaugural act of personality formation. Malraux thus granted a prophetic quality to certain fabulations, where the legend leads to the materialization of its imaginings.

Malraux's own experience bears this out. The belief that Malraux was a factor in popular uprisings in Canton, Annam, or Shanghai is due to the

legend he created through his early novels and fabulations, yet this reputation would suffice to earn him a conspicuous role during the Spanish
Civil War. With his experience in Spain retroactively lending credence
to his Asian legend, Malraux would command enough respect to be able
to declare himself captain among resistance fighters in the Lot. From
the Spanish Civil War onward, in other words, Malraux *would become* (his
tardy Resistance commitment notwithstanding) what he had previously
only pretended to be. Far from being an example of bad faith, Malraux
considered this trait to be one of the marks of the true creator, citing
Victor Hugo and de Gaulle as models: "This metamorphosis, one of the
most profound that man can create, transforms a destiny endured into a
destiny directed." [40]

Gary's conception of art revolved precisely around the idea that what
is normally taken as a purely figurative transformation can in fact literally pass into reality. Romain Kacew and his uncertain origins—Gary can
say it with confidence in 1960 because Kacew has already been legally
buried for nine years—were things of the past from the moment a novel
appeared bearing the name Romain Gary. *Promise at Dawn* makes this perfectly clear; upon learning of Cresset Press's acceptance of *Forest of Anger*,
the narrator simply states, "I was born" (*PD* 374).

Throughout his career, Gary was adept at creating a play of mirrors between the plot dynamics in a given novel and his own situation as author.
If we return to *The Roots of Heaven*, we see that Morel, in being named,
judged, and defined by others, undergoes a sort of doubling. He begins
to exist *for the public* only from the moment that he becomes a legend;
that is, a fictional construction *narrated by others*. His double, once it enters
into the public domain, takes on an existence of its own, becomes active
in spheres independent of Morel himself. Thus, the legendary figure of
Morel cannot be considered identical to Morel himself, just as Partisan
Nadejda corresponds to no known individual. In *The Roots of Heaven*, in
other words, Morel, as he is reconstructed through various accounts, is
never supposed to represent a realistic depiction of a human character:
"I wanted to create a legendary persona," Gary states. "Malraux told me,
'Critics were wrong to judge Morel as a fictional character. He's a mythical character. Your book is not a novel, it's a myth'" (qtd. in Guth 4). By
citing Malraux as his authority, given Malraux's well-known penchant for
mythomania, Gary as much as suggests that what applies to Morel in this
regard applies to himself as well. In an interview organized by longtime
friend François Bondy, Gary is even more explicit:

Bondy: I have the impression that you have deliberately allowed a completely inaccurate image of yourself to gain credit . . . Let's take, for example, the Spanish

Civil War. You have never set foot in Spain—not before, not during and not after the civil war. Yet from *A European Education* up through the Goncourt, the newspapers have repeated that you are a former pilot of the España squadron. To the best of my knowledge, you have never denied this . . .
Gary: It's wonderful to have a legend. (Bondy, "Le moment de la vérité" 3)

The timeliness of *Promise at Dawn* for this project can be measured by the assumptions we find in various reviews. For example: "[Gary] is famous enough that we more or less know his background . . . This long book of confidences will give more precision to the general features. It interests us because it is a varied, unpredictable and eventful story. But most of all, it brings us closer to a man no longer protected or disguised by fiction." [41] On the contrary, as we have just seen, *Promise at Dawn* accomplishes a consolidation of Gary's new identity, putting the truth about Kacew's origins out of reach. It fixes the points of reference in Gary's legend and provides the narrative that allows the public to assemble the disparate adventures around a coherent, unified persona. Having drawn his civilian identity from his literary production in a most concrete way, Gary has succeeded on every level in his attempt at self-invention. *Promise at Dawn*'s complex narrative structure, consisting of overlapping flashbacks, refines the catalogue of images associated with his public persona and rehearses the sequence of key episodes: the disadvantaged youth struggling under the weight of his mother's unreasonable expectations; the hardships of a young foreigner in Paris during the thirties; the patriot, more-French-than-the-French in his dedication to the Resistance; the soldier's sacrifices recompensed by the diplomatic career; the novelist crowned with success. Using the means of fiction, he has invented himself in the real world, giving himself a past that serves to explain his present.

Although in truth it deals only tangentially with the craft of writing, *Promise at Dawn* nonetheless presents Gary as a writer who only happens to be a war hero and diplomat. This reverses the priorities revealed by his correspondence in the Calmann-Lévy period. The fact that *Promise at Dawn*'s overarching narrative is a *literary* biography means that the legends of the bastard child, soldier, and diplomat are trotted out in the service of the author, and not the other way around. *Promise at Dawn* scripts Gary's identity *as an author*. The creation of this marketable identity is complete. Not coincidentally, this consecration of his image is the most durable contribution to his personal legend and corresponds to the peak of his literary reputation. [42]

The Satirist

> *Mother Peep: To demystify, you must first mystify. We need a new mystification . . .*
> *Voice from the crowd: Up with the mystification of the demystifiers! . . .*
> *Up with the new mystification!*
>
> *Ionesco,* The Killer *76*

Thus far, we have focused on the three key moments of Gary's ascension, each tied to a period of intensive media interest generated by his most acclaimed works: *A European Education* (1945), *The Roots of Heaven* (1956), and *Promise at Dawn* (1960).

One can say with some justification that the Prix des Critiques for *A European Education* was in recognition more of the novel than the novelist, a celebration of the Resistance and of a humanistic longing for a reunited Europe. It crowned the values expressed, not the individual expressing them. (Similarly, the Goncourt Prize of the same year went to a novel on the German Occupation by the then-unknown Jean-Louis Bory.) Henceforth, however, Gary would be a writer with a reputation. In reviews of *The Roots of Heaven,* he was "the writer to watch, whether he wins [the Goncourt] or not" (Berchet). Thus, when the Goncourt Prize did come his way, it could this time be considered an acknowledgment of Gary's status as an author; it rendered official a certain rank in France's literary hierarchy. The third stage, *Promise at Dawn,* capitalized on this consecration. By presenting Gary's life under the guise of autobiography but in the mode of legend, it accelerated a move from the restricted field of literary recognition to general celebrity.

But a curious feature in this career trajectory is the inability of Gary's popular works to drag along in their wake his other books. Gilbert Ganne's essay on the phenomenon of best-selling authors states that once writers settle onto the highest sales plateau, they are thereafter assured a minimum audience of fifty thousand in immediate (i.e., sight unseen) sales for each new book (Ganne, *Messieurs les Best-Sellers* 19–20, 25). While *The Roots of Heaven* would come much closer than *A European Education* to reaching the sales threshold identified by Ganne, it is nonetheless surprising that the first runs of *Tulipe, The Company of Men,* and *The Colors of the Day* did not come close to exhausting the stock of their cautious first editions, a mere five thousand copies each. Moreover, it is clear from surveying the reviews of *The Roots of Heaven* that rare is the critic who remembered any of Gary's books other than *A European Education,* conveniently reissued right before *The Roots of Heaven* appeared.[43] The other works, already out of circulation by 1956, would essentially be edited out of Gary's collected works in just a matter of years. Two other works bracketed around *Promise at Dawn*—*L'homme à la colombe* (1958) and *Johnnie Cœur* (1961)—would meet with the same fate.

The question then arises as to why these particular books were so quickly erased from Gary's corpus. What is it about these novels that ostracizes them? Is it really that they are so definitively inferior to Gary's acclaimed works?

Clearly, it would be an understatement to say that some of the commercially unsuccessful publications failed to find favor with the critics. Theater critic for the *Figaro* (with its wealthy readership) and former Goncourt winner himself, Jean-Jacques Gautier was influential enough to make or break a play in Paris during the fifties and sixties. In his review of the stage adapatation of *Johnnie Cœur*, he can hardly find words for his outrage, calling the work, "a sarcastico-lyrical hodge-podge, a pretentious 'scribble-fest,' a nonsensical, juvenile meli-melodrama."[44] Even by Parisian standards, the abusiveness of the criticism goes to extremes, sliding quickly from aesthetic assessment to personal insult: "Like all wordsmiths, that is to say starving artists, I regularly fall prey to envy. It devours me. Ah! But here is a play—*Johnnie Cœur*—that I am most happy not to have written, and I pity Romain Gary, a man of culture, refinement and integrity, for having to reread his own work (if only to proof the galleys)!"[45] Directed by François Perier, the play would open the following year to a chorus of boos from both national and regional dailies: *Le Monde, La Libération, Le Parisien Libéré, Combat, Le Bulletin Critique*, and *La Résonance Lyonnaise* all panned it.[46]

Given the virulence of these responses, one wonders if the rejection of these works is also due to other factors. In the remainder of this chapter, I will explore the hypothesis that these works' subject matter and their incompatibility with Gary's legend contributed equally to their failure, and I will explore the consequences of the omission of these books for an interpretation of Gary's work and image.

The process of selection between Gary's well-known and his forgotten works cuts along surprisingly simple lines. Beginning with the first part of his career, one easily detects the significant difference in nature between *A European Education* and its three successors. Though bleak in its depiction of the partisans' suffering, *A European Education* remains a novel dedicated to what one could call "highest" in humankind, a novel of humanism's victory over fascism. The follow-ups, on the contrary, are mired in a profound state of pessimism, focusing on the negative repercussions of World War II. Catonné succinctly summarizes *Tulipe*, for instance, as taking place "in the postwar ruins and rubble with humanist faith veering off into charlatanism" (*Romain Gary* 135). *The Company of Men* argues against the facile Manicheism and retributive mentality of post-Liberation France, while *The Colors of the Day* points dejectedly to the fighting in Korea as an indication that the peace after World War II is only a brief pause in a continuing series of potentially global cataclysms. This contrast persists at later stages of Gary's work. *The Roots of Heaven* and *Promise at Dawn* are strong affirmations of romantic idealism, while *L'homme à la colombe* and *Johnnie Cœur* are diatribes against the failure of the UN to defend the values upon which it was founded, thus cutting into hopes for a peaceful future. The group of failed works, in other words, casts serious doubt on the society dreamed up by his three top sellers.

As is perhaps often the case, Gary's cynicism seems born of disappointed optimism, a dashed hope that the euphoria at the end of World War II would change not just the political tables but humankind as well. One can argue, then, that his satires grated on readers' nerves for more reasons than just their literary imperfections: Gary's works were among the first to call into question the heroic character of the victorious Allied populations, and did so at a time when France was seeking to heal the wounds suffered in the military defeat of 1940 and the moral defeat of the ensuing collaboration.

At first glance, the harsh contrast between the idealist thematics of the humanist novels and the bitter, iconoclastic mockery of such idealism in the satires is confounding. Gary seems to be shooting himself in the foot. Whereas the legendary hero is endorsed as a vehicle of humanism in *The Roots of Heaven*, the revised version of *A European Education*, and *Promise at Dawn*, the vicious satires of self-promoting charlatans and false messiahs tear that same model to pieces.

In *L'homme à la colombe*, for example, Johnnie, disgusted with the UN's inertia and the exploitative indifference of the media, dreams of committing "some immense moral con job or prodigious abuse of confidence to avenge his lost illusions and show that he [is] completely cured of his idealistic aberrations" (46–47). Wanting to prove that he is no longer taken in by the diplomats' gesticulations of indignation and calls to action, Johnnie sets out to beat them at their own game, staging a bogus hunger strike from within a room hidden in the depths of the UN Building. Johnnie surrounds himself with agents and publicists in order to program the evolution of his campaign and orchestrate each self-serving protest action. Reporters on the political beat, too saturated with UN pontification to be moved by expressions of sincerity, perk up their ears only when Johnnie's promoter explains that his client is a fraud:

"But are you sure that he's really a scumbag?" asked [a journalist].
"Kids, . . . what we have here is an authentic abuse of confidence in the grand old tradition of our fathers, a young man ready to make us laugh while he makes himself a little money" (*HC* 64).

The journalists are seduced by the novelty of this candid approach and become accomplices in Johnnie's social manipulation. Along similar lines, the parody of Christlike social crusaders in *Tulipe* attacks the establishment of legends in its oldest, strictest sense of the term: it borrows a pseudepigraphical format to sort out the "truth" in the legend of a Resistance hero-cum-social activist.[47]

Not only do these shams exploit the same types of cause championed by the heroes of *A European Education* and *The Roots of Heaven,* but they exploit the same strategies. *Tulipe*'s explicit parody of the sanctification of a social crusader poses problems for readings of *The Roots of Heaven,* since the latter consists of a Jesuit priest collecting testimonials about Morel's deeds (the archetype of a hagiographical record). Moreover, Morel himself is already walking in the footsteps of Father Charles-Eugène de Foucauld, mentioned by name in the novel (*RH* 31) and candidate for sainthood since 1926. Symbols closely tied to these heroic figures are now turned into derision. In *L'homme à la colombe,* Johnnie eats during his hunger strike in order to find the strength to continue fasting. Gary also attacks other prominent postwar figures, deflating, for instance, Sartre's "L'existentialisme est-il un humanisme?" by citing it in an inappropriate context (*JC* 140). The use of the press to amplify one's message follows the same pattern as in the heroic novels, where Morel, like de Gaulle, carefully weighs the symbolic effects of each "outlaw" action—Johnnie, however, does it with utter cynicism: "I need some collusion . . . I need the press, television . . . A few thoroughly-corrupt journalists, ripe enough to be squeezed, always at my beck and call" (*JC* 33). The reading public is not spared either. Learning that his cause is gaining momentum, Johnnie exclaims, "[The public] bought it! That's what they're there for. Whenever it's a question of believing, hoping and buying into something, . . . the public can always be counted on" (*JC* 57). This troubling reversibility of Gary's heroic themes even extends to his most cherished of sacred cows, de Gaulle and the Resistance. In *Tulipe,* Gary commits the heresy of imagining a time in the future when historians, lacking sufficient documentation, will have inadvertently switched the roles of some of World War II's principal figures:

Resistance: action brought by the German people from 1940 to 1945 against the invader, during the period in which French armies occupied Germany under the command of a "leader" named Charles de Gaulle. The latter was finally defeated at Stalingrad by the Chinese and committed suicide with his mistress Eva Braun in the ruins of Paris.[48]

One can easily imagine that this passage failed to raise any laughter at Colombey-les-Deux-Églises, all the more so given that one of the most hostile reproaches against de Gaulle's vision of the executive office was that it was too "dictatorial." Gary's point here, of course, is quite the opposite. By providing a satirical account in which the heroes and villains have been reversed, an account in which fascism and the Holocaust are completely absent, he is seeking to warn that the lessons of the war and Nazi Germany have not been learned and that history must be heeded.

These controversial and unpopular works thus have the merit of zeroing in on several key ethical questions, looking at the social and personal uses of legends and what gets swept under the carpet in their creation. They examine the risks in the public's susceptibility, as well as the tendency of legendary figures to fall dupe to their own images. These satires only partially resolve these questions and leave us uncertain of how to evaluate Gary's positions in these contradictory branches of his literary production. One can attribute the public's refusal to accept the pessimistic portion of Gary's work to any number of factors, but because his own legend is anchored in tales of idealism, victory, and rebirth, it clearly is difficult to integrate into this legend the dismantling of the *topoi* that grounded its creation.

This is what is unfortunate in the dismissal of these novels, for they in fact address the contradictions that are at work here. Taken together, these overlooked works are a scathing critique of modern myths, particularly with respect to their sociopolitical roles. They announce a suspicion of a postwar infatuation with legends at the very moment that Gary's own would take on significant dimensions.[49]

No doubt a great deal of this angst reflects Gary's experience in postwar politics. He moved through a succession of posts that confronted him with the shortcomings of his contemporaries in power. Following the tragic debacle witnessed in Bulgaria, Gary spent two years working on European reconstruction only to see it unexpectedly dashed when the French themselves cast the fatal vote against a common European defense project. When he wound up at the UN as spokesperson for the French delegation, he found himself in the role of ventriloquist, part statesman, part press attaché. He was required to present policies dictated by others and was in the sensitive position of eloquently defending stances at times contrary to his own views, particularly with respect to the French colonies in Indochina and North Africa. The vehemence of Gary's criticisms of the diplomatic milieu and the UN reveals an awkward doubling, an acute bout of guilty conscience. His writings on the subject are of such violence that they could have seriously compromised the standing of the French delegation in New York.[50]

But while the outrage is patent in his sociopolitical critiques, it would be a mistake to restrict the scope of this satirical venom to his diplomatic disappointments. As we have seen, Gary could marshal the components of his own legend with tremendous ease. In fifteen years, he had consolidated a coherent but varied ensemble of elements where biography, novels, and public persona were mutually reenforcing. At the same time, however, Gary was growing aware that this facility with role-playing spelled a definite danger for him. It is one thing to be recognized as a convincing disciple of André Malraux; it is another to find oneself feeding the elephants at the Vincennes Zoo as part of a *Paris-Match* photo promotion for *The Roots of Heaven*.[51]

Gary's reputation had reached beyond literary circles and taken on new connotations and a different momentum. In 1951, the Gallimard publishing firm struck up a joint venture with *France-Soir*, whose peak circulation in this period set a new record at more than 1.1 million daily copies (Charon 101). Thus, when the newspaper's director, Lazareff, and Gary became friends in 1956, the agreements were already in place to facilitate Gary becoming a regular contributor. This collaboration would continue into the seventies, with *France-Soir* first printing *Les trésors de la mer Rouge* in serialized form. In other areas, the handful of big-budget film adaptations derived from Gary's works (see Bibliography) would also prove a decisive factor in this transition. Prominent directors and producers like John Huston, Darryl Zanuck, Peter Ustinov, George Cukor, and Jules Dassin; and stars such as Errol Flynn, Juliette Greco, Orson Welles, Henry Fonda, Melina Mercouri, Gina Lollabrigida, Sophia Loren, Paul Newman, Leslie Caron, Charlotte Rampling, and David Niven were of an entirely different order of celebrity, and they boosted Gary's status through an effect of contagion (which was facilitated by the fact that Gary lived in Hollywood as French consul during those years). The daily media updates surrounding the production and release of these films often exceeded anything generated by the original books.

At this point, the development of Gary's image would be taken largely out of his hands. It would shift to another model of celebrity, from that of a literary type to that of an entertainment figure. Even when Gary put an end to his high-profile assignment in Southern California in 1959, he did so only to begin an equally high-profile relationship with American actress Jean Seberg. Beginning in the year of her role in *Breathless* (1960) and leading to the disintegration of their respective marriages, their romance was frequently documented by paparazzi working in Italy and on the French Riviera.

Gary's literary reputation would be compromised in proportion to the extension of his general visibility. He was, of course, far from innocent in this process. As his correspondence with Calmann-Lévy demonstrates, he actively pursued literary prizes. When he did finally break through with *The Roots of Heaven* and *Promise at Dawn*, he willingly developed his image, as if it were an external facet of himself whose marketing would leave him unscathed. Upon learning of the latter's great popularity, he requested sick leave from his post in Hollywood in order to return to Paris for additional promotional operations (Catonné, *Romain Gary* 224). It was especially *Promise at Dawn* that, in rehearsing Gary's image *too* effectively, further enabled this transformation in his status. Gary can hardly be cast as a victim at this juncture, for he all too clearly paved the way for his own commodification.

An underlying assumption in many of the most vitriolic attacks on Gary is that he excluded his own persona from the barbed critiques in the satires. In looking at Gary's early literary failures, however, one is struck by an unmistakable pattern. Right on the heels of his first success, *A European Education* (1945), comes *Tulipe* (1946), which satirizes the production of public images for propaganda purposes. Similarly, the next work after his Goncourt Prize for *The Roots of Heaven,* which features a veteran of the Resistance launching a conservationist campaign, is *L'homme à la colombe* (1958), which looks at how a disillusioned war vet mounts a fraudulent social movement. Lastly, two years after the publication of Gary's most explicit self-mythologization (*Promise at Dawn*), the stage production at La Michodière of *Johnnie Cœur* ridicules its hero's attempt to incarnate his legend. *Each satire is the exact inversion of its successful counterpart.* This obstinacy in tearing down each success is all the more revealing in that these parodies are essentially the same text reworked according to different genres (hagiographic tale, novel, and play). It is as if Gary were stubbornly trying to draw attention to something that his readers and critics did not wish to acknowledge.

A closer examination of the texts confirms this. There is a pastiche of Gary's own self-invention, for example, in a scene from *L'homme à la colombe* in which Johnnie brainstorms with his assistants. With plans for his scam completed, the narrator remarks: "All that remained was to reach an agreement regarding the name under which Johnnie would take the front pages by storm" (*HC* 72). It is difficult not to hear the echo with the passage cited above from *Promise at Dawn,* which shows Gary and his mother mulling over possible pen names with an eye toward finding the one that will ensure his fame as an author.[52] This connection between Gary's manipulation of his image and that of the con man appears from another angle in *Tulipe.* Not only does the legend reveal Tulipe's scam but the *record* of that legend turns out to be fraudulent as well (*T* 124). The author is included in the wave of counterfeiting, à la Gide.

Gary's gesture is an attempt in part to slow down his own participation in this process. He would soon demonstrate a profound ambivalence toward his own image, creating parallels between himself and some of his most reprehensible characters. This is most striking in *Talent Scout,* published in 1966 but written in the wake of the fanfare surrounding *Promise at Dawn,* beginning in 1960 (Huston, *Tombeau de Romain Gary* 114). In this flighty, suffocating novel, nearly every male character—a motley collection of sadists, circus freaks, and frauds—is derived partially from a facet of Gary's identity. Take, for instance, the indictment of the televangelist Dr. Horwath, fatally blind to his own hypocrisy; one can detect a grain of self-consciousness concerning Gary's own ease with the press:

For two years now, a prominent advertising agency was making sure that [Horwath's] name was as familiar to the public as their daily bread. The Truth: should one hesitate to use modern methods in order to guarantee its dissemination? . . . Horwath felt no shame in premeditating his effects or in fine-tuning the presentation of what his detractors cynically called his "show" . . . But one does wonder whether the means he employed were compatible with the dignity of his calling and whether there was not a good dose of pride and egomania entering into his exhibition (*TS* 15–17).

In all of the satires, the perpetrators of scams are ultimately the victims of their own illusion. Having gotten everyone else to believe in them, they end up seduced as well. Martyrs for their legend and ideas, each dissolves into complete abstraction: "It's wonderful . . . My body is disappearing . . . I don't feel anything any more" (*JC* 174). The risk one runs in substituting a legend (or legends) for one's past is that one loses oneself, ending up like Malraux's Clappique, "the only man in Shanghai who doesn't exist" (Malraux, *Man's Fate* 192).

Who is, after all, Romain Gary? In their interview for the Swiss journal *Preuves,* Bondy launches into an uncompromising, column-long assessment of Romain Gary's dominant personality traits and concludes, "Is this more or less the truth?" Gary responds: "The truth? What truth? The truth is perhaps that I don't exist. What exists, what might begin to exist one day, if I'm very lucky, are my books, a few novels, a body of work" ("Le moment de la vérité" 7). Gary moves us back and forth between the "I was born" of *Promise at Dawn* and the "I don't exist" proclaimed in this interview from 1957. It is an attempt to play out a persona that he sees as indistinguishable from his literary production, yet at the same time to resist the desire for "incarnation" that he sees in the followers of "Gaullocentrism" or in his idealists' imitations of Christ.[53]

These texts thus aim to awaken Gary's readers to the stakes of these legends, their possible abuses, and especially their "constructedness." These are reminders that, as with any other prominent figure, Gary owes his fame to processes of distortion—be they intentional or accidental, harmful or anodyne. In a sense, it is a dangerous admission on Gary's part, for unveiling his formula for success could potentially be at his professional expense. He is trying, in essence, to draw the public's attention to the falsifications that have seduced them, the creative liberties that have made Romain Gary possible where before there was only Roman Kacew.

This is not to say that Gary roundly condemns the activity of mythification. Throughout Gary's career, the Cheshire mutability of Malraux or the symbolic stagings of "Gaullist Resistancialism" are preferred to the quest for authenticity that drives Sartrean existentialism.[54] In the space of public representation, where every act becomes symbolic or staged, authenticity is judged impossible. As Catonné writes with regard to one of Gary's activists, the simple fact of being caught up in a wave of popular support suffices to warp one's self-definition: "transformed into a guru by the media and an object of fervor for dazzled beautiful souls, [Tulipe] quickly takes on the mask of imposture" (*Romain Gary* 136). But by continually reviving an awareness of the artificial composition of these symbolic figures, Gary hopes to break down the effect of blind fascination that they exert, not just on the public but on the sources of these legends as well.

It should be clear by now that, cynical as these texts may be, all is not nihilism in them. In fact, Gary pushes his satires one step further. Bondy points out that the abuses of confidence depicted in these works are not really fraudulent protests, but rather *the fraud is in and of itself a means of protest* (*NSC* 67). In other words, the essential objective in these satires is not to protest against abuses of confidence but to use an abuse of confidence against the functioning of certain institutions, to question *their* legitimacy. For Gary, this is an "authentic" means of attacking social institutions. It is, in fact, central to his writing from as early as *Tulipe*, as shown by his last-minute request to change the work's title to *The Protest*.[55] In later years, his approach would only grow in clarity and emphasis. In *Johnnie Cœur*, for instance, Gary writes: "Painting, literature and politics no longer suffice; they've been left behind. One must truly commit oneself to go all the way, to live one's opinions, to live one's protest . . . A beautiful moral con job, it's damn difficult" (*JC* 27). Having found his project, Johnnie concludes: "What I've got here is a great way to express myself, an esthetically-perfect demonstration of sarcasm and scorn. I'll answer absurdity with buffoonery, I'll mime my disgust and liberate myself through parody and satire lived and breathed" (*JC* 56). The frauds and misrepresentations contrived by Gary's characters take on a different meaning in this light, and certainly one catches a glimpse of the path that would lead to the creation of Émile Ajar.

It is easy to get entangled in Gary's convolutions, but in these pairs of contrasting works he is trying to present the two faces of the same operation, its potential and its pitfall: "I thereby obtain two characters who accompany each other in my novels. In reality they are but one, but I divide them into two because it procures a rich source of conflict from a novelistic point of view . . . It goes without saying that the method of splitting man into two conflicting characters was invented by Cervantes and that I will limit myself to using it in a different manner, a manner that I have always employed in my novels, and which explains why, ever since *Tulipe*, all of my 'dominant' characters have been accompanied by their contrary" (*PS* 212–13). In nearly every novel, Gary's characters show an acute awareness of the institutions that are susceptible to manipulation, be it for altering public opinion or the contours of their social identity.[56] The satirical works serve as timely reminders concerning the three interlocking parts of this process: the public's gullibility, the press's cynical insouciance, and the legendary figure's narcissism. Or, to put it another way, Gary's ethical concerns focus on the line that differentiates the production of a fiction aimed at realizing certain ideals in a given social context (de Gaulle, Nadejda, Morel) from a misrepresentation that exploits a social problem for personal gain (Tulipe, Johnnie).

A distinction between *mythification* and *mystification* is helpful. In the first instance, the protagonists of *A European Education, The Roots of Heaven*, and *Promise at Dawn* remain conscious of how they have constructed a myth and thus have an awareness of the myth's imaginary character. They act with an understanding of what its role could be within the community. In this passage from *The Roots of Heaven*, for instance, Morel recounts how he and his comrades invented various symbols during their detention in concentration camps to help bind them together: "We all sensed confusedly that, given the point we were at, if we didn't find some rule of dignity to keep us going, if we didn't latch onto some fiction or myth, all that remained for us was to give up the fight, to agree to anything, even to collaboration. From that moment on, an extraordinary thing took place: the morale of K block suddenly went up several notches" (*RH* 207). The device corresponds to the partisans' invention of Nadejda in *A European Education* and summarizes Gary's understanding of de Gaulle's significance in World War II. In the satirical novels, however, the reader encounters intentional mystification where an antihero subverts the media and betrays communities for personal gain.

Through the combination of his heroic novels and satires, Gary wants to engage in social demystification without falling into the demythification of society. It is not to do away with the symbolic order, but to recognize the *composition* of the symbolic order, to recognize that it is partly grounded in myths. We can now see the stakes of overlooking these satirical works in a consideration of Gary's work. Without them, one neglects the running dialogue that Gary maintains among *all* of his works, whose individual conception is often a comment upon or foil to prior works. Recognizing the mutually articulating nature of his texts allows one to understand that many of the positions adopted are relative to opposing views developed elsewhere.

Chapter 3

Strategies of Mobile Identity, 1961–1973

In the United States for most of the late fifties, Gary missed the greater part of the buildup to the Algerian Revolution. He would publish an article in Life *that was largely sympathetic to the Colonels' rebellion ("The Anger That Turned Generals into Desperados"), a choice that would annoy Gaullists and Leftists alike. After de Gaulle opened the door to Algerian independence, however, the partisans for French Algeria in the Secret Army Organization (OAS) repeatedly targeted de Gaulle and even Malraux for assassination. Upon Gary's return to France, he was in contact with some of the more extreme sectors of Gaullism. His friendship with Dominique Ponchardier, a former Resistance hit man, undercover agent, and de Gaulle bodyguard, who formed an anti-OAS group of* barbouzes *(unofficial counterterrorists), may have led to Gary's recruitment: in January 1962, at a time when he was no longer actively serving in the diplomatic corps, Gary received authorization to carry "a concealed automatic weapon for the execution of special missions to which he might be assigned" (document qtd. in Larat 117; apparently nothing came of it). In 1963, his divorce from Lesley Blanch officialized, Gary married Jean Seberg. According to David Richards, the marriage had been precipitated by Seberg's pregnancy. She gave birth to Alexandre Diego Gary in Barcelona on July 17, 1962. Because Seberg and Gary were not yet married, Diego's birth and the first years of his life were hidden from even the Garys' most intimate friends and family. Using contacts in the diplomatic services, Gary established Diego's birth certificate to list him as being born in the French village of Charquemont on October 26, 1963, after his parents' wedding (Richards 123–26). Now husband and wife, Gary and Seberg dined with the Kennedys and lunched with de Gaulle at the Élysée. Gary traveled to Morocco, Peru, Colombia, Poland, and Hungary. He published articles in a variety of American and French venues on diverse current event topics (the UN, the effects of cinema on literature, censorship, etc.). In 1967, his Gaullist ties led to a position in the Ministry of Information. Scarcely a year later, however, during the uprising of May 1968, Gary abruptly resigned in support of the students, thereby burning his bridges on the Right without convincing anyone on the Left. His position appeared even more contradictory after he penned an impassioned attack on the French population for abandoning de Gaulle in 1969. Gary was invited to Israel on an official visit, created a small scandal at de Gaulle's funeral in November 1970 by wearing his Free French air force uniform, and was named commander in the*

Legion of Honor for Cultural Affairs in 1971. In the years after de Gaulle's death and Malraux's departure from the government, Gary made it clear that his attachment was to de Gaulle and not the Gaullists. Prior to the 1974 presidential election, for instance, he declared his support for François Mitterrand against Giscard d'Estaing. Meanwhile, Gary's marriage to Seberg had ended in separation. After their divorce, Gary and Seberg maintained a difficult but important friendship. In the United States, Seberg's generous contributions to African American civil rights groups made her a highly visible figure in Hollywood's liberal community. News of a Seberg pregnancy reached the public through Los Angeles Times *gossip columnist Joyce Haber (May 19, 1970) and* Newsweek *(August 24, 1970). The articles asserted that the father was an important member of the Black Panther Party, one of Malcolm X's cousins. Greatly distraught over these articles, Seberg was found unconscious on a beach in Majorca after an attempted suicide. She eventually gave birth prematurely to a Caucasian girl. The child, most likely fathered by Gary and named for his mother, did not survive. To satisfy the morbid curiosity of onlookers at the child's funeral, held in Seberg's hometown, Seberg ordered an open casket service. Although Gary and Seberg won a slander suit against* Newsweek, *Seberg's psychological equilibrium crumbled and she sank into severe depression and addiction (Richards 254–57; Seinfelt 335–36). Gary shot a controversial film,* Kill, *in 1971, and a number of reviewers and friends were angered to learn that Gary had cast the fragile Seberg in the lead role as a hysterically desperate woman. After its premiere in Marseilles in 1972,* Kill *closed quickly in France and was not released in North America. (This came on the heels of another disturbingly violent film he directed in 1968, also with Seberg in a problematic lead role,* Les oiseaux vont mourir au Pérou.*)*

Responding to the "Marcel Proust Questionnaire" was something of a rite of passage for French writers on their way to celebrity. Gary participated with more or less goodwill, naming Bob Dylan as his favorite musician and "running away" as his most admired military feat. To the question, "Where would you like to live?" he answers: "Everywhere and in everything, with a million lives" ("Romain Gary," *Cent écrivains* 139).

But, even if Gary possessed the material means in the sixties and seventies to maintain residences in Majorca, Switzerland, and Paris and on the French Riviera, living a million different lives is precisely the one thing that he felt he was no longer able to do. After the success of *The Roots of Heaven* and *Promise at Dawn*, Gary's relationship with the press had soured, for political, social, and personal reasons.

Throughout the sixties, Gary was one of de Gaulle's most frequent and steadfast defenders in the world of French letters, publishing pieces in *Le Figaro, Le Monde, France-Soir*, and *Life* (among others). Pigeonholed by factions on the Right and the Left as a diehard Gaullist, Gary would feel the ill effects of this political engagement in the aftermath of the Algerian Revolution. As one of Gary's supporters notes, "Doubtless because he expressed his loyalty to General de Gaulle in *Promise at Dawn,* Romain Gary did not receive the same chorus of accolades for his latest novel."[1] Even so, Gary maintained his ideological independence and hardly passed for an orthodox team player within the general's inner circle. Though Gary would stand by an idealized vision of the Resistance, the irreverent character of his texts often touched on political dynamite. This nonconformism made him an unwelcome presence in the upper echelons of the Quay d'Orsay and the Élysée.

Largely for political reasons, then, Gary's poor reception was no longer restricted to his satires. Rather than succeeding in relativizing and nuancing his image, he found that everything that did not conform to what the press expected of him was discarded. The weight of his commercial image became greater than that of argument, with the result that his mythification was always taken in the first degree, his irony and sarcasm overlooked. Remembered Gary: "I felt like I was being farmed out to the circus, music halls and vaudeville. I was being treated like a vulgar amusement, a provider of minor literary distractions. People weren't buying my books any more because critics greeted them with silence" (*Ench* 72). Moreover, as with Johnnie Cœur, when Gary lied, journalists believed him; when Gary told the truth, no one listened. He became hostage to the very processes he tried to reveal. There developed a continual and significant gap between his intentions and how the critical press interpreted his actions.

Over the next decade, Gary would take stock of the failure of his satirical works. He embarked on a more diversified effort to devise literary strategies for regaining control of his authorial image and communicating his vision of the artistic process. His activity became aimed primarily at promoting what I term "concepts of mobile identity": through a renewal of the picaresque genre; a conception of *autofiction* that allows a "transcendence" of the first person; and the development of clandestine identities. It marks a stretch of theoretical reflection on and deliberate experimentation with the novel's formal possibilities that is unique in Gary's career.

The Picaro

> *All novelists are outlaws, be they tolerated or not.*
> Gary, qtd. in Gaède, L'écrivain et la société

As we know from *The Roots of Heaven,* on the one hand, and *Johnnie Cœur,* on the other, Gary often linked the author's activity with that of his socially committed protagonists. After 1960, the emphasis would shift markedly from political figures and social activists to figurations of the novelist and of artists in general.

On most occasions, the novelist appears as a disreputable character: "How did Tolstoy dare be everywhere and in everything, taking the place of a thousand minds and souls, seeing into all of their thoughts and hearts —in short, playing God? Such knowledge of others can only be an imposture . . . [Novelists] *invent things* that are not *true*; they tell tales. The whole lot are charlatans, liars, and pipsqueaks" (*PS* 47–48).

These remarks appear in the context of Gary's rejoinder to the New Novel and Alain Robbe-Grillet's critique of traditional narrative modes, but Gary's (only partly) ironic description of the novelist's activity also ties in well with the concerns he developed in his satirical works. As he continued that project in the sixties and early seventies, we encounter an entire gallery of figures embodying his conception of the modern artist, none of whom bring to mind the noble calling of the forty Immortals of the French Academy. *Talent Scout* (1966) assembles sundry varieties of entertainer for a dictator's bemusement: false prophets, impostors, jugglers, magicians, hypnotists, circus freaks, and lounge acts. Rooted in a long tradition of popular arts and pseudoscience, *The Enchanters* (1973) presents the eighteenth-century equivalent: alchemists, spell casters, charlatans, medicine men, and acrobats. The thesis is simple: "Art and talent consist in creating illusion" (*TS* 302).

The resulting figure puts the art back in con artist. One of Gary's direct inspirations in this respect is Thomas Mann's work. Mann describes the writer's art as one of making people believe in things that do not exist, or of attributing to oneself knowledge and adventures that one has never had. In *The Confessions of Felix Krull* and *Tonio Kröger*, or to a lesser extent in *The Holy Sinner* and *Joseph and His Brothers*, the artist is portrayed as a *Hochstapler*, or confidence man. Mann creates a problematic figure of the author that mixes, in the case of Felix Krull, an aristocratic confessional discourse with tales of petty crime (Feuerlicht 92–107). Krull is an unusual swindler, a purely literary one, since his activities are not really motivated by material gain. He pulls off a series of frauds in which the pleasure of the disguise is his primary reward. He slips easily from one social identity to the next, equally comfortable at both ends of the social scale. Krull's impersonations, effecting as they do a "transformation and renewal of [his] worn-out self," are not simply masks but fundamental alterations of his identity.[2]

While there is much to Felix Krull that suggests Gary's project, Gary sees Mann's treatment of the question as too limited and well-heeled. Gary refuses to concede Krull as a mere character in the novel, with the aristocratic novelist's dignity and authority still safely outside. To this end, Gary proposes another emblematic figure in 1965, Don Juan's valet Sganarelle, recast here as a factotum in the service of the novel, situated somewhere between author and protagonist. Sganarelle does, in effect, bring together several features of Gary's project. His name is derived from the Italian verb *ingannare*, to dupe, fitting in well with Gary's collection of tricksters. The role of Sganarelle was usually played by Molière himself, a stage equivalent of screenwriter-director-actor Willie Bauché presented in Gary's *The Colors of the Day*. Used in five of Molière's plays in five different roles, Sganarelle possesses a Protean flexibility, where each appearance is independent of the previous incarnation. As a result, there is no possible narrative contiguity to reconcile the ensemble of Sganarelle's adventures.[3]

Though these ideas have a significant place in his vision of the novel, Gary does not pursue specific parallels to Molière's character very far, uprooting Sganarelle rapidly from his theatrical context. What really tempts Gary in this figure is a certain way of surviving by one's wits, and it is for this reason that Gary draws a connection between Sganarelle's adaptability and the rootless lifestyle of the picaro: "[Sganarelle] has always been unscrupulous, indecent, and in complete bad faith. He will resort to any scam when it is a matter of best serving the interests of his Master [the novel], even if it means using trickery, ruses and lies . . . Sganarelle strikes me as combining all of the essential characteristics of the picaro; he is inescapably bound to all of the characters in our picaresque adventure" (*PS* 66–67).

The picaresque harks back to an era when not just the protagonist but the novel itself was the bastard offspring of the arts. It is Felix Krull without the bourgeois breeding, a poor man's Count Saint-Germain with neither leisure nor letters of introduction. Perpetually involved in minor scams, a teller of tall tales and a master of lending reality to what does not exist, characterized by dissimulated identities and gypsylike migrations, the picaro possesses all the colors necessary for Gary's protagonist-author: "I'm going to force myself to build *Frère Océan* [Brother Ocean] around a character who will be neither painter, musician, nor even novelist. With as much violence as possible, he will play . . . that essential role occupied by art throughout time and which makes art a natural enemy of any 'order of things': my character will be an *agent provocateur*" (*PS* 94).[4] The picaro is the ideal embodiment of this literary vision, and Gary's most intriguing novels from this period are attempts to imagine modern incarnations of this figure who dates back to the origins of the novel. As Gary proclaimed already in 1956, "The modern novel will be picaresque — or won't be at all."[5]

Lady L. is an excellent example of how these themes play out. Written first in English as a tribute to his wife Lesley in 1958, Gary translated it himself for a French audience in 1963. It was thus written in the period of Gary's greatest success, in the years following the Goncourt Prize. The parallels of the novel's plot with Gary's own situation are unmistakable. The heroine, one of England's most distinguished aristocrats, decides on her eightieth birthday to confide the truth about her origins to an associate. It turns out that the revered Lady L. was in fact born Annette Boudin to a Parisian washerwoman and an absinthe-soaked father. After her mother's death, Annette worked the streets until a chance meeting changed her fate. Charismatic anarchist Armand Denis recruited her as part of a plan to steal his way into the wealthiest safes of Europe. A corrupt calligrapher rechristened her Mlle Diane de Boisérignier by crafting artificially aged documents authenticating her noble heritage and by placing her nonexistent family in *Burke's Peerage*.

To assume her new identity, she underwent an intensive apprenticeship on demeanor, fashion, and conversation, all of which she absorbed with undeniable talent. Her true birth certificate was destroyed, as were all other traces of her past. Her lessons fully rehearsed, she entered the social world of the Swiss aristocracy, casing castles for Denis' anarchists to plunder. She then married into a succession of powerful families, her path eventually leading to England, where her offspring rose into the ruling class.

As one gathers, her adventure is not a tale of genteel socialization but a burlesque fable of complete self-invention. Even authenticity, it turns out, is fabricated: "[Lady L.] began to inspire admiration not just for her beauty but for those innate qualities that aristocrats recognize immediately. She possessed that inimitable *on ne sait quoi* in her ease and self-assurance that one cannot acquire; rather, one must be born with it . . . Yes, she had an innate sense of authenticity" (*LL* 110–11). In this respect, *Lady L.* reads like a parody of Gary's own story as presented in *Promise at Dawn*. Both use a flashback reconstruction of a highly organized and willful passage from illegitimate origins to official consecration, falsifying their identities and taking on new social roles with brio.

Gary's fullest realization of the picaro character, however, is Genghis Cohn in *The Guilty Head*. Having fled undivulged difficulties encountered under another identity and taken up hiding in Tahiti, Cohn is explicitly identified with the picaros from the very first pages.[6] In addition to its isolation and exoticism, Tahiti is also the site of Paul Gauguin's tragic final years, which serve as Gary's paradigm in this novel for the artist's struggle with the powers-that-be. Cohn takes it upon himself to avenge Gauguin, cooking up a scam that involves turning artistic fame against the institutions that had refused to recognize Gauguin's genius in the first place: "Tahiti was living in worship of Gauguin, with a curious mixture of remorse and pride. They had let the painter die, alone and wracked with misery, overrun by administrative and legal woes, not to mention the fierce hatred on the part of the missionaries . . . In other words, it was a surefire meal ticket, and Cohn had quite comfortably cashed in on it. He was making Tahiti pay what he called 'a Gauguin tax,' and despite the competition he was getting by just fine, thanks to his appearance and deplorable lifestyle" (*GH* 13).[7]

The plan is an unusual one: Cohn impersonates the painter's legend in every element, shamelessly mining it to exploit the Tahitian tourist trade and authorities. He sets up a studio full of art students cranking out Gauguin "originals" (which Cohn later signs as Gauguin and puts up for sale) and flaunts a debauched existence living with his Tahitian girl-friend in a reconstruction of Gauguin's beach cabin. Cohn is helped in this endeavor by travel agent Hervé Bizien de La Longerie, who plans to stimulate island tourism through the creation of a sort of cultural Disney-land, with each site consisting of the reconstitution of some legendary scene. Promises Bizien, "You'll tour the grounds in a bus, going from the Original Sin up to Gauguin and Van Gogh. There'll be Victor Hugo on his rock at Guernesey, and I can extend it bit by bit as the funds come in, with a downsized replica of Chartres Cathedral and a miniature Ver-sailles" (*GH* 40).

For Cohn and his associates (Verdouillet plays Van Gogh), the cre-ativity of their art lies in the means they find to reproduce these legends. "Authenticity"—Cohn's term—thus lies in the perfect imitation of one's model. Cohn even manages to beat out Gauguin's illegitimate son for the role of imitating the painter, achieving a dubious realism when sores break out on his legs much like those that decimated Gauguin's health in his final years: "It's as if I had a guarantee of authenticity stamped on me!" exclaims Cohn; "I'm going to double my prices" (*GH* 111). Being the artist *is* their art; the only work produced is their public persona. Once again, there are strange echoes of *Promise at Dawn*, where creating his image as an author is shown as more important than his written work.

This marks one extreme in Gary's desacralization of the figure of the author and the ways in which legend and authorial persona overshadow actual production. At the other end of the spectrum from Genghis Cohn, *The Enchanters* presents a far less cynical incarnation of the picaro in the form of Fosco Zaga. Gary's literary apprenticeship as presented in *Prom-ise at Dawn* is still the model, but here it rediscovers its innocence and with it its vocation: "I cried out . . . that henceforth everything I would experience would depend on my will alone because I was the first Zaga to discover the art of fabricating the eternal with the ephemeral, real worlds out of dreams and gold from counterfeit coins" (*Ench* 371–72). Contained within this delirious declaration of artistic faith is a riddle of sorts: Fosco will create the eternal (art) from the ephemeral (man), reality from dreams (art is a reality owed to the imagination), and gold from false currency (as a novelist he is paid for producing make-believe stories). At once prophet, magician, and alchemist, Fosco brings Gary full circle. In the movement from *Lady L.* and *Talent Scout* to *The Enchanters*, Gary plots the scoundrel's rise to respectability, the long climb from circus act to cultural icon. Says Fosco: "[My father] dreamed that his sons might attain new heights, heights within reach if one acquired a pickpocket's skills, a juggler's dexterity and the flexibility of a contortionist—and then learned how to apply those qualities to the realms of thought, politics and literature" (*Ench* 138). When we recall that *Promise at Dawn* refers to Malraux as the greatest juggler of them all (*PD* 132), it suggests that this is more than just a passing image for Gary.

This art of creating imaginary characters to circulate in one's stead may seem a far cry from the real-life legends that Gary himself admired—until one recalls that de Gaulle compared himself to Tintin and Malraux to children's storybook characters like *Puss in Boots* (Malraux, *Felled Oaks* 32, 25). Gary clearly has such figures in mind. Having referred to de Gaulle as "a fantastically clever and gifted impersonator of ten centuries of French history," Gary did not hesitate to reveal to a national television audience aspects of de Gaulle's personal staging such as the hiring of Jean-Paul Belmondo's makeup man Charly Koubeserian for the president's appearances on the small screen.[8]

Malraux is present in another extremely important manner in Gary's thought. As individuals, we confront circumstances—historical, material, and metaphysical realities—that preexist us. Malraux terms the ensemble of these conditions *le destin* (fate, destiny). Encompassing both natural reality and the powers-that-be (the social forces and institutions that intervene in our lives and assign our official identities), "destiny" indicates the ensemble of obstacles opposed to our free self-invention. We can either passively endure our individual fate or we can attempt to produce our own, an *antidestin*. An "antidestiny" is thus the result of a concerted effort to conceive oneself against a preestablished condition, to try to bend it to one's desires or resist it.

Malraux's definition of art as antidestiny appears nearly verbatim in the mouth of one of Lady L.'s husbands: "[The Duke of Glendale] saw art as a revolt against the human condition, against the brevity of one's destiny" (*LL* 120). Elsewhere, what Malraux terms destiny corresponds to Gary's use of *la Puissance* (the powers-that-be) or *le réel* (the real, reality). The "Powers-that-be" are necessarily accompanied by their "Ceremonial," comprising a court, protocol, and reigning myths—in other words, the particular authorities, rituals and values one comes up against in a given cultural or social domain, the institutional rituals displaying and conferring power (*PS* 295). In the following passage from *Pour Sganarelle*,

Gary defines the mission of his protagonists as a picaresque odyssey combating or subverting these very forces: "Mime, parody, and attack all the deformations and misformations that the Powers-that-be impose on man from one end to the other, all the while giving vent to one's particular form of fraud" (*PS* 122).

The battle thus is a resistance against definition, the established order, against the fixity and finitude of an attributed identity: "My protagonist will always elude the Ceremonial. Though he will attack it, he is not an anarchist; he is a man who is constantly changing identities, in the midst of 'becoming.' He is mobile, temporary and always on the verge of leaving (but without ever arriving). He refuses to be tied down to anything, to be immobilized or contained. He can neither be completed nor identified definitively. None of his provisional identities can be enthroned in that Escorial where the sinister immobilization of man in an identity of circumstance takes place" (*PS* 306). In keeping with the picaresque, Gary's construction of alternative, permutating personae is designed as an episodic activity, with no single incarnation of the protagonist ever constituting the whole of an individual's identity.

Autofiction

Up until 1960, Gary's novels participated in the elaboration of his legend indirectly, by encouraging the reader to infer a connection between what was known of his life and what was recounted in the novel. *Promise at Dawn* is the first work in which Gary appears as a novelist, and we have seen the crucial role it would play in determining the long-term contours of his public image. Gary would continue to use this device, appearing by name regularly in works that identify him as their author: peripherally in *The Dance of Genghis Cohn* (1967) and *The Enchanters* (1973), centrally in *White Dog* (1970) and *Les trésors de la mer Rouge* (1971). Despite the presence of concrete, personal referents, these works cannot properly be considered autobiographical but rather must be placed within a genre known as *autofiction*. Autofiction is a literary form originating by most accounts in the twentieth century (see Colonna 2–3).[9] It brings together all the formal features of autobiography but uses the author's name and personal circumstances as a departure point for the production of deliberate fictions. It typically depends on a highly visible authorial persona located at an ambiguous intersection between fact and fiction, where the narrator is both protagonist and implied author. It is the literary genre that corresponds most directly to projects of authorial self-invention, in that the reader can be easily led to interpret as autobiographical what is in fact imaginary.

There are as many variants of autofiction as there are authors writing it, though typically they tend to build an authorial persona cumulatively, across a number of works. To take opposing poles, there are those, like Cendrars and Henry Miller, who engage in their episodic fabulations with considerable gusto, while Céline and Jean Genet distort their lives into caricatures of their own public condemnation. Gary falls almost exactly in between, deflating his persona through doses of self-deprecatory humor while nonetheless enumerating its heroic attributes. Gary explains his motivations for using this approach in *Promise at Dawn*: "This is not about me. It is about the *I* we all have. Our poor little kingdom of the *I*, so comical with its regal interiors and fortified enclosure" (*PD* 184). More than ten years later, the approach would be the same: "To understand the role that humor plays in my works, you must realize that it is one way for me to settle scores with the *I* we all have" (*NSC* 11–12). His ironic personal accounts are conceived as a type of self-sacrifice in which "Gary" becomes an exemplary self, but exemplary only insofar as he exposes weaknesses he has in common with other egos. The discussion of personal identity is thus directed toward universal concerns: "The truth is that *I* does not exist. *Me* is never the goal; it is just something that I *pass through* when I turn my favorite weapon [self-deprecation] against it. I am trying to get at the human condition . . . , a condition that was imposed upon us from without [i.e., our identities, metaphysical condition, destiny]" (*PD* 161).

These disinterested claims can be disputed, of course, particularly in the case of an inveterate media hound like Gary. But it is important here precisely to separate the biographical person from the literary strategy. Gary, after all, is claiming to use the latter to dissect the *faults*—vanity would be one of the first attributed to the *I*—of the former. An attentive reading shows that Gary's fiction does in fact move in the direction he indicates. In rewriting his own life to expose the shortcomings and ambitions of a modern individual, he develops into a more and more generalized, caricatural version of his public image. His use of autofiction, for instance, usually includes a list of the elements that have led to the legend of Romain Gary. In *White Dog*, a confrontation with the CRS security forces during the May 1968 rioting allows Gary a chance to run off a short list of his official administrative identities: "I take out my diplomatic passport, my Companion of the Liberation identification card, my card of second aide to the Minister of Information . . . '—Commandant Gary de Kacew' " (*WD* 192). A page later, the same litany is recited, reducing his public biography to its most condensed form: "Emigration is quite an ordeal. It makes you General Consul of France, a Goncourt laureate, a decorated patriot, Gaullist, and spokesperson for the United Nations French delegation" (*WD* 194–95). By dealing only with the nametags attributed to him, he reduces his persona to an amalgamation of types. It is a way of reminding us of their classificatory role. This is all the more evident on those occasions in *White Dog* when he goes out into the streets during the civil unrest, dressed up in the wardrobe of his legend—the red Legion of Honor bow, the green and black ribbon of the Companions of the Liberation, and his War Cross (*WD* 193). These are identities one dons, and their elements are conducive to the production of a stereotyped portrait. To disrupt a civil conflict based in large part on such generalizations, Gary presents his garish ensemble as a provocation to both the students and the forces of order.

Thus, while Gary continually draws attention to his own self-portrait, the push in these works is to move *through* the genre of autofiction toward an analysis of what is common to the "I" in all of us, to the role played by this sense of self, incarnated in a variety of social identities. This "passage *through* the I" ("*Me* is never the goal; it is just something that I *pass through . . .*") is a key concept in Gary's vision of writing. *La nuit sera calme* provides some suggestive images concerning this use of the first person: "My self-esteem does not get defensive at the idea of opening up to a perfect stranger . . . , because my *I* does not constrain me to any regards toward myself—quite the contrary . . . *Gari* in Russian means 'burn!'; it's an imperative form . . . I want to test myself, a trial by fire, so that my *I* is burned off, goes up in flame" (*NSC* 11–12). That the author's pseudonym (and by extension his self-fashioned authorial identity) can be considered a reference to this "self-sacrifice" underscores the notion's centrality to Gary's literary aesthetic. By the same token, it also clarifies his relation to his pseudonymous alter ego. In associating the process ("Burn!") explicitly with his pseudonym, he stresses the self-consuming nature of his own persona in much the same way as Blaise Cendrars.[10] It is an identity through which Gary passes to enter a text, to begin writing. Such an attitude is consistent with his effort to draw attention to his use of a pseudonym in *Promise at Dawn*. After all, there is a seeming contradiction in this gesture: if the very fact of seeking a new name tacitly admits trying to orchestrate his image, why draw attention to what he has chosen to dissimulate? It signals that the mediagenic construction is just that and should not be confused with an actual person.

Whereas a writer like Cendrars invests his literary fortunes in the creation of a self-portrait that also reenforces his social identity, in the seventies Gary does not use autofiction to invent an all-encompassing authorial subject. The play of identities being carried out here is complex and ultimately demonstrates that Gary holds true to his claim to be breaking away from autobiographical genres. Contrary to the habits of autofiction, for instance, which in most cases uses personal detail to create the illusion of a biographical subject, Gary eschews this sort of disclosure in favor of the identity-types mentioned above. The break with conventional autofiction is absolute, since the focus of the narratives, and of the ensemble of his work for that matter, is not on the concentrated elaboration of the same underlying self (Colonna 11), but rather on the continual reinvention and metamorphosis of a succession of alter egos. Gary's work thus escapes the fetishization of the *I* that some critics reproach in autofiction. The specificity of the writing subject is never the work's principal topic.

We are now seeing movement in the opposite direction from Gary's earlier activity of mythification. Rather than constituting an authorial presence that takes on increasing consistency and is interchangeable with his social persona, Gary is producing a disposable straw model on his way to other identities. In theory, then, the pseudonymous figure *Gary* could take on any number of identities: "When I begin a novel, it is to run where I am not, to go see what other people are up to. It's a way of escaping and reincarnating myself" (*NSC* 258).

This attitude is not confined to Gary's novels. Bondy sees Gary's continual fabrications as a sort of provocation and makes the observation during one of their interviews that, much like the character La Marne in *The Colors of the Day*, Gary produces new versions of himself for encounters with the press: "Each interview paints with great verisimilitude a completely different character. One presents you as some sort of trumpeting elephant, another shows you as being hypersensitive and fragile in nature" ("Le moment de la vérité" 3–4). Gary's response states clearly that this is part of his conception of being a writer: "I'm a novelist. I can't resist the desire to create new characters, especially when, in essence, people are asking me to" (4).

An episode from Gary's published travel journal, *Les trésors de la mer Rouge*, is a textual illustration of this transformation of identities. In the course of a motorcycle excursion through Yemen, Gary is separated from his knapsack, and thus from all of the indicators of his European identity (passport, Western clothing, luggage, etc.). Obliged after a few days to shed his dirty pants and shirt for Yemenite garb, he is mistaken for a local by a Chinese tourist. Exultant, Gary poses for a photograph: "Never had I experienced to such a point the feeling of being no one, that is to say, of finally being *someone* . . . The habit of only being oneself ends up completely depriving us of the rest of the world, of all the others. *I* is the end of possibility . . . Now, finally, I have begun to exist outside of myself, in a world so utterly stripped of that familiarity which allows us to find ourselves . . . I had finally pulled off my transhumance" (*TMR* 102).

Later, when a young Russian girl passes by—in principle a compatriot —she looks a travel-weary Gary over disapprovingly and announces in Russian to her companions, "What a disguuuusting mug!" (*TMR* 103). The anecdote is Gary's way of signaling that if his own people do not recognize him any more, he *can* in fact evade even the most fundamental traits of his identity—be it the outward signs by which others recognize him or the Proustian veil of habit that blankets him in comforting continuity. Gary sees these moments as triumphs against an all-too-constraining identity: "Pent-up with hands and feet bound, buried inside myself like all the rest of us and hating the limits thus imposed upon my appetite for life — or, rather lives — I had now managed to escape from the penal colony that condemns me to only be myself. I felt like I had finally succeeded in life. One of my *lives,* at any rate" (*TMR* 103–4). The important thing in these passages is not just to be able to determine one's own identity but especially to be able to change or transform that identity. This term of *transhumance,* of migration, is what leads me to my own phrase, "strategies of mobile identity." Autofiction, as we see it used here, is Gary's means developed throughout the late sixties and early seventies to adapt first person narration to his poetic and philosophical goals.

Writing is the means to this multiplication of selves, with his reworking of autofiction ultimately meeting up with his renewal of the picaresque. Driven by "[an] imperious desire to compete . . . with the Powers-that-be," Gary scripts a fictional social persona whose "life" he can then play out in writing: "[I am] consumed by a need to diversify myself through new and multiple identities, to live *through these identities* an integral experience of what I must *first create in order to be able to discover it for myself thereafter.* By this means I can break free from the habits and claustrophobia of my individual state, my little kingdom of the *I*" (*PS* 9–10; emphasis added). This is a key passage defining his relation to his authorial persona (so much so that he initially planned to use *Le royaume du Je* [The kingdom of the I] as the title for the book that would eventually be published as *La nuit sera calme*).[11] The need to climb into the skin of another ("[that] I must first create") in order to trace out the novel corresponding to that character ("to be able to discover it for myself thereafter") would be the model employed both for first- and third-person novels.

Gary lays out the theoretical underpinnings of this approach in *Pour Sganarelle.* He notes first that any authorial figure, regardless of the degree of accuracy or sincerity involved in self-examination, becomes in turn a literary creation, a reinvention: "When Proust peers into himself, he invents himself: he is not uncovering his psychological truth, he is creating Proust, a character" (*PS* 114). As Proust himself argues in *Against Sainte-Beuve,* writers experience themselves in the act of writing as a sort of fictional character that can depart in any number of ways from an author's actual biography and personality. However, contrary to the attitude of many other modernist writers, Gary does not see this alienation as a problem. For him, it is the most desirable facet of the practice of literature. Gary sees this figure as the "author-character," in opposition to the picaresque "protagonist-character" that we examined in the first pages of this chapter.

This pairing of "author-character" and "protagonist-character" allows him to stress the fact that *both* are literary constructs. After all, in many respects, the issue is not just a problematic of writing but one of reception as well. An important divorce exists between how authors understand their persona and what the public sees in them: "Tolstoy confirms my idea that not only is there no identity between a work and its author but sometimes the two are even worlds apart. One writes what one is: but one does so with resentment at times or nostalgia for another identity. In those instances, one is writing *against* what one is, but those who deduce [authors] from our works fail to spot the deception and imposture" (*PS* 14). The result is an authorial figure constructed piecemeal on both sides of the equation, but the writer and reader do not and will not arrive at the same figure, even though in both cases this figure is located more properly on the side of the text.

The gap is felt by Gary in at least two areas. First, the author experiences these novels as a transformation, but the public and the press hold on to the established image of an author. Second, where Gary treats this persona as an imaginary production, the public assumes it corresponds to an actual being. Gary's response to this miscommunication is to try to direct the process of public construction by dragging his image into his fictions. It is here that Gary adds his own touch to what otherwise might be a fairly common portrait of the "paper author," for Gary combines third-person picaresque and first-person autofiction within the same work. Since the authorial figure is situated on the side of the text, Gary employs it as another fictional element. This literary model is based on a partial identification between the author-character and the protagonist-character, in which the interplay between the two is the catalyst for each new novel. Thus, his prior identity as an author is acknowledged but is taken only as a departure point. The process is envisioned as a means of establishing contact with his characters, of bridging the gap that exists between him and the fictive identities he wishes to take on and explore: "This is how I created [the character Fosco Zaga], attentive foremost to his 'literary enchantments,' pimp and parasite, poxed and predatory though he be. To draw myself as close as possible to this character (who struck me as fairly distant from myself and my life), I wrote the novel in the first person. I even gave Fosco my Paris apartment on the rue du Bac, to try at least to have something in common with him. Based on these details . . . , Mme Jacqueline Piatier concluded in *Le Monde* that the novel's hero—charlatan, pimp and pox-ridden—was me" (*NSC* 260).

Decrying what he deems the critics' "refusal of fiction," Gary reminds us that the use of existent referents in a novel does not make the work factual or biographical (*NSC* 261). It is in this sense that Gary's practice, even if it borrows amply from his real life, must be classified under the genre of autofiction. The objective is not the production of a more advantageous, colorful, or coherent persona. Rather, he is attempting to remind us that any social identity is a fabrication, that there is no single base identity existing "underneath" the social trappings. The author-character "Gary," a figure possessing certain traits (Resistance hero, Russian Jew, husband of Jean Seberg) and a certain voice (lyric, ironic, etc.), loans these features to a new protagonist-character for each work. Writing then becomes a series of contacts between author and protagonist, where the vicarious involvement with the hero gradually transforms the authorial persona. The identification is thus a complete departure from the one usually imagined (in biographical criticism, for instance), for it posits no set identity on the side of the author.

The activity is formulated as a mental acting-out, a theatrical exercise of sorts: "I 'think myself' through my characters; I let myself be hypnotized by them, caught up in that craving I have to live a multiplicity of lives as different as possible from one another. It's a process of mimeticism which in the end is that of an actor . . . Moreover, I believe that all novelists are author-actors" (*NSC* 255). The link between Bondy's evaluation of Gary's behavior during interviews and Gary's understanding of the literary process is explicit. The formation of an authorial persona is inseparable from the act of writing, just as there is no preexistent "I," singular and inalterable, serving as a point of departure.

The example of *The Dance of Genghis Cohn* helps clarify what is meant here. One of the questions this novel raises is whether Gary should be considered a Jewish writer.[12] On the one hand, Kacew is a common Jewish surname and by genealogical standards Gary was officially Jewish, since his mother was Jewish. On the other hand, he was not a practicing Jew, and the initial use of his pseudonym served partly to distance his Semitic origins.[13] While *Promise at Dawn* makes light of this latter decision, after Gary's experiences in Russia and Poland, and during the German Occupation, one suspects that it is tied up in far more ambivalent reactions. Scenes such as the troubling episode in *A European Education* in which the child narrator, Janek, first rescues and then drives to his death a gifted young Jewish violinist make it particularly difficult to gauge Gary's feelings about this facet of his identity, since *both* characters — the child persecuted and the child persecuting — could be identified with depictions of Gary found later in *Promise at Dawn* or *Talent Scout.* But while for the earlier parts of his career we can only guess at Gary's attitude toward his name change, *The Dance of Genghis Cohn* displays a double desire: to affirm publicly his Jewish identity and to discover *for himself* precisely what it means to him to be Jewish.

This project is fully revealed only in the closing paragraphs of the novel. Without transition, the novel casts aside its fictional characters and the reader must quickly decipher that the scene that interrupts the narrative is based on a trip made by Gary and Seberg to Poland in 1966. Gary has apparently fainted at the foot of a memorial to the victims of the Warsaw Ghetto and is just beginning to regain consciousness as the novel ends. We are led to understand that the entire novel has played itself out in his mind during his fainting spell, like an elaborate, highly charged dream, a personal revelation that immediately transforms his sense of identity. Gary alludes to this metamorphosis with a bit of Groucho Marxian irony in snippets of conversation supposedly overheard as he comes back to his senses:

> "Mother, who's the gentleman that fainted?"
> "He's not a gentleman, my dear, he's a writer . . ."
> . . . .
> "I never knew he was Jewish . . ."
> "Neither did he." (*DGC* 272)

Prior to visiting this monument, Gary was traveling in Poland as a humanist writer, French dignitary, and Resistance hero. When he emerges from his fainting spell (*when he comes back to himself,* one could say), he is a changed man: he is now a *Jewish* humanist writer, French dignitary, and Resistance hero.

Thus, on one level, the novel continues Gary's self-invention by moving to redefine his public authorial image in terms of being henceforth a Jewish French Resistance writer, but also in the course of writing he wants to explore this side of himself, which he had formerly repressed or ignored. What questions does his Jewishness raise for him? What literary approach can he use to think it through? How does it change his thoughts about his experience in France, in the Resistance, or as a writer? Will he reorient the direction of his work?

The novel in which this discovery occurs centers on a Jewish comic (Genghis Cohn) who has come back from the grave to haunt a former SS officer (police commissioner Schatz) who directed Cohn's execution.[14] Gary's own metamorphosis is acted out in the novel as resulting from his interaction with the book's characters. Gary devised an unorthodox narrative mode to convey this facet of the writer's experience, using occasional abrupt shifts between speakers or parenthetical dialogues to address the relationships between author and characters. As the characters comment on their status vis-à-vis one another and the author, we witness a confusion of selves as they struggle to sort out a topology of voices. Who inhabits whom? Who speaks through whom? At several points, for example, the disgruntled protagonist Genghis Cohn remembers that he exists only in Gary's imagination: "I had completely forgotten where I was. This guy [Gary] is a real shit and his subconscious is a vipers' nest . . . I'm not going to stay a second more. But I'm no longer certain of anything. I don't even know if it's me who is thinking or if it's him. At any rate, at least there's one thing I'm sure of, and that's my yellow star [i.e., the Magen David]" (*DGC* 248).

The only fixed point of identity for the protagonist is the Star of David, since it links him to the author by their common Jewish heritage. The hierarchy of author over characters is not absolute, however, for Gary recognizes that Cohn has something of an independent existence within Gary's imagination. The author-character remarks: "I smile, my eyes closed. I'm know that bastard Cohn suspects I'm here. He figured out a while ago where he's ended up" (*DGC* 269). The characters can be seen as representing different stock identities—the comic Cohn as a personification of the mythical millenary Jew (Kauffmann 85) and Schatz as the unrepentant SS officer—that are negotiating Gary's thoughts on the aftermath of World War II and his own sense of identity.

This psychic entanglement ultimately leaves all of these characters transformed by their contact with one another. This goes from the comic scenes of a drunken Schatz startled to find himself shouting in Yiddish (which Cohn has been teaching him while the former Nazi sleeps) to Gary as author, regaining consciousness with Cohn's voice now inhabiting his writing persona. Judith Kauffmann reasons convincingly that Cohn is also *Gary*'s dybbuk and serves as a guide initiating the neophyte (since nonpracticing) Jew into his heritage (Kauffmann 77). Where there is initiation, there is transformation, and indeed Gary's return to consciousness can be seen as a sort of rebirth.

Here the author has been invoked in a very different mode than in the other novels where Gary appears by name, for the author's subconscious is presented as a psychic space in which the author's sense of self continually evolves as a result of frequenting other characters' identities. It is another attempt to suggest an *episodic author*, in the sense of one who lasts only the duration of the given work, one who is transformed by the writing of each work.

This process of transhumance thus enables Gary to exist, for the duration of a book, in the skin of another "person," albeit of his own invention. Writing can either be a means of exploration of certain features of one's identity (in the case of *The Dance of Genghis Cohn*), or a means of realizing the dream of multiple identities (in the instance of *Les trésors de la mer Rouge*): "Thus, as a novelist, I write in order to learn about what I don't know, to become what I am not, to enjoy an experience or life that eludes me in reality" (*NSC* 324). For Gary, the literary experience is one of trying out different identities, as a vehicle to literary renewal and a way of destabilizing those labels that are imposed on oneself.

Clandestine Resistance

The whole of Gary's writing career unfolds against the backdrop of the Resistance. Often, the reference is quite literal: his first six novels contain characters identified as formerly in Resistance outfits. On a thematic level, Gary participates in the Gaullists' metaphorical extension of the historic phenomenon of the French Resistance to a generalized humanist notion of "Resistance." For instance, in *The Roots of Heaven, Promise at Dawn*, and the later editions of *A European Education*, this term provides a conceptual umbrella for a range of strategies resisting what is seen as a dangerous debasement of human values.

As a result, the basic vocabulary and themes of the Resistance—clandestineness, refuge, hidden identity, subversive action—play an important role in organizing different facets of Gary's literary imagination. Various types of hideaway figure in nearly every one of his novels, be it the requisitioned apartment in *The Company of Men*, the hidden room in *L'homme à la colombe*, the stack of lumber that shelters the child narrator of *Promise at Dawn*, or the underground chambers of *A European Education* and "A Humanist." [15] These are literal and symbolic spaces of retreat.

In terms of identity, the equivalent of these hideouts is the pseudonym. Gary's first sixteen works contain dozens of pseudonymous characters. In *The Company of Men, Lady L., The Colors of the Day*, and *The Guilty Head*, nearly every single character, significant or secondary, turns out to be using an invented name. [16]

After the publication of *Promise at Dawn* forefronted Gary's own use of pseudonyms, dissimulated identity would take on a more complex role in his writing. An insistent link would remain between the establishment of legends and clandestine efforts, but now the references would change registers, breaking away from most connections with the Gaullist project. The initial reference was heroic, always grounded in the attempt to shore up faltering idealism: Nadejda, mythical captain in the Polish Resistance (*A European Education*); Viauque de Montjoli, Resistant and Buchenwald survivor (*Tulipe*); La France Libre comrades Rainier and La Marne (*The Colors of the Day*); and Morel enduring solitary confinement during his deportation (*The Roots of Heaven*). Beginning with *Lady L.* and *Promise at Dawn*, clandestineness would still mean going underground, but in order to reinvent oneself more than to fight for a cause.

A related distinction concerns the status of these characters. Todorov notes that Gary only writes about the *Resistance* and never about *war*; in other words, disdaining the aggressors, Gary focuses on the means of struggle that typifies the underdog, what Todorov calls the "strength of the weak" (Todorov 243). Thus, while the small group of Gary's best-known protagonists enjoy public consecration in their novels, the vast majority of his characters are in fact outsiders, nobodies in every sense of the term: orphaned, without proper papers, petty thugs living on the run. The paranoid philosophy of La Marne, Genghis Cohn, Lenny (*Ski Bum*), and Gluckman ("The Oldest Story Ever Told") is neatly summarized in Gustave Vanderputte's motto: "In life, you want to slip by unnoticed . . . It's a real art. Don't let yourself be spotted, young man, that's the first thing you should learn" (*CM* 44–45). These characters exist in a strange margin outside of all legitimacy where their dreams of becoming "someone" are more a flight from what fate and circumstances designated them to be; in the words of Luc, the young hero of *The Company of Men*, "I was clandestine, illegal . . . I had to avoid any publicity and dedicate myself wholly to my job, which was to try to become someone" (*CM* 94).

These strategies of clandestine resistance can thus aim for high visibility or complete anonymity, but in both cases the foundations are the same. It is a concept that allows Gary to bring under the same umbrella the opposing faces of his own existence, the Resistance hero and the bastard child, the two archetypal figures that lie behind all of his different incarnations.[17]

These attitudes toward life leave us with a cast of characters who invent all aspects of their life stories, changing their names and nationalities and tossing off wild improvisations whose contradictions leave the reader never knowing a character's true identity. This is a facet of self-invention Malraux explored briefly in the character of Clappique, only to back off from it in later works. Not so with Gary, whose presentation of Willie Bauché in *The Colors of the Day* is much in the same tradition: "His ancestors had all been gardeners for the Counts of Illery in Touraine. His father died of a broken heart when Willie told him of his intention to emigrate to America . . . [Willie] often made up entire outlandish biographies of this sort for himself . . . He carefully hid the fact that he was one-quarter black. His hair was a bit frizzy and his features had a certain roundness . . . but nobody suspected anything. Maybe this explained his mythomania: a constant need to bury something, to confuse the issue. Moreover, he didn't have any black blood; this, too, was invented" (*CD* 43–44). Even the interpretations that we might be tempted to give to Bauché's lies are thwarted by further fabrications. At no point do we get behind the mask. When *The Colors of the Day* later develops a story line based on the assumption that Bauché grew up the child of a prostitute in New Orleans, we know not to trust this information either.

Along similar lines, instead of an attempt to affirm a freely chosen self, Cohn's activity in *The Guilty Head* consists of the dogged dismantling of any fixed identity. Most of his traits, for instance, are negative: we learn that he is only pretending to be American and that his real name is not Cohn, yet nothing will ever be put in the place of these voided features.

The reader is alerted to the fact that Cohn's identities are all impersonations from the outset: "[Cohn] had managed to disappear without
leaving any traces whatsoever, hidden inside of a character of his own
invention" (*GH* 119).

Cohn appears to have realized the dream of Willie Bauché and Gustave
Vanderputte, to disappear into a completely clandestine existence. Cohn
cannot escape quite so easily, however. Circumstances conspire against
him to impose a new identity. All along, unbeknownst to him, someone
has been on his trail, tracking him and his secrets. Perhaps no one knows
his true name or nationality, but the CIA thinks it does. Cohn's facial features and fingerprints had been surgically altered in Caracas to help him
out of a prior jam.[18] Now, it appears that the surgeon accidentally gave
him the appearance of a French nuclear physicist who has fled Europe in
a panic after discovering the means of producing a bomb capable of de-
stroying the planet. Confused by Cohn's resemblance to the scientist, the
superpowers think that they have found the missing researcher. At first,
Cohn happily embarks on this new existence, calling it "an absolutely
unprecedented coincidence that opens up all sorts of possibilities" (*GH*
272). In the novel's busy conclusion, however, Cohn discovers that he is
not the only one in disguise. He is nearly killed by undercover operatives
on several occasions, and his Tahitian companion, attractive precisely for
her lack of connection to European identities and institutions, turns out
to be a carefully disguised anthropology student from Tübingen, fleeing
the same world as Cohn—and playing her hand one card better.

Gary has extended the mutability of identity well beyond the terms set
by Thomas Mann in my discussion of *Felix Krull*. Whereas Mann's reader
is always certain of the protagonists' identity (only the other characters
are in the dark), here Gary reminds us that the stability of fictional identity depends primarily on the author's whim. Gary mocks literary conventions with the presentation of a spy "who wasn't named Victor Turkassi"
(*GH* 224; the device is repeated with the characters Mahé and Tamil).
Later, in his dying moments, it seems we are given his real name: Nikolaï
Vassiliévitch Ordjonikidzé (*GH* 229). Upon reflection, however, we notice
that this name is siphoned off of other people's names (the first names
are those of Gogol, the patronym that of a leader of the Bolshevik Revolution). It, too, is more of a "pseudoname" than a pseudonym. The result
is a hollowing out of identity that at times endangers the very readability
of the text (see also *Europa*). More interestingly, however, secondary characters drawn entirely by stereotype (Cohn's Tahitian girlfriend, Tchong
Fat, Callum, and Meeva) suddenly take on a new breadth when we realize
that their clichéd appearances are alibis hiding other identities.

An example of how these problematics of clandestine resistance affected Gary's vision of authorship can be found in one of his own pseud-

onymous precedents. *L'homme à la colombe,* because it ridicules the UN at a time (1958) when Gary was still active in the French diplomatic corps, was of necessity published under a pseudonym: Fosco Sinibaldi. What is interesting in this case is the way the use of a pseudonym, imposed or not, mirrors the novel's dominant themes. Recall from Chapter 2 that *L'homme à la colombe* centers on an idealist (Johnnie) who succumbs to cynicism. To avenge his disappointed dreams, he cooks up a scam to exploit the public's gullibility. Having discovered an unknown room that exists in the UN building by dint of an architectural glitch, Johnnie settles in as a "clandestine tenant," a voice of idealism issuing from the belly of a vast bureaucratic machine. Deliberately depicted in the tradition of the American everyman, Johnnie harangues the political establishment, a David against Goliath, but safe and anonymous in his hiding place. The pseudonymous author Fosco Sinibaldi, unknown and untraceable, mugging the diplomatic community with impunity, doubles Johnnie's gesture. Through the parallel of the hidden room and hidden name, Gary created an element of collusion between the figure of the clandestine tenant and his pseudonymous publication.[19] Moreover, the name itself announces its true colors: *Fosco* (dark, in Italian) casts Sinibaldi as Gary's shadowy double, the flip side of authenticity, his first clandestine alter ego, while Sinibaldi is an allusion to *Gari*baldi (frequently mentioned in Gary's catalog of patriotic legends). This doubling between Gary's own use of pseudonyms as an author and their role within his fiction has received surprisingly little commentary, even after the revelation of Émile Ajar's identity. The author's protest doubled that of the protagonist; Gary's authorial strategy participated in the same argument.

A Critical and Theoretical Impasse?

It is easy to see where the story of Cohn in *The Guilty Head* imitating the artistic image of Gauguin would send Gary down a path that would lead to Émile Ajar. Looking at Gary's career in retrospect, the Ajar episode emerged as a logical conclusion to the trajectory of the literary vision developed here. On the eve of the Ajar episode in the early seventies, however, Gary's impending creative burst and high-wire act were much more difficult to foresee.

Gary's efforts to transform his image ran into stumbling blocks on two planes. As indicated at the outset of this chapter, his image took a beating in the press during this period. Hostility toward de Gaulle, attacks on the Resistance legacy, Gary's failed films and the tragic events destabilizing Seberg more than tarnished Gary's formerly heroic and debonair persona. At this juncture of his career, good fortune, political savvy, and personal judgment all seem to have abandoned him. Similarly, on the literary front, his capacity to stay one step ahead in the game of self-creation seems to have waned. He very nearly broke with Gallimard over quarrels about the firm's advertising techniques, techniques that struck Gary, after his exposure to American marketing strategies, as outdated (Larat 104). The press, posed as an intermediary between Gary and the public, refused to take note of his objectives. Success on the best-seller lists with more conventional efforts (*White Dog, La nuit sera calme,* and *The Enchanters*) served to ensure that challenging works like *The Dance of Genghis Cohn, The Guilty Head,* and *Europa* did not receive substantive consideration.[20] Each new novel was passed off as the work of someone the public knew too well already. Comments Gary: "In Paris the literary world is condensed to the dimensions of a pinhead. Moreover, it bears an extraordinary resemblance to socialite circles, both on the Left and on the Right. Under these conditions, everything is *personal.* As soon as you become what people call today a 'personality,' it is no longer your work that is judged but you—... and this without even knowing you. What comes into play ... is your image, an ensemble of psychological and political factors that have nothing to do with your book or film" (Gary, "Je suis un irrégulier" 1). For most critics at this time, Gary was judged to be on the decline and was not expected to make contributions of note to French literature.

Gary's project in *The Dance of Genghis Cohn* gives us a specific example of how this process failed to come off properly. The writing of this novel produced a new mythic scenario for Gary. Whereas early in his career he deliberately mystified inquiries into his origins, hushing in particular his Jewish background, *The Dance of Genghis Cohn* shows him embracing this identity. Ideally, then, a change in his image as an author would occur as a result of his changing stylistics, themes, and self-portrayals. Though Gary's gesture elicited a variety of responses, none corresponded to what he was hoping to communicate. While the French press on the Right laced its reviews with scarcely veiled anti-Semitic slurs, conservative Jews rejected Gary's designation as Jewish because he was not a practicing Jew in a religious sense. During this period, for instance, Gary stated that he received a letter informing him of why he was refused a listing in the *Who's Who in World Jewry*: "Those cuckolds sent me a letter in which they awkwardly explained that I don't possess the characteristics necessary to be considered Jewish," comments Gary. "[They're] a lot pickier than Rosenberg and Himmler were" (qtd. in Catonné, *Romain Gary* 46). An article published in *Information juive* after Gary's death explains the reasons for refusing Gary's "affiliation." Arnold Mandel wrote: "[Gary is] is a hybrid if there ever was one. He is not at all Jewish. Born of a Jewish mother, according to the Halakah he was officially Jewish. But in such matters the Halakah legislates without necessarily deciding the outcome ... [Gary] never experienced the destiny of the Jews, was not considered Jewish and did not consider himself as such" (qtd. in Catonné, *Romain Gary* 45).

Particularly telling here is the fact that Gary's detractors preferred to search for confirmations of his Jewishness in the form of public behavior—that is, in performances of his authorial identity.[21] Even this cannot really be defended. Gary's childhood migrations strongly suggest that he was subjected to "the destiny of Jews." In his moves from Russia, Poland, France, North Africa, and England, his youth spent moving from school to school, he very much endured the status of "a pariah deprived of homeland" (Larat 23), barely staying one step ahead of the eastern pogroms and Nazi madness. He used his public roles on a number of occasions to denounce the French government's attitude toward Israel and French Jews (see Gary, "Lettre aux Juifs de France" 8–9). Gary was even willing to break with de Gaulle on these questions, taking issue wryly, for instance, with de Gaulle's controversial phrase: "When [de Gaulle] called the Jews 'an elite people, sure of itself and domineering,' he somewhat confused Auschwitz with Austerlitz" (Gary, "Je suis un irrégulier" 6).

Gary would find himself stuck in a strange middle ground: he was Jewish for anti-Semites but not for certain important sectors of the Jewish community, just as his Gaullism was held against him by the Communists, moderates, and the right wing, but he was ostracized for his lack of orthodoxy by de Gaulle's closest advisers. Though in the latter case it is a matter of individual opinions that can be judged variously, in the former, Gary could no longer even integrate factually demonstrable autobiographical elements into his public image. Another confirmation of this comes with the fate reserved for *La nuit sera calme*, a book-length interview with François Bondy published in 1974. In it Gary seizes the opportunity to set the record straight on a number of hot topics (his feelings about Algeria, post–de Gaulle Gaullism, Communism, etc.), and his remarks make it clear that Gary is not easily classifiable within the usual political categories. There is a mixture of social progressivism and "Old Europe" that has prodded critics to nuance some of their portraits of him. But even this recourse to a nonfiction genre like the interview is not as innocent as it seems. At Gary's death, Bondy revealed a hidden element of this book's conception: "This too was a joke, a trick, a hoax if you will. The manuscript of the book was quite complete when he gave it to me and suggested only that I insert some questions of my own in order to fill it out" ("On the Death of a Friend" 34). The cleverness of this maneuver is farther reaching than one might initially think. Clearly, it allowed Gary to direct which topics would be discussed and on what terms. But it also allowed him to place autobiographical material in a way that it would pass unquestioned. It was common knowledge that Bondy had known Gary for years and thus would be familiar with many aspects of his past; who would think to challenge the veracity of information presented by the *interviewer*? A fictional Bondy became the means to fine-tune the legend. Thus, Bondy "reminds" us of the respect Claudel and Martin du Gard expressed for Gary's early novels, Georges Bidault's patronage of Gary's diplomatic career, and Gary's impassioned defense of John F. Kennedy to a hostile French audience shortly before the latter's assassination (*NSC* 56, 115, 152, respectively).

While much of Gary's inability to nuance the contours of his image is due to the political and sociohistorical climate of the period, it can also be argued that the failed connection with the press is inherent in the literary strategies employed in these works. One clear shortcoming in *Pour Sganarelle*'s theoretical stance is that it adopts at times the position that literature constitutes a realm separate from reality, in seeming contradiction with the founding principles of *A European Education, Lady L.*, or *Promise at Dawn*: "[Literature borrows] all of its means from the Powers-that-be in order to create a realm to which the latter would no longer have access" (*PS* 128). In 1965, dragging his own fictions into reality apparently struck him as out of the question: "[My protagonist] signifies his point of view. Everyone is free to imagine him savoring a cigar in Switzerland or to transform culturally-informed impulses into an adherence to a political party . . . *But my protagonist does not exist outside the novel.* What the novel will or will not produce from its contact with our culture is a problem that concerns those who are primarily interested in concepts . . . My picaro *can only signify* his attitude toward the Ceremonial through his mime: he acts out his point of view" (*PS* 319; emphasis added).

In other words, Genghis Cohn is only a character in a novel, *acting out* resistance to institutional prescriptions and the symbolic status quo. Cohn's strategies and irreverent attitude may strongly resemble those of the later Ajar, but here confrontations with the Powers-that-be are in effect only pantomimed. They remain representations of resistance safely contained within the text.

We can see how this translates into Gary's choices with respect to his image. *The Dance of Genghis Cohn, The Guilty Head, White Dog, The Enchanters*, and *Les trésors de la mer Rouge* all differ in their approaches, but each ultimately boils down to a *representation* of changes in personal identity. How an artistic creation—the author—would compete with reality is *described* but not *performed*. To put it another way, the root of the problem lies in the fact that these works focus on fluctuations or transformations of the protagonist's identity, but they do so in novels where the identity of the implied author remains relatively constant for the reader. Again, this fixity is due in part to the stubborn reading habits of the press, but it must also be recognized that it is one of the dangers of Gary's frequent use of autofiction, where the implied narrator plays off of a stable, historical reference outside of the fictional account. The reader is thus led to incorporate new works into the old portrait.

Gary's basic tenet conceived of art as the attempt to impose imagination upon the circumstances of existence, yet as we see here his problematization of authorial persona passed primarily through experimentation with fictional frames. Thus, his prior skillful manipulation of interviews and biographical rescripting notwithstanding, Gary's own understanding of how his novelistic practice could participate in his ideal of self-invention remained in many ways circumscribed by the conventional boundaries of modernist literary technique. Fosco Sinibaldi, for instance, remained merely a paper author, with no accompanying support.

Gary was still seeking how best to conflate his literary and media practices for a new stage of creative self-renewal. But as long as Gary was losing the battle *outside* of the novel, any new elements he would introduce *within* the novel were powerless to threaten reality. Thus, the problem of how literature could compete with reality—how it could, in other words, *alter* reality—remained for Gary unresolved. Thus, the novels during this period would eventually come to something of an impasse. He succeeded on one level insofar as his sense of himself as a writer had been substantially transformed by the conception and execution of these works. But he failed to shake the press in its view of him as a writer possessing a certain force in his passionate defense of humanist themes but of limited literary range. Gary's own sense of identity had changed dramatically, as had the forms and themes of his works, but the parameters of his public image remained static.

Where would Gary find his solution? *Pour Sganarelle* is a meandering, disorganized essay. It is a confusing but rich reflection, a sort of work-in-progress in which we can follow Gary as he gropes toward the realization of his vision. In a sense, the answers are already there, but Gary has not yet recognized the full extent of his own argumentation: "Every contact with the world constitutes itself as reproach, frustration, provocation or desire. Men die for no reason; victories and suffering, peoples and ideologies all go to waste as they fail to suffice . . . The Powers-that-be in the real world beat me down and triumph on all fronts in this Rivalry. Under my very eyes, they impose themselves as masters of the situation. If I don't constantly bury this manure in the roots of a new work, it ends up infecting my conscience instead of fertilizing it. I no longer exist: I start to dissolve" (*PS* 9).[22] Because man does not seem able to bring art and ideas directly to bear on reality—the ideals for which people sacrifice their lives continue to fail to be realized—Gary must try to embroil reality in art. He is not in any way advocating escapist art.[23] Nevertheless, his approach continues to eschew the demands for authenticity that accompany Sartre's vision of committed literature, for Gary wants to undermine and rewrite reality by "burying it" within a work of fiction.

What Gary offers instead is this notion of "rivalry" as an updated form of his prior experiments with literary protest. As I noted in Chapter 2, fraud in Gary's early satires was conceived as a means of protest. It is here that the logic of Gary's own argument pulls him out of this impasse toward a new formulation. Instead of explaining the ways in which reality is constructed from artifice (and thus can be altered through symbolic realms), Gary must *prove* it. Gary's conception of the novel has shifted; he has moved away from seeing it simply as a space of representation, a place for staging philosophical truths (his penchant for allegory and philosophical tales), to seeing it as a weapon of sorts: "[I would like to point out] the misunderstanding which limits the notion of technique in art . . . to arrangement and form: *the novel is itself a technique,* the form[;] the content, values, truths, sincerity, source of inspiration are all supplies. *All of these are part of the arsenal, processes of seizing power* . . . The genres themselves—literature, painting, music, theater, philosophy, cinema—are only arrangements or realizations of a choice of means, artifice and the nature of the psychic terrain. They do not mark a difference in goal or aspiration" (*PS* 10–11). Considered from this angle, it is no longer simply a question of a literary aesthetic but of a literary *practice* or *performance* in a very literal sense of the term. Furthermore, it is clear from these remarks that this process pertains to facets of Gary's life that extend well beyond the novel, for his very sense of self depends on (or is constructed out of) successfully maintaining this creative relation to reality (where he fails, he "no longer exists").

Gary would discover the resolution to this artistic problem right under his nose. A principal element of the constant transformation of his characters' identities is the proliferation of pseudonyms within his novels. *It is one of the primary devices for maintaining a mobile identity within his narratives.* Why not do so himself as a way of introducing his own fictional constructions directly into the course of daily reality and the French literary "Ceremonials"? What was judged an important step in the creation of his postwar persona thus returns to mind: if he cannot transform Gary, he will become someone else altogether, a new persona entirely of his own invention, one that can be molded at will. The devices of autofiction and the picaresque characterization will be put in the service of this new clandestine alter ego. If Gary's protagonists are actor-authors, Gary the novelist will take his role as an author-actor to another level.

Chapter 4

The Invention of Émile Ajar, 1974–1975

Retired from the diplomatic corps, divorced from Seberg, and disappointed by politics, Gary now focused on his literary activities, publishing works under four different names during this period. His cousin Dinah passed away, leaving her son Paul Pavlowitch with few living relatives. Aside from a summer spent in Majorca, Gary spent these years close to Paris.

Shatan Bogat

> *I now had . . . to forge the soul of a terrorist and move on to direct action.*
> LL *163*

Looking to pursue his aesthetic vision on a more ambitious scale, Gary began plotting a new pseudonymous episode. It is clear from biographical and textual evidence that a project was already under way in 1972. A longtime friend of Gary's, Sacha Kardo-Sessoëff, recalls that Gary proposed a collaboration in which Kardo-Sessoëff would sign his name to detective novels written by Gary. A Bulgarian friend was also solicited (Bona 318). The fact that Gary sought the participation of friends implies that he planned to have another person play the role of this pseudonymous invention. In other words, Gary was planning to pass off his new incarnation as a real author, a literary *and* social persona. Faced with two refusals, however, Gary reduced the scope of his plans and acted on his own.

In the spring of 1974, an unknown writer named Shatan Bogat published *Les têtes de Stéphanie* (Direct flight to Allah). Somewhat in the tradition of Gallimard's detective thriller collection *Série noire*, this spy novel reached a French audience thanks to a translation from American English by Françoise Lovat. Abundant review copies won it unusual critical exposure, and reviewers in the popular press were nearly unanimous in praising this seemingly uncomplicated but fast-moving work. Christine Arnothy wrote, "Sadistic and droll, sparkling with humor, Shatan Bogat . . . writes with the stroke of a master."[1] Jean-Pierre Amette, critical of a poverty of literary talent in the espionage genre, also saw Bogat's writing as exceptional: "Style? Tricky, taunting, brisk, icy, peppery, charming, fast. Imagine the panache of a Lucien Bodard combined with the deadly elegance of a James Hadley Chase."[2] Another reviewer even congratulated Gallimard on their excellent translation.[3]

A press release unveiling Bogat's striking life story accompanied the publicity materials. Reviewers picked and chose from this curriculum vitae, each recomposing a figure according to the tone best befitting their paper's audience. *La Nouvelle République du Centre-Ouest,* for instance, offered a compact but intriguing portrait: "Thirty-nine years old, son of a Turkish immigrant, Shatan Bogat was born in Oregon. He directs a fishing and shipping business in the Indian Ocean and Persian Gulf. The black market arms trade inspired one of his novels. He won the Dakkan Prize in 1970 for his coverage of international gold and weapons traffickers."[4] *Nostradamus* relayed the same combination of colorful anecdote and social commitment: "A former journalist turned writer then sponge diver in India, the author dedicated himself in his previous works to exposing the networks of the illegal arms trade. With a touch of the great Lawrence of Arabia, this book deserves a prime spot in your crime fiction collection."[5]

Although spy novels of this ilk are usually known for the relative anonymity of their authors, Bogat's biography oriented the assessment of the book in most of these brief articles. Having repeated Bogat's credentials as a known combatant of arms traffickers and a longtime resident of the Persian Gulf region, one critic concluded, "This should be enough to convey how well he knows this setting and how important *Direct Flight to Allah*'s themes are to him."[6] The author serves as guarantor for form *and* content in Henri Collard's piece for *France-Soir*: Bogat possesses "a style that is 100% American, both explosive and relaxed, but with an appreciation of the Persian Gulf's local color that is not from the eye of a tourist."[7]

The problem here, of course, is that not only did Bogat's prior publications not exist—nor for that matter the Dakkan Prize nor even the translator—but Shatan Bogat himself was a fiction. Good journalistic practice—in this case, a verification of Bogat's supposed bibliography—would have revealed the hoax. Details like the anomaly of a pulp fiction thriller published as a Gallimard novel or its extensive promotion could also have alerted the press to a suspicious endeavor. What of the Dakkan Prize (from an alternative spelling of *Deccan,* thus "corroborating" Bogat's ties to India)? Moreover, on literary grounds, these critics established their analysis based upon an authorial persona every bit as roundly stereotyped as the characters normally found in the spy genre. This hardboiled, "100% American" thriller was in fact written by a European author who spoke Russian, Polish, French, British English—and even some

German, Bulgarian, Hebrew, and Arabic—before he ever tackled the colloquialisms of American English. Finally, having recently completed a serialized travelogue in Yemen for *France-Soir* in 1970 (*Les trésors de la mer Rouge*), Gary possessed a knowledge of the Persian Gulf that was precisely that of a tourist.

Of all the reviewers, only author-lawyer Jean-Claude Zylberstein voiced an inkling of something awry: "An exceptional success in the difficult art of the thriller: a political masterpiece, this story of a provocation in a Persian Gulf nation; a novelistic masterpiece, the misogynistic narrative of pretty Stephanie's agony; and, finally, a stylistic masterpiece, the flowered evocation of an Arabia full of furor and mystery. Bogat is a master. But which one? This too is a mystery."[8] While one suspects that Zylberstein perhaps knew more than he admitted here—director of foreign literature and detective collections, he also served as Paulhan's secretary during the Gallimard years and still practices as a renowned specialist in copyright law—his colleagues failed to heed his suggestion that this spy mystery warranted some detective work of its own.

No doubt Bogat's true identity would have remained unrevealed were it not for Robert Gallimard's impatience with the book's sluggish sales. He brought an end to the masquerade by disclosing in a radio interview that Gary was responsible for the text and pseudonym. Even after the revelation of Bogat's identity, though, reviewers neglected to reexamine the novel's contents; however, dimensions of the text that went unnoticed by those reading "Bogat"'s work are more evident when one compares it with Gary's literary production.

Bogat's authorial persona—sponge diver in the Indian Ocean, tracking down black market arms traders—was in fact created in the image of the exotic espionage novel he was supposed to have authored. In reflecting upon this mimetic relation between author and text, an interesting complicity also emerges between Gary's pseudonymous tactic and the protagonist's covert adventures. Gary gives a very different meaning to the Balzacian injunction that writers should compete with the *état civil*, for the true undercover operative here is Gary himself, carrying out his literary mission under a falsified identity.

This last point requires a look at the novel itself. *Direct Flight to Allah* does not attempt to break any new ground from a formal point of view, since stylistically it is little more than an agreeable pastiche of adventure fiction. But behind the cover of its superficial suspense plot, Gary has smuggled in his own arms: a deceptively rich scenario that touches on many of the topics that preoccupy him. In his preface to the paperback edition, for instance, he affirms that the use of a pseudonym has nothing to do with working in a discredited genre: "One would be mistaken to think that I chose a pseudonym . . . because it was for a book that one might somewhat disdainfully call 'an adventure novel.' I did it because I sometimes feel the need to change identities, to break free of myself, if only for the duration of a book" (*DFA* 6).

We encounter a similar words expressed by the male protagonist, a CIA operative known only as "Rousseau": "[Rousseau] had a soft spot for what he called his 'escapes' from himself. He could not resist the temptation to take on for the duration of a mission identities as far as possible from his own—he knew it a bit too well and expected nothing new from it" (*DFA* 168). The method and goals are identical. "A man who saw himself as a past master in the art of living in the skin of another" (*DFA* 176), Rousseau takes on these alternative identities in an episodic manner the same way Gary as pseudonymous author sought to do so. Both shed previous identities in order to find renewal in disguises of their own concoction. Reminiscent of Gary and his enjoyment of his encounters with the Chinese and Russian tourists in *Les trésors de la mer Rouge*, Rousseau finds this sense of constant transformation pleasurable in itself: "He would sometimes catch himself hamming it up and would chastise himself for the pleasure he took in assuming a disguise or playing a role well-suited to his physique. Without a doubt, he enjoyed it thoroughly" (*DFA* 147).

The experiment with Bogat triumphed to the extent that the final result was a seamless artistic ensemble; the novel *and* biography were literary efforts cut from the same cloth. Gary's pseudonymous persona was briefly thought to circulate in the real world, since the alleged Dakkan Prize, prior publications and family tree seemed to confirm Bogat's existence. It marked a move one step closer to the realization of the exploits dreamed up by Willie Bauché, Lady L., and Genghis Cohn in Gary's prior novels. Gary as much as recognized this progression in *Direct Flight to Allah*, since he slyly slipped in a number of veiled references to his own preoccupation with these techniques. When Rousseau muses over his previous undercover guises, for instance, we are in fact looking at a list of some of Gary's past and future incarnations: "[Rousseau] had already played so many roles in his professional life that he wondered at times if he had any personal life left at all. He had been Jewish, Cuban, Puerto Rican, Italian, black Caribbean, an Arab terrorist and Brazilian" (*DFA* 142). While the first few terms allude to prior protagonists (in *The Dance of Genghis Cohn*, *Talent Scout*, *Europa*, and *The Guilty Head*), the last two announce Gary's *next* pseudonymous metamorphosis, a reputed Algerian terrorist exiled in Brazil.

Émile Ajar, Act One

> *I wasn't daring enough!* . . . *This time I'm going to double the dose!*
> HC 75–76

Shatan Bogat's *Direct Flight to Allah* stands ultimately as a cursory and essentially ludic warmup of sorts, a text performed in a throwaway genre with limited literary stakes. Six months prior to the publication of *Direct Flight to Allah*, however, in January 1974, Éditions Gallimard received a manuscript sent from Brazil by an equally mysterious Émile Ajar. Pierre Michaut, a French businessman operating out of Rio de Janeiro, explained that his friend Ajar instructed him to deliver the text because Ajar was unable to come to France.

The manuscript, eventually titled *Gros-Câlin*, is of a completely different tenor and literary importance from *Direct Flight to Allah*. *Gros-Câlin* is charming and offbeat, yet at the very limit of coherence. Given that no one had ever heard of Ajar, the stylistic mastery displayed in the novel raised suspicions among Gallimard's preliminary readers. Despite skepticism from Claude Faraggi and Queneau, Christiane Baroche and Colette Duhamel succeeded in having the manuscript recommended to the Readers' Committee. At this next level, a couple of readers were tempted to take a chance on it, but Queneau curbed their enthusiasm and this time turned the tide against Ajar. To the trained eye of a fellow prankster, the unusual circumstances surrounding this work looked like trouble.[9] Noted Queneau, "The letter that accompanies the manuscript suggests an author who is awfully impressed with himself and most certainly a pain-in-the-ass" (qtd. in Bona 322). Under the gun because of a forty-eight-hour ultimatum issued via Michaut, Claude Gallimard eventually got cold feet and in February 1974 decided to pass the manuscript along to one of Gallimard's subsidiaries, Mercure de France, directed by Claude's wife, Simone Gallimard. In need of a strong seller, Mercure de France was only too glad to seize the opportunity. Its editors amputated its final chapter (which Ajar, confined to an intermediate role, was not able to prevent), and the release was timed for the fall prize season of 1974 (Bona 321–23; Pavlowitch, *L'homme que l'on croyait* 20–22).

The first reviews show a majority of critics quite seduced by this newcomer. Trade papers such as the *Le Magazine littéraire, Les Nouvelles littéraires, Le Figaro,* and *Le Monde* all strongly supported Ajar's novel. A rising young talent himself at the time, Didier Decoin offered extremely high praise: "[French letters] have found their most ruthless moralist since La Fontaine. They have found their most tragically joyous poet since

[François] Villon and Rabelais."[10] Populist dailies like *France-Soir* and *Le Parisien libéré* followed suit, though they were soon distracted by the quest to uncover Ajar's identity. Standing apart were the weekly news magazines, with begrudging endorsements from *L'Express* and *Le Point* and a dismissive review from *Le Nouvel Observateur*.[11]

Ajar's well-placed admirers made him a leading candidate for several important awards. Once Ajar was swept into the prize derby, however, the issue of establishing his identity became more urgent. Critics were laudatory but increasingly wary: most feared the involvement of a known quantity behind this faceless name. Michel Cournot, literary director of Mercure de France and prime suspect for many, could only pass along the scant biography that accompanied the original manuscript. It announced that Ajar was born in Oran in 1940 and that his childhood acquaintance with Camus was his reason for initially seeking to be published by Gallimard. On Gary's instructions, Michaut had also added a few sordid details to fuel Ajar's notoriety but especially to justify why the maverick writer could not meet his publisher or cooperate in promotion: an illegal abortion performed by Ajar, a former medical student in Paris, had attracted the attention of French authorities and led to his exile in Brazil. This was scarcely reassuring for Cournot and Simone Gallimard.

Meanwhile, Gary had also maneuvered discreetly to prop up this biography. The novel provides internal "evidence" in the form of asides that echo Ajar's presumed biography. *Gros-Câlin*'s narrator, Michel Cousin, remarks at one point, "I sometimes tell girls that I'm studying medicine"; or, "What's more, I don't even look Algerian" (*GC* 58; 117). In addition to these allusions scattered throughout the novel, Gary orchestrated occasional news items, such as a press release identifying Gisèle Halimi as Ajar's attorney. The Tunisian-born lawyer had engineered the much-admired defense in France's precedent-setting abortion rights case (the Bobigny Affair in November 1972) and had founded "La Cause des femmes" (The women's cause) a year later, both social issues featured in *Gros-Câlin*. Moreover, Halimi brought further credibility to Ajar because she had largely made her reputation providing legal aid for the Algerian National Liberation Front (FLN) and counted among her clients politically committed authors like de Beauvoir and Sartre. In other directions, the connection Ajar claimed to Camus is evocative as well: the narrator's disjointed and self-enclosed character in *Gros-Câlin* brings to mind a burlesque incarnation of Meursault or Dr. Rieux. The combination of these factors—internal textual "evidence," the unknowing collaboration of independent public figures, and the beginnings of a literary genealogy—granted Ajar greater consistency in the press's eyes.

By the same token, Ajar's work repeatedly calls attention to the fact that as readers we do not know who Ajar is. *Gros-Câlin* purports to be a zoological essay by a socially ill-adapted narrator on his pet python's life in Paris. Gary, however, repeatedly pushes his wry sarcasm in a number of passages to the point that his lines can hardly be given meaning unless one links them to the question of *Ajar*'s uncertain identity: "Pythons are not really an animal species, they're an awakening of consciousness" (*GC* 117). Or, more playfully (with a teasing allusion to *The Roots of Heaven* for future readers): "Physically, Gros-Câlin [the python] is beautiful. He resembles an elephant's trunk a tiny bit, it's quite friendly. At first sight obviously, people mistake him for someone else. But I sincerely believe that people will really like him once they get to know him" (*GC* 54). That Ajar is hidden, well hidden, is true, but he is also an author who leaves clues to the fact that he is hidden. This is an aspect frequently overlooked in recent assessments of Gary's work: elliptically, Gary entices critics into a game of literary hide-and-go-seek.

This challenge created an unusual situation for reviewers. Ever since the decline of the New Novel, there had been few surprises or discoveries on the French literary scene. Critics had grown accustomed to dealing with known quantities. Yet now they found themselves obliged to formulate an interpretation without the comfort of the author's identity. If it is a writer in hiding, who is it? Critics are powerful in Paris, wielding as much influence as many writers. What if by chance Ajar is in fact Queneau or Paulhan? Attacking this unknown figure could have unforeseen consequences in the small world of Parisian letters. Therefore, while waiting to uncover Ajar's identity, in what literary tradition should they place him? What profile should they give him? Ajar's style was so quirky, so resolutely resistant to traditional categories, that it demanded interpretation but refused to provide many easy handles. Daunted by the elusiveness of Cousin's strangely opaque monologue, critics took the safe way out and contented themselves with vague summaries of the novel's haphazard plot. The end result is that *Gros-Câlin* was subjected to surprisingly little probing analysis.

There are nonetheless a number of recurrent thematic details in this relatively sparse novel, and these would seem to indicate interpretive paths worth exploring. One noteworthy instance concerns the narrator's somewhat obsessive but unexplained adulation for Jean Moulin and Pierre Brossolette. In referring regularly to these heroes of the French Resistance, Gary plays on Ajar's supposed fear of being identified: "Maybe I express myself with veiled allusions but the Parisian conglomeration includes ten million customers, not counting vehicles, and it is advisable, even in taking the risk to cry out with one's heart on one's sleeve, to hide and not expose the essential. Moreover, if Jean Moulin and Pierre Brossolette were caught, it's because they showed themselves outdoors and went to meetings on the outside" (*GC* 16).[12]

Several reviewers picked up on this recourse to clandestine existence as a defensive gesture in modern-day urban living. Thus, the link Gary established in *The Roots of Heaven* and elsewhere between his vision of a humanist Resistance and metaphors for postwar social struggle would also be perceived in Ajar's work: "Jean Moulin and Pierre Brossolette regularly appear throughout the narrative as a way of symbolizing [the narrator's] recourse to a clandestine existence. In other times, Cousin would have been an underground Resistant" (Mohrt 13).[13] Since Ajar was also in hiding, critics almost by reflex attributed the narrator's attitudes to the author. As a result, they increasingly overcame their initial skepticism and believed in Ajar. That is, they opted for the notion that *Ajar existed but was in hiding*, turning away from the idea that he could be the pseudonymous fiction of an established writer. Despite the fact that the objective of many critics was to flush out the identity of the author of this book, no one seized on the possible parallels between the theme of clandestine existence and pseudonymous authorship.

Though in retrospect we can easily recognize Gary's playful irony, a related theme that would receive no attention from the critical press is that of ventriloquism. Midway through the novel, the narrator decides to seek the help of a ventriloquism instructor. The elderly teacher, Mr. Parisi, had been an entertainer in the past and even now "his hands always seemed on the point of pulling aside a curtain to reveal something hidden behind it" (*GC* 92). The art of learning to project one's voice so that it appears to the public that another person is speaking neatly fits Gary's enterprise. The teacher reassures the narrator and his fellow pupils: "We all have identity problems . . . Sometimes you have to recycle yourself elsewhere" (*GC* 96). The narrator is particularly impressed by a fellow student, Achille Durs, who has decided late in life to make some big changes: "It takes a lot of courage to change lives at an age when others don't even dare think about it any more" (*GC* 102).

Mr. Parisi promises the narrator that he will "be able to make [his] python speak by the end of six weeks" (*GC* 96). What of this python, the central recurring element of the novel? In the reviews, it is subjected to all manner of banalities. "Don't we all shelter a python within us?" asks one critic.[14] On the rare occasions when the python is discussed in relation to literary problematics, one falls back on mentions of Ajar's "serpentine" style, his convolutions and digressions like so many coils enveloping and suffocating the reader. Such unchallenging readings concerning a writer who has aroused great controversy and curiosity is puzzling. Is it really, as the narrator claims, a zoological treatise on pythons? This novel is definitely an effort at classification, with its narrator himself to be placed somewhere between buffoon and naturalist Buffon. But the real project here of course is not to study animal behavior in urban settings. Rather,

Gary wants to examine for himself the formation of that strange reptile that one more commonly calls an authorial persona. In other words, *Gros-Câlin* is first and foremost an elaborate riddle about the experience of writing under an identity that one is in the process of inventing. As a matter of fact, the reader has only to substitute *pseudo* for *python* in some sentences to decode otherwise incomprehensible passages: "It's impossible for me to express here everything that a man who lives clandestinely with a python feels at times in our circumstances. In truth, it's a way of throwing up a wall" (*GC* 58). It is conceived, in other words, as a protective device for his dealings with others: "My principal problem isn't so much my at-home as it is my at-others" (*GC* 63).

Considered from this angle, several features leap out at us. What is one of the narrator's favorite things about pythons? "All that is just tales of molting, in order to start over with a fresh skin, but always the same one, pseudo-pseudo . . . I'm a specialist on this subject, you can trust me on that . . . Pythons are permanent. They slough off their skins but they always start over . . . They get a new skin, but it boils down to the same thing, just a bit fresher, that's all" (*GC* 40). It is a bit like certain aging writers and their pseudonyms, one might say. After all, these remarks are far more pertinent for an author like Gary, who has already passed through a number of disguises in his career—"I'm a specialist on this subject" and "They get a new skin"—than they would be for a novice like Ajar. The narrator continues: "The experience of renewal is a profound moment in the life of pythons . . . They feel like they are on the point of acceding to a new life . . . All observers of pythons know that the slough awakens in this agreeable reptile the hope of acceding to an entirely different animal domain, another species, fully evolved and with lungs" (*GC* 101).

The connection between the python's shedding and the birth of a new writer is in fact explicit. In the following paragraph, Gary presents what can be read as an account of the transformation of his authorial persona, the birth of Ajar as Gary's new pseudonymous incarnation: "I also noticed that Gros-Câlin began his first slough in my home at just about the same time as I started taking these notes. Of course, nothing happened—he became himself again, but he tried quite courageously, and produced a fresh skin. The metamorphosis is the most beautiful thing that has ever happened to me" (*GC* 17). The writing of this work begins, in other words, with a joyous experience of shedding an old skin, or, rather, with the observation and narration of this joyous experience. The simultaneity of the writing and the metamorphosis makes one wonder if Cousin's act of taking up his pen does not in some way participate in if not instigate the snake's molting. As suggested by *Direct Flight to Allah* (176), losing oneself in the course of writing is akin to shedding one's skin and taking on another. Moreover, one is hard-pressed otherwise to explain why the narrator places the disjunctive pronoun in the first person: "the metamorphosis is the most beautiful thing that has ever happened *to me*." Ajar may be little more than a new skin on the old beast, but this new incarnation of Gary is different enough to provoke a rich new voyage through the imaginary (the novel *Gros-Câlin*).

It is in this transformation that the writing experience provides its momentum for Gary. The relationship between Cousin and his python is thus a camouflaged mirror of Gary and his pseudonyms. In this reading, Cousin stands as a relatively fixed reference point, his job and coworkers attesting to his social being. In contrast, the python (i.e., a pseudonymous alter ego) exists primarily in Cousin's own mind, when they are at home alone. What we have in essence is a literary performance of *Pour Sganarelle*'s arguments, the step-by-step story of Gary's transmutation into Ajar. For it is the dialogue between Cousin and Gros-Câlin that is presented as the subject of the book; it is the relation between the two that produces the story.

If Cousin wants to record his python's existence in Paris, he must loan it his voice, but in the process he appropriates its existence, puts himself in its place. As the novel advances, Cousin identifies more and more intensely with his python, to the point of losing his bearings. Here is the danger in assisting this other: as with Gary becoming a caricature of his legend, one risks becoming absorbed in and by one's own creation. By the end of the novel, the reader is no longer sure whether there ever was a snake in Cousin's apartment, but what is certain is that Cousin now takes himself for a python.[15]

Gros-Câlin pursues the difficulties involved in the birth of a new authorial persona in another figurative register, one that somewhat incongruously borrows its metaphors from contemporary debates on abortion rights. The book's epigraph, for instance, is an excerpt from a newspaper clipping citing Dr. Jean-Louis Lortat-Jacob, one of the central figures opposed to liberalizing abortion and president of France's Medical Association at the time: "The National Council of the Order of Medical Doctors reaffirms its hostility to free abortion. In the event that legislators authorize it, it is their opinion that this 'chore' must be performed by a 'specified personnel of execution' and in 'places specifically effected for this purpose: ABORTORIA [les AVORTOIRS]'" (*GC* 7). Ajar's running critique of the French Medical Association's opposition to improving access to abortions recalls his supposed legal difficulties and his ties to Halimi, thus giving a biographical orientation to these references that precludes other interpretations by the press. Doubtless Gary himself takes issue with the article in part out of outrage at the doctor's choice of vocabulary, for Lortat-Jacob's inflammatory allusions to butchery and concentration camps are intended to turn public opinion against abortion clinics through rhetoric rather than reason.[16] But if we continue to examine these passages in *Gros-Câlin* with respect to the rest of Gary's work, we see that Gary employs this vocabulary in other contexts as well.

"I also respectfully agree with the Order of Medical Doctors," remarks Cousin. "There is in fact life before birth, and it is toward this goal that I dedicate my efforts" (*GC* 38). The response is cryptic, for what Cousin understands of another's speech usually has only a partial relation to what the speaker intended. Nevertheless, Cousin states that his effort (the book on his snake) is aimed at recording this "life before birth." The allusion, for those who have read *Gary* carefully, takes us back to the opening argument in *Pour Sganarelle* on the formation of authorial personae, which depends, in Gary's opinion, upon the dialogue created between writer and protagonist, the "author-character" and "protagonist-character." In this passage, for instance, Gary is speaking about his struggle to bring a new writing self to "eclosion": "I feel surrounded by a *latent life whose birth I am preventing*, a sap that I fail to assist in spreading and taking form. I am no longer answering to life. *I feel like an abortionist and I feel aborted. I could almost accuse myself of genocide.* A neurosis, a state of absence, for both the protagonist and the novel. And yet, this latent presence exists outside of me: I can't manage to grasp it, to render it concrete, to allow it to be. I can't get beyond this sketchy state. Mutilated, feeble, incomplete . . . a novelist without a novel" (*PS* 9–10; emphasis added). Gary drew on this natal imagery in 1965 to find a means to describe, from the author's point of view, the author-character he feels taking form in his mind when he writes, and of the ensuing effort to coax it into being, to allow it to take on its own independent existence. It reiterates the vital link Gary insists upon between the writer and the second, created persona of the author, without whom for Gary there can be no novel. This genesis is a delicate process in which Gary finds himself as much midwife as mother.

Nine years later, in *Gros-Câlin*, the same dynamic is being described, but within a fictional discourse, and this time it is being seen from the opposite angle, that of a protagonist-character who is struggling to distinguish himself from his progenitor, the author-character. A repetition in this respect of Genghis Cohn's combat with "Romain Gary" in *The Dance of Genghis Cohn*, Cousin turns both rhetorical and medical terminology on their figurative heads in his quest to construct an identity of his own:

To take the decisive step, all that remains is for me to overcome this state I'm experiencing of being absent to myself. The sensation of not really being there—or, more precisely, of being a sort of prologomenon [*sic*]. This word applies perfectly to my case, for in "prologomenon" there is a prologue to something or

someone, which gives me hope. These states of sketchiness or erasure are very trying . . . It was in the course of one of these prenatal bouts of consciousness that I
wrote to Professor Lortat-Jacob . . . I even thought of sending a letter to Cardinal
[François] Marty, but that prospect truly frightened me: he, on the other hand,
was fully capable of telling me the truth. That I was prenatal, premature and by
way of the urinary tract. (*GC* 82–83) [17]

Mere pre-text for Gary to produce a new writing persona (*prolegomenon*
more properly indicating "the way into a work"), Cousin-Ajar is stranded
in a strange no-man's land, existing only insofar as the novel begins to
exist.

But exist it does. On the Parisian literary scene, as mid-November drew
closer, Ajar emerged as a strong candidate for the Renaudot Prize. This
success would bring some unexpected complications, however. With Ajar
in the running for honors aimed at helping young writers make their
way in the literary world, Gary's maneuver now entailed other ethical dilemmas. Robert Gallimard, one of Gary's trusted friends and the only
member of the publishing world in on the secret, informed Gary that he
thought it would be unfortunate for an established writer like Gary to
deprive a true beginner of the Renaudot.[18] Gary reluctantly acquiesced,
and letters withdrawing Ajar's candidacy were sent to two members of the
Renaudot jury, Max-Pol Fouchet and Alain Bosquet. Other juries took
note and soon removed Ajar from their lists of contenders (Bona 327).
It is nonetheless clear, however, that in the eyes of the critics Ajar was as
talented as any of his contemporaries inside or outside of the "Hexagon."

The speculation surrounding the prize derby served to stir up more
curiosity about Ajar, and journalists directed the greater part of their interpretive skills at the effort to decipher his personality and background.
Though no one really considered Gary the possible author, some of the
readings detected traits very much specific to Gary's literary vision, particularly with respect to authorship. Given the role attributed to Sganarelle in Gary's theoretical manifesto, Decoin's review in *Les Nouvelles
littéraires* was somewhat close to the mark when he wrote, "Several centuries later, Émile Ajar's approach meets up with that of Molière." By far
the most striking, however, are Christine Arnothy's brief reviews of *Gros-
Câlin*. Writing in nonliterary contexts (the populist *Parisien libéré* and a
television guide), she all the same would see through the Algerian biography and single out with uncanny accuracy Gary's true literary influences:
"Ajar, the 'Oranian' with a Czech sense of humor and Russian angst, describes Paris with subtle touches like no one has ever done"; "If [Pierre]
Daninos was Russian, . . . he would have written this gem."[19] Though substituting Kafka for Gary's Polish roots, Hungarian-born novelist Arnothy
would nonetheless be the only critic to situate Ajar in Gary's mixed eastern European/Russian heritage. In the second notice, she would come

closer still: "Ajar is a Gogol of the Left Bank, a Pushkin of the Parisian shadows."[20] Though *Gros-Câlin* itself makes no allusion to Russian authors, nor to anything else from the Soviet Union for that matter, nearly every novel signed *Romain Gary* testifies to a great admiration for Pushkin and Gogol.

With one novel, Gary succeeded in many respects in realizing the literary program he set out for himself in the *Pour Sganarelle* projects. The reworking of his Resistance heritage into a metaphor for social resistance was effective with his readers, now that it had been freed of its associations with the older generation of Gary (and de Gaulle), and his treatment of mutability of identity and the writing relation found new, "fertile" models. But most importantly, Gary succeeded in escaping his authorial identity and producing a new one in its place. As Ajar, Gary would have a new readership and a new rapport with the critical press. The lessons of *The Dance of Genghis Cohn* and *The Guilty Head* bore fruit: in order to alter his identity, Gary had to camouflage not just his identity but the transformation of that identity.

Romain Gary

> *Time does not age you, it just compels you to use disguises.*
> LL *19*

One of the most remarkable aspects of Gary's feat is that Gary continued to publish under his own name during this period. This productivity served at once to discourage anyone from suspecting Gary of writing the Ajar novels, but it also served as a foil reinforcing the distance that separated the two writers. For if Michel Cousin in *Gros-Câlin* is struggling to be born, in Gary's *Your Ticket Is No Longer Valid* Jacques Rainier is on the brink of suicide, disheartened by the onset of professional decline and sexual impotence. Already killed once in an earlier Gary novel (*The Colors of the Day*), Rainier returns to die a second death here, a symbolic one in that the stakes are principally tied to the viability of Gary's image in the seventies (a theme already touched on in the French edition of *Ski Bum*, published under the title *Adieu Gary Cooper*).

Your Ticket Is No Longer Valid was publicized not as a literary event for 1975 but as a topical psychosexual study. Its subject matter clearly titillated certain audiences, further confirming Gary's reputation as a writer who could sniff out timely themes. The novel worked its way up the best-seller list, though at the expense of some uncomfortable promotional appearances. In addition to an October 16, 1975, visit to the television program *Aujourd'hui Madame*, Gary also found himself on the twenty-third installment of *Apostrophes* seated with Dr. Gérard Zwang, author of *Lettre ouverte aux mal-baisants* (An open letter to lousy lovers), and Dr. Michel Meignant, the self-proclaimed "apostle of masturbation."[21]

Similar to Bogat's *Direct Flight to Allah* in this respect, the novel presents the simple surface of an easy-reading romance, underneath which lies a deceptive number of layers for interpretation. Bertrand Poirot-Delpech focused on the parallel Gary established between Rainier's "andropause" and the European energy crisis, which had begun a couple of summers before, taken here as symptomatic of the Old World's fading prestige in the global economy.[22] Daniel Oster added another layer to the reading, zeroing in on Gary's sociopolitical critique (money = phallus = power).[23]

Encouraged by biographical references such as Rainier's tours of duty in the Spanish Civil War and the Resistance, many critics would conclude that the protagonist was a fictional projection of Gary. The resulting self-portrait inferred of Gary reduced his world-view to an obsession with virility, for Rainier is displayed throughout the novel with war medals clanking and his morale sagging (to say nothing of the rest).[24] Hostile critics would revel especially in Rainier's struggles with sexual impotence, which they would take to be by extension an admission on Gary's part of the loss of his creative spark. Many, of course, had come to the same conclusion several novels earlier. Showing little regard for Gary's *amour-propre*, one reviewer linked these themes in an article that refers to Gary as "the tired stallion of the Gallimard stable": "What? Everything is going wrong in his business and romantic affairs? One wonders if there might not be some pernicious links between these forms of decline . . . If it isn't simulated, Gary's anxiety is that of a mediocre novelist . . . Let us not forget Victor Hugo who at eighty still had more working for him than just a strong heart."[25]

While arguably the tone of some of these reviews crossed the line into mean-spiritedness pure and simple, one must nevertheless recognize that *Your Ticket Is No Longer Valid* seems itself to encourage this line of interpretation. In a conversation with his son, for instance, Rainier declares that it is time to "close up the books and settle his accounts." Explains Rainier, "Let's just say that I've entered a twilight zone in which one attaches desperate importance to sexuality . . . The moment of concessions and confessions: it comes down to the same thing" (*YT* 237). For those critics opting for a biographical vein in their interpretations, Rainier's remarks can be seen as Gary's own surrender to declining literary and sexual performance.

How does this play out in the text? At a key moment in the novel, Rainier wakes up during the night to find a handsome foreigner in his room. The intruder's virility and youth make a strong impression on Rainier, and it is not insignificant that the thief steals only Rainier's watch. Time has run out, it would seem, for Rainier. The thief flees, but a vivid image remains in Rainier's mind. Somewhat perversely, Rainier transforms the image of this thief into a fantasy figure (whom he names "Ruiz"), a sort of macho stand-in that he invokes mentally to help him make love with his substantially younger girlfriend, Laura (*YT* 141–43).

Reading on the surface, critics considered this plot a pathetic confession of the lengths to which Gary would go in order to maintain his virility. Some in fact were offended by the sexual politics implied by Ruiz's image. Gilles Rosset would write, for example, "There is a curious air of reverse racism floating through this novel. By that I mean, Gary's hero has some complexes about the sexual power of people of color."[26] These readings are, as we will see, the result of traps tendered by Gary. A warier interpretation reveals other possibilities.

Just exactly where does this avowed impotence lie, and does the novel propose a solution to it? According to the novel, Rainier's problem is located in his self-image, his self-perception; however, although Rainier may well be the focus of *Your Ticket Is No Longer Valid*, curiously he returns only to yield his place to another (Ruiz). In other words, one could argue that Rainier is not giving up on love but is retiring a sexual and social identity that he has outlived. If there is to be a biographical link extrapolated between Rainier and Gary, then, one question we can ask is whether it is Romain Gary the writer who has lost his spark or, rather, is it his image, his authorial identity, that has worn thin? In considering this substitution in terms of problematics of writing, we can argue that Gary is admitting to the sterility of his own authorial identity but is determined to continue his creative life. If his authorial identity can no longer engender innovative fictions, he will attempt to recover his literary spark as someone else.

This reading finds confirmation when Rainier runs into Ruiz again by chance, this time at a party where Ruiz is working with a catering crew in order to rob the guests. Driven by fascination to learn more about his fantasy double, Rainier sneaks into the cloakroom and makes off with Ruiz's passport and driver's license (which identify him as Antonio Montoya, residing in the *Goutte d'or* district of Montmartre's predominantly North African neighborhood). Rainier now disposes of Ruiz's identity in a literal sense, insofar as Rainier has Ruiz's papers and can finger him for several crimes.

Using this threat for leverage, Rainier meets up with Ruiz and imposes an odd arrangement in which Ruiz must merely remain available for those times when Rainier requires his presence (whether actual or imaginary is unclear). Initially, Rainier seems to exercise complete control over this situation: "In the course of the first nights that followed my pilgrimage to the source [Rainier's visit to Ruiz], my imagination recovered all of its evocative power. My phantasms exploited Ruiz with a mastery . . . that seemed inexhaustible. There seemed to be no limit to the speed with which my regenerator agreed to obey me in spite of himself" (*YT* 213). But this arrangement in fact leads to a precarious relation, for Rainier becomes dependent upon Ruiz-Montoya for imaginative and sexual vitality. Later, for instance, the tables have already begun to turn: "If Ruiz now refused to serve me and left me entirely resourceless, it was not only because he felt exploited . . . He wanted to become my master. He had understood that I could no longer do without him" (*YT* 214). At once antagonistic and cooperative, this duo of master and slave find their positions to be potentially reversible.

Rainier's dependence on Ruiz forces him to admit to himself that he has been living off of his own legend for too long. Though he gives up on an elaborately planned suicide, Rainier still dies a symbolic death insofar as he realizes that he can no longer go forward in his life without Ruiz or some other fantasy foil performing in his place.

At novel's end, we are left hanging with a suspended conclusion in which Rainier, Montoya, and Laura leave together on a journey to parts unknown. A few details help us decipher a resolution to the plot. Rainier's girlfriend comes from Brazil, which is the most probable destination of the trio at the story's end (*YT* 247). But Brazil is also, one recalls, reputed to be the home of one Émile Ajar. In other words, a conclusion is not given in *Your Ticket Is No Longer Valid* because a new story is beginning elsewhere, in *Ajar*'s works. Along these lines, the negotiations between Rainier and Ruiz strongly resemble those between Gary's "author-character" and "protagonist-character." In those situations as well (*The Dance of Genghis Cohn*, for example), Gary did not hesitate to blacken his own image. An interesting parallel emerges: whereas Rainier is thought to resemble Gary, the portrait of Ruiz, scarcely more than a caricature, bears a definite likeness to Ajar, caricature himself of the dark-skinned immigrant and delinquent. Gary has created his new picaro in the image of the stereotypes of the day.

In the otherwise mournful appearance on the *Apostrophes* edition dedicated to male sexual dysfunction, Gary provides an explanation of what he is up to here, albeit in his usual covert manner: "In *Your Ticket* when I have the third character [Ruiz] intervene, . . . he intervenes first in the form of a phantasm and then becomes a reality. But what does this third partner become when he becomes a reality? He becomes a substitute, an artifice, a prosthesis. It is a return to *The Roots of Heaven* and everything that I have written up to the present: the extraordinary invasion of artifice in our rapport with life" ("La sexualité masculine," Archives of the INA). The claim here is that Rainier's invention of Ruiz is linked to Morel's efforts in *The Roots of Heaven* to produce a legend, where both testify to the ambition that products of the imagination can rival and transform reality. The project is really more specific, however. Gary mentions *The Roots of Heaven* because he is not yet willing to disclose his ongoing experiment with Ajar. But as Gary explains here, what interests him is how an imaginary creation or projection can pass into reality. (Ruiz-Montoya, after all, came to Rainier while Rainier was asleep, perhaps as a dream, since Laura was not awakened by the scuffle and burglary.) Just as with Ajar in *Gros-Câlin*, Gary's focus is on this process by which a writer takes a phantasmatic image, nurses it along in his imagination, and sees it come to life in the "real" world. In the end, one can ask oneself whether Ruiz-Montoya exists any more than the boa constrictor Gros-Câlin.

The "prosthesis" that Rainier needs to remedy his impotence is Ruiz-Montoya; the substitute Gary needs to renew his literary career is Ajar. Why choose Ruiz or Ajar as the new image? Gary's mechanism for escaping his worn-out authorial identity was to seek out an Émile Ajar, a Ruiz, from the parts of Paris where, in a sense, Gary located the young, vital part of himself, a young man, in other words, who faced the same obstacles of alienation and exclusion that Gary encountered as a Russian immigrant newly arrived in Paris.

With the Ajar project successfully under way, what Gary did with *Your Ticket Is No Longer Valid* was to provide critics with a portrait that corresponded to how they *liked* to see him. Though derivative of the legend originally set in motion by Gary himself, this negative portrait of Rainier represented for Gary in 1975 the *media's image* of Gary, "the mug they've stuck me with" (*LDEA* 16). The procedure was repeated with Ajar, for the racial typing of "Ruiz"—a sort of rogue matador, half-thief, half-Latin lover—served as a double for the image endured by Gary throughout his youth and public life. At the same time, the use of the sexual metaphors in *Your Ticket Is No Longer Valid*, in satisfying the press's expectations about Gary, was a camouflaging technique that Gary used to lull them into looking no farther. The critics' harsh judgment of the novel's racial and sexual characterizations was in fact a reading of the various stereotypes that had plagued Gary personally and professionally. Gary provided a few general traits, and the press completed their interpretations along the most predictable lines, thereby overlooking the various subtexts.

The objective thus was double: Gary wished to lead the critics into eventual ridicule by giving them what they were looking for, knowing that they would therefore miss the real objectives of the book; he also wanted to discard this burdensome authorial image. This novel, so apparently unassuming, is impressive in its richness insofar as it manages to bring together many of Gary's preoccupations and, under the very noses of the critics, transform Gary's creative dilemma into a passage out of a literary cul-de-sac.

Gary's own hostility to the idea of surrendering, voiced in these same sexual metaphors, could have served as a clue to incite alternative readings of *Your Ticket Is No Longer Valid*. In the highly polemical *Pour Sganarelle*, for instance, Gary labels the writers of the New Novel "capitulary 'novelists' letting the novel go soft" (*PS* 117). He even takes his idol Tolstoy to task, accusing him of having betrayed his creative genius by giving in to reality in his old age: "Never had the bad faith of inexpression more loudly proclaimed the reign of the impotent than when a faltering Tolstoy condemned sexuality at the age of seventy in *The Kreutzer Sonata*. This attitude is typical of the anti-novel, the non-novel and pseudo-novel produced by the non-novelists of novelistic capitulation and agonizing death rattles at this halfway point in the life of literature" (*PS* 117).[27] *Your Ticket Is No Longer Valid* is Gary's rejoinder to Tolstoy not because it proposes a highly dubious technique for escaping impotence—after all, can one truly take seriously the idea that Gary wrote a novel to promote the use of Ruiz as a sexual aid? Rather, *Your Ticket Is No Longer Valid* answers the challenge because of the literary solution it constitutes: Gary's use of this sexual metaphor *within* the novel allowed him to achieve his ends *outside* of the novel (to mislead critics in order to rediscover creative liberty). The use of Ajar as a "substitute" provided a new wealth of novelistic resources in the face of strong institutional pressure to retire from the literary scene.

The success of Gary's dissimulation is all the more amusing given that it is owed to ploys elaborated in prior Gary novels. In works as varied as *The Company of Men, The Colors of the Day, Johnnie Cœur, The Guilty Head, The Dance of Genghis Cohn,* and *The Gasp,* characters expound on the advantages of inventing slanderous stories about themselves in order to lead people away from secrets the characters wish to protect. In "confessing" his professional and sexual decline in *Your Ticket Is No Longer Valid,* Gary thus smears himself as a smoke screen to shield his creative rebirth, his nascent second career. The same technique is used with Ajar's biography: the rumors of a shady past connected with illegal abortions keep the press at a respectful distance. Never mind that the same false biography has already been presented in two Gary novels: Mahé, a pseudonymous con man, poses as a repentant ex-abortionist as part of a scam in *The Guilty Head,* while a mysterious character in *The Company of Men* known only as Rapsodie flees to Paris from Czechoslovakia because of a medical past supposedly compromised by wartime abortions.

Émile Ajar, Act Two

Your Ticket Is No Longer Valid saw Rainier go into a tough neighborhood in North Paris seeking a young, disreputable character to rejuvenate his imagination. If there is any doubt that Gary's novel is a staging of his own search for literary renewal, Ajar's second novel, *Madame Rosa*, published the same year as *Your Ticket Is No Longer Valid*, situates its young Algerian narrator in Belleville, an equally tough, primarily immigrant neighborhood in East Paris.

We find several themes characteristic of both Gary's and Ajar's works. One of the protagonists, a former madame named Madame Rosa, now operates a fraudulent daycare center for the children of prostitutes, collecting money from the government for each child she takes in. The themes of abortion and clandestine existence that were featured in *Gros-Câlin* occupy an even more important place here. The narrator of *Madame Rosa*, Momo, is one of these semilegal babies, a "*clandé*" (a "clandy," from "clandestine"; *MR* 70). He knows nothing with certainty about his origins, and official sources are unable to resolve the issue. As with Gary in real life and the majority of his literary protagonists, "the certificate proving that I was born and legal was fake" (*MR* 35).

The strongest clue to Momo's origins is a rumpled receipt signed by Madame Rosa that a man presents one day when he comes to pick up his child after an absence of many years. Momo reads past the man's elbow and tries to reason out what this means for him: "*Received five hundred francs from Mister Yoûssef Kadir as an advance for little Mohammed, of Muslim faith, October 7, 1956.* Well, that was a real shock but now it was 1970 and I quickly did the math, that made it fourteen years ago so it couldn't be me (*MR* 185)."[28] The reader understands from other information that Momo is in fact the child in question, though the date is a surprise, given that Momo thought he was only ten. But October 7, 1956, is also significant for Gary, since it corresponds to the exact day of the original release of *The Roots of Heaven*. We have come full circle from Gary's *Apostrophes* appearance, which included a veiled reference to Ajar tucked behind the explicit mention of *The Roots of Heaven*, to a reversal of those positions (a veiled reference to Gary's *The Roots of Heaven* tucked into a discussion of Momo's birth).

While this receipt clears up some of Momo's questions about his origins, Kadir's difficulties are just beginning. Madame Rosa does not want to relinquish Momo, so she presents Kadir with another child in her care, a certain Moses. Kadir leaps to his feet: "Moses is a Jewish name . . . I entrusted you with a Muslim son, three years old, first name Mohammed. You gave me a receipt for a Muslim son, Mohammed Kadir . . . I gave you a duly registered and certified Arab son and I want you to return an Arab son . . . Under no circumstances do I want a Jewish son, Ma'am— my health won't allow it" (*MR* 195–96).

Madame Rosa feigns astonishment and rummages through her papers. After a few moments, she announces that she has located the problem:

she had received two children on October 7, one Jewish and one Muslim. She breaks down what remains of Kadir's composure when she concludes: "It all makes sense now! . . . I must have raised Mohammed as Moses and Moses as Mohammed. I received them the same day and I got mixed up. The little Moses, the right one, is now with a good Muslim family in Marseille . . . and your little Mohammed, here with us today, I raised him Jewish. Bar mitzvah and all. He has always eaten kosher, you can rest assured . . . Identities, you know, can make mistakes, too . . . A three-year-old doesn't have a lot of identity, even when he's circumcised" (*MR* 198). The entire novel hinges on this haphazard coexistence of Jewish and Muslim cultures, rendered all the more operative by the fact that the protagonist's name, Momo, is the diminutive of both Mohammed and Moses, prophets of their respective religions. By playfully presenting the two children as potentially interchangeable, Gary insists upon the *constructed* nature of their social identities, at the expense of stereotyped notions of innate identity—in this case, of Arab and Jew.

While the neighborhoods of Belleville may belong to an entirely different world from the elite circles of the Quay d'Orsay and the French literary scene, texts from the same period as *Madame Rosa* indicate clearly that Momo and Ajar are not to be seen in opposition to Gary. On the contrary, there exists a strong identification. As Tzvetan Todorov notes, if Momo was born in 1956, that makes him the same age as Gary when he arrived in France (Todorov 237). This parallel is already incorporated into passages of *La nuit sera calme* that discuss Gary's difficult student years in Paris. In this book of interviews published two months after *Gros-Câlin* was sent to Gallimard, Gary recalls his encounters with racism, the experience of no longer being Russian but not yet French, and his constant worry about money and his future. These "starvation years," as he would later refer to them in his correspondence,[29] are an element of his past overlooked by many reviewers who saw only a wealthy Gaullist diplomat living off film and translation rights. In seeking a contemporary parallel to convey better what his own early years as a Russian immigrant were like, Gary offers the example of a *Beur* (slang for a French-born child of North African immigrants) growing up today in Paris's Twentieth District. Gary insists on this equivalence throughout *La nuit sera calme*, to the point of metonymically substituting one for the other. Recounting how he came to know one of his first girlfriends, he remarks, "We met on rue Mouffetard, when I was just a young Algerian of today—and back then, there wasn't even the prestige of the oil reserves" (*NSC* 38). It would become a sort of refrain punctuating Gary's reminiscences: "In the thirties, an Algerian—back then they said *métèque* [mestizo]—in Paris without a dime really had it tough" (*NSC* 28). The message is clear: if Roman Kacew, the immigrant youth we see in *Promise at Dawn*, had had the same humble origins starting out in Paris in the seventies, he would most likely be Algerian. As one of Gary's relatives would later write: "[Gary] didn't give his author [Ajar] an easy time of it. Algerian, abortionist and pimp for his own personal well-being, this unscrupulous, itinerant and unstable picaro, author of tender and slightly smutty books, was definitely Romain's younger brother" (Pavlowitch, *L'homme* 84). The character of Ruiz in *Your Ticket Is No Longer Valid* serves as a phantasmatic double for both Ajar and the young Gary: the first time Rainier sees him, he believes Ruiz to be an Arab, whereas later it occurs to him that Ruiz may have Mongol blood in his ancestry — just like Gary (*YT* 128, 209).

As a result, the identifications offered are of Gary with Ajar, and of the young Russian student Roman from *Promise at Dawn* with Momo from *Madame Rosa*. In fact, *Madame Rosa* is in many respects a deliberate remake of *Promise at Dawn*. The two novels, far and away Gary's most popular, are structured by the same coming-of-age story of a fatherless immigrant child reacting to the death of an all-important maternal figure; even their titles have a certain similarity (the original French title of *Madame Rosa* was *The Life Before Us*). Both heroes are on the brink of delinquency, yet Momo voices ambitions just as extravagant as those entertained by Roman in *Promise at Dawn*. In this scene from *Madame Rosa*, Momo daydreams about what he would do if he had money: "I'd send all the sons of whores and their mothers to luxury palaces in Nice where they'd be sheltered from life and could later become heads-of-state on official visit to Paris or members of the Majority who express their support or even important factors for success" (*MR* 105). It is Gary's life transposed into Ajar's, sometimes ironically (as here), at other times poignantly, allowing Gary to refigure a part of his youth in a way that he could not writing under his own name.

This parallel between Momo and the young Roman of *Promise at Dawn* is not an isolated moment in Gary's writing. As it turns out, this character is a staple throughout the different stages of Gary's fiction. His very first hero, Janek, is orphaned and forced underground where he fends for himself as best he can in *A European Education*. The war orphans of *The Company of Men* (which include its child narrator, Luc Martin) are presented in a chapter entitled "Les Ratons," *raton* being a slang term defined by the *Larousse Argot* as a "child brought up stealing." In one of Gary's novels written just prior to the creation of Émile Ajar, *The Enchanters*, yet another child narrator, Fosco Zaga, takes us back to eighteenth-century Russia, referring to himself as "a child born of chance, practically a gypsy" (*Ench* 18–19). This recurrent figure has the force of an archetypal character for Gary, each time conceived in the guise of a different period. If Kacew the impoverished immigrant of 1930 is the equivalent of a struggling North African in France today, Kacew's Russian ancestor would be precisely this young Zaga, following his nomadic father in a flight from Pugachev's rebellion.

Fosco, Roman, and Momo, centuries and cultures apart, are in effect the same child, constituting three different portraits of Gary: the first derived from his ancestry, the second mythologizing his own youth, and the final one a projection into today's setting. Gary was writing essentially the same book, each recast according to the circumstances and era of its imagined author. The link to writing is made explicit in every case, since all of these protagonists undergo improbable apprenticeships toward literature, from Momo's and Roman's shared desire to be the next Victor Hugo to Fosco's ambition to raise his family's art of showmanship to that of literature.[30] In other words, these novels all elaborate a tale of the origins of a writer, the ensemble of which are cast as permutations within a family of related identities.

Along similar lines, Gary's authorial inventions strike one as springing from the same lineage, a family of international misfits and outsiders whom one could consider the adult transformations of these child narrators: Romain Gary, Russian émigré who adopted his Resistance nom de guerre; Fosco Sinibaldi, possibly of Turko-Italian origins but writing in French; Shatan Bogat, the American wayfarer grappling with his Turkish origins; and Émile Ajar, the Algerian who has fled France to Brazil. On an onomastic level, these pseudonyms form series of pairs. Gary is matched up with Ajar, not just by their publishing adventures but because they share common linguistic origins (with *gari* meaning "burn!" in Russian and *agar* meaning "embers"). A second pair is found for *Direct Flight to Allah*, with Bogat listed as an American author of the French text but a French counterpart, René Deville, credited with writing the English edition.[31] Here, too, they share a semantic link, since Bogat's name opposes Russian terms for Satan and God (*Shatan* and *Bog*), while the Frenchman can be broken down into *René* (from *renaître*, to be reborn) and a French pronunciation of the English word "devil." Moreover, I have uncovered a previously unknown instance of this same pattern occurring even earlier in Gary's career. Fosco Sinibaldi was intended to have an alter ego, who never materialized only because Simon and Schuster turned down the projected translation of *L'homme à la colombe*: "Jack Ribbons" was presented by Gary in letters to one of his American translators as having a novel provisionally titled *Man with a Dove*, which sharply criticized the United Nations.[32]

On a referential level, Gary respects the supposed cultural horizons of each of these author-characters. As Jeffrey Mehlman notes, Gary represents an immigrant completely assimilated into French culture, while Ajar stands for "total alienation from the France in which he lives" (Mehlman 224). Thus, in his novels, Gary, as man of letters, humanist, and diplomat, draws on the whole of Western art and entertainment for his field of reference (e.g., El Greco, Pushkin, Maurice Dekobra's *The Madonna of the Sleeping Cars*, Gary Cooper, Nostradamus, William Blake). He casts his tales on a global scale and his protagonists move amongst all levels of society. Even a claustrophobic novel like *Clair de femme* bears the possibility of its narrator running off to Caracas for the weekend. In marked contrast, the author Ajar, in the economic and skewed prose of Gary's Algerian picaro, shares neither Gary's culture nor his social aspirations. He largely confines both of his novels to a few square blocks in the poor sections of Paris. Ajar is a third world author, with a postcolonial backdrop imported for *Gros-Câlin* (the boa was purchased in Morocco, Mlle Dreyfus is from Guyana) and *Madame Rosa* (with its supporting cast of Hamil, Driss, N'Da Amédée, etc.). The few specific cultural references here are to Haroun al-Rachid or to French grade school textbook figures (Hugo, Brossolette). And the language of Ajar's novels, so strikingly disjointed in its dissection of institutional euphemisms, is derived from the journalistic and legalistic parlance used to describe and police the immigrant quarters of Paris, but always applied inappropriately by a narrator too young to master the peculiar ways of speaking that are one of the tools employed by the Powers-that-be.

In the course of *Madame Rosa*, however, the disparate worlds of Gary and Ajar are brought together. Momo has a few privileged adult interlocutors who turn out to provide these links. Dr. Katz, the reassuring authority figure who cares for both Momo and Madame Rosa, contains an echo of "Kacew" (pronounced "Kat-seff"; see Bellos 59). More important, we discover that the entire narrative is being retold by Momo to a specific audience: the representatives of Gary's milieu (the bourgeois couple Nadine and her psychoanalyst husband Ramon, whose first name is an anagram of Roman). Gary thus closes the circle: just as Rainier makes a foray into the *Goutte d'or*, Momo in return concludes his tale by wandering into the pricy and historic First District.[33]

While Gary worked through these intricate explorations of his authorial identities as a means of restarting his career, the press's squabbles over Ajar's identity were still limited to interpreting a paper author who had cleverly resisted their investigative efforts. With the critical and commercial success of *Madame Rosa*, however, Ajar would soon embark on an adventure unique in literary history.

Chapter 5

The Consecration of Émile Ajar, 1975–1980

Gary's personal life was marked by several significant losses. After de Gaulle's death in 1970, it was Malraux's turn in 1976. Meanwhile, Seberg, never having fully recovered from the loss of her infant daughter, slid deeper into her suffering and depression. Gary and Seberg spent part of the summer of 1978 together at the Connecticut home of William Styron, but Gary was struggling with depression and Seberg was also in very poor health (Styron 36–37). On September 8, 1979, in the wealthy Parisian suburb of Neuilly-sur-Seine, Seberg's naked body was found on the floor of the backseat of her car, next to a container of barbiturates. From her blood-alcohol level, doctors deduced that it would have been impossible for her to reach her car without assistance. Gary also noted that Seberg's glasses were missing. Judge Guy Joly opened an investigation "against X for non-assistance of a person in danger" (Bona 379). The circumstances of Seberg's death remain unclarified to this day (though it is certain that Gary played no role whatsoever in her death). Gary dropped a bombshell at a press conference, however, announcing that through well-placed contacts he had uncovered the source of the rumors concerning Seberg's pregnancy: under J. Edgar Hoover, the counterintelligence program (COINTELPRO) of the FBI had undertaken a campaign of psychological warfare to destabilize Seberg, creating the rumor that her sociopolitical commitment was motivated by a sexual appetite for black men. In an unusual move, the new FBI director, William H. Webster, admitted the involvement of Washington, D.C. and Los Angeles FBI divisions and made public a number of edited documents related to the affair (see Wendell A. Rawls Jr., "FBI Admits Planting a Rumor to Discredit Jean Seberg in 1970," New York Times September 15, 1979). Gary was greatly shaken by the implications of this discovery and had difficulty maintaining his composure during the press conference. The French press was critical of Gary's handling of the revelation.

Émile Ajar

> *One has to get away from abstraction. What counts in art is the part that is alive.*
>
> JC *13*

Gros-Câlin had garnered enough support to be a serious contender for the 1974 Renaudot Prize. When *Madame Rosa* surfaced the following year, Ajar's adventure escalated another notch. One of the first to review the book, Jacqueline Piatier, set the bar very high. Reminding readers that *Gros-Câlin* had been "the most original and seductive novel of [last] season," she went so far as to speak of *Madame Rosa* as being a *Les Misérables* for the twentieth century, while Max-Pol Fouchet compared Ajar's second novel to Céline's *Journey to the End of the Night.*[1] Ajar also made converts of some of the critics who had initially been reluctant to embrace him: Jean Freustié, for instance, one of the few reviewers to snub *Gros-Câlin,* admitted to having been won over by *Madame Rosa.*[2] The appearance of a second work of quality confirmed Ajar's talent and his name was once again at the top of many lists, but this time it was the Goncourt that was at stake.

Ajar's triumphant return also taunted the press with its inability to uncover his identity. Despite early readings like Arnothy's, which came quite close to the truth, critics were now stymied. Mentions of Gary's use of "Shatan Bogat" popped up as reminders of the frequent incidence of pseudonymous pranks, but no one presented Gary seriously as a possible culprit. The most persistent hypothesis favored Queneau, but the names of Aragon, Pierre Bénichou, Jacques Lanzmann, Maurice Pons, and Claude Faux (Halimi's husband) were also thrown into the rumor mill. Cournot bore the brunt of much speculation as well, given that his novels had been awarded the Prix Fénéon in 1949 and the Prix des Deux Magots in 1958 by prestigious literary juries. The scrutiny only intensified with the discovery that the first of Cournot's works, *Martinique,* featured a narrator who became a tree at the end, recalling Cousin's tenuous hold on reality in *Gros-Câlin.* Still others surmised the possibility of an American author, despite the intricate, untranslatable linguistic play demonstrated in these texts. Journalists going through police records turned up no Ajar, though the name of Hamil Raja, an alleged Lebanese terrorist, briefly fired their imagination. With the failure to solve the mystery, the guesswork turned farcical: Pivot, tongue in cheek, wondered if Ajar were not perhaps Pauline Réage's illegitimate son, while a few papers passed around the idea that Gary's own child Diego could be the culprit—despite his mere thirteen years of age.[3]

Securing a major prize is of great importance to a medium-size publishing house like Mercure de France, which had not won the Goncourt since 1918 (Georges Duhamel received it for *Civilisation*). As the Goncourt decision approached, Mercure de France was eager to capitalize on its success with Ajar, but its staff was in the awkward position of promoting an author who they were not even certain existed. Because Cournot was suspected of being in on the mystification (in one capacity or another), he found himself reassuring journalists that he knew no more than they did. Simone Gallimard was even reputed to have hired a private detective in an attempt to locate her reticent star.[4]

In addition to the positive reviews in the press, Gary saw that the public had embraced Ajar. *Madame Rosa*'s first printing of fifty thousand copies evaporated rapidly, and in little time the novel had worked its way up the best-seller charts (it would reach the top slot of *L'Express* by the end of November). Gary even managed to consult some of the fan letters sent to this "young" talent. Marlene Dietrich expressed great admiration for *Madame Rosa* and requested a copy of *Gros-Câlin*. Ajar's only detractor at this point seems to have been a certain Prince Momo, a lumberjack in the Ivory Coast, who claimed that his life story had been told by Ajar without authorization (Pavlowitch, *L'homme* 75).

Ajar's success far exceeded Gary's expectations, but he knew that Ajar could not win a major prize unless jurors and the press were persuaded of his legitimacy. Michel Tournier, for instance, an important member of the Goncourt jury, reportedly contacted Simone Gallimard to express his desire to back Ajar but complained that it would be impossible to convince the others without some form of verification of Ajar's identity (Bona 339). In the workings of modern-day celebrity, this necessarily meant a public manifestation. Pressed by the escalation of events, Gary either had to up the ante or renounce.

Gary in fact had already chosen the former. The narrow miss with the Renaudot in 1974 made him realize the potential for even greater stakes for his experiment. In April 1975, he took steps to provide Mercure de France with the physical presence it so sorely needed by enlisting his distant cousin Pavlowitch to play the role of Ajar.[5] Gary first asked him to call Cournot and renegotiate the terms of Ajar's contract. Despite the fact that Mercure de France was already receiving dozens of phone calls each month from would-be Ajars, the conversation went without a hitch. Michaut met one final time with Cournot and Simone Gallimard in order to smooth the way for Pavlowitch's entry onto the scene, describing Pavlowitch as a drifter who had squatted at Michaut's Rio de Janeiro apartment for several months. Michaut added that things were now going a bit better for Ajar and that Ajar would soon settle in Switzerland with his girlfriend (Pavlowitch 80–84).

Gary then prepared a couple meetings, plotting out Pavlowitch's role in minute detail. The impersonation would be something of a high-wire act, for Pavlowitch had to improvise his demeanor and remarks within the boundaries of Gary's prearranged script. Pavlowitch began by sending Mercure de France a blurry photograph of himself for promotional use (the photo, taken years earlier in Guadeloupe, had the advantage of showing him prior to the growth of the bushy, long hair and extravagant moustache that he was sporting in 1975). Next, still playing the card that Ajar could not travel to France owing to his troubles with the law, Pavlowitch went to Gary's apartment in Geneva and invited Cournot and Simone Gallimard to meet him there to settle a number of professional matters. In preparation for this visit, Gary borrowed an idea from one of the rumors circulating in the papers, that of the supposed Lebanese terrorist. Gary gave Pavlowitch a contact in Paris who furnished Pavlowitch with fake identification papers: a driver's license and an insurance certificate made out to one "Hamil Raja, rue du Cygne, Geneva." These were to be casually displayed in front of Cournot if the opportunity presented itself (Pavlowitch 87).

The first meeting fell through owing to a miscommunication on Pavlowitch's part, but eventually Cournot was able to hook up with Pavlowitch. Pavlowitch signed contracts, collected a check, and even made changes in the manuscript of *Madame Rosa* in response to Cournot's editorial queries. A revolver left out in plain view discouraged inquisitiveness on Cournot's part (Bona 337). A month later, Pavlowitch and his wife, Annie (posing as Ajar's girlfriend), undertook an even more elaborate test: Simone Gallimard, disappointed at the failed first meeting, insisted on meeting her new star. Gary decided that Ajar and his "girlfriend" would host Simone Gallimard for a weekend in Copenhagen. The Pavlowitchs decided on the proper setting for Ajar, with Paul favoring a furnished flat inhabited by Greek immigrants but Annie ultimately convincing him to take a small cottage in the suburbs. Simone Gallimard was delighted to meet her mysterious author, and the visit went extremely well. She brought several dozen copies of *Madame Rosa* for Ajar to sign and suggested phrases for personalized messages to members of the Goncourt, Renaudot, and Médicis prize juries (Pavlowitch 112–18).

Impressively, Pavlowitch's performances were flawless, with Gary having correctly anticipated many of the hurdles to clear. Pavlowitch's age, persona and handsome but slightly disreputable appearance fit the bill perfectly. His haunted eyes and thin, watery voice matched wonderfully the vulnerability one senses in Ajar's writing. Only under the force of inspiration or conviction did Pavlowitch become assertive and energetic in demeanor (see "*La Peau de l'ours*: Ajar . . . et après," Archives of the INA). Moreover, he possessed detailed knowledge of Gary's books and literary preferences and had a strong interest in writing. Neither Simone Gallimard nor Cournot doubted for a second Pavlowitch's authenticity. Cournot recollects: "[Pavlowitch] had, if you'll pardon the expression, the right look for the job . . . At once bandit and crazy, bizarre and un-nerving . . . this man had the physique, voice and style of Émile Ajar . . . When I asked him to change a word here and there, he never hesitated. He had no difficulty making the changes and his additions were often for the better. He struck me as being very seasoned, a real 'pro' in his impro-vised corrections" (qtd. in Bona 334–48). Pavlowitch had previously held a rewriting job at Gallimard and had done ghostwriting for an encyclope-dia publisher, experience that clearly aided in his chores with Cournot.

As long as the only confirmations of Ajar's authenticity came from his publisher, the press remained petulant and suspicious. Thus, having re-assured Mercure de France, Gary now presented Pavlowitch with another challenge. Gary and Pavlowitch set up an interview with the *Monde*, which conveniently (for them) selected a relatively young journalist, Yvonne Baby, to visit the Copenhagen cottage for an interview with Ajar. It was now a question of a different exercise. Pavlowitch had to make Ajar con-vincing and appealing, in the image of the works already published, but without divulging information concrete enough to risk verification. Pavlowitch's task was facilitated somewhat by the fact that the literary press is a press that for the most part *wants* to believe in these colorful figures. Once the complicity of the press entered creatively into the equa-tion, whatever lapses may have occurred in Pavlowitch's performance were more often than not unconsciously smoothed out in the journalist's final account.

The resulting article, "La Maison d'Ajar," was a big scoop for both the *Monde* and Mercure de France. Pavlowitch, acting as Ajar, discussed the genesis of the novels and gave an explanation (albeit inaccurate) for what was now openly acknowledged as a pseudonym: "*Gros-Câlin* was a bit like me trying to open a door without opening it completely . . . *Gros-Câlin* is Ajar, from the English 'ajar,' as in 'a door is ajar.'"[6] Pavlowitch also abandoned the Algerian biography on this occasion, supplying a more down-to-earth version of his past. Cournot then rendered official the new biographical sketch by releasing it to Françoise Ducout of *Elle* magazine:

Born in 1940. French. Childhood in Nice in the "musicians' quarter." Of Russian and Yugoslavian origins, his mother was in the French Resistance. Ajar remains very strongly attached to his mother (who died young) and to the idea of Resis-tance. He finished his baccalaureate and started medical school in Toulouse (four years). To earn his living, he worked at the same time as a monitor in a center for pre-delinquence and later as an assistant on film crews. In 1963, he left France to try life elsewhere: Spain, Morocco, the West Indies, the United States, Brazil. He returned to Europe in 1975.[7]

Less sensational than the previous bio-sketch, it traded the outlaw image for that of a rootless outsider. This new version presented several advantages. Though the original biography now had the status of a fictional diversion, the mentions here of the Resistance, medical studies, contact with the movie industry and travels in Brazil all establish bridges with the initial profile, allowing one to see how "Ajar" could have invented it in the first place. The effect created is that the first one was fiction, thus the new one is the truth. With a more plausible background of odd jobs and wanderlust, Ajar thus became individuated, passing from the status of simple mask to disguise.[8] As for Pavlowitch, the references to Nice, Russia, and Toulouse wove in his own background so that he could better fend for himself if interviewers asked specific questions, but the information was distorted enough to conceal his true identity: for example, he did attend one of the universities in Toulouse, but it was for law school.

Gary and Pavlowitch had now given Ajar support in the necessary arenas. The texts, biography and photograph were mutually reinforcing, Mercure de France had put its publicity and advertising departments into motion with a clear conscience, and the press confirmed Ajar's talent and existence. In the final run toward the Goncourt, a snowball effect thus took place. Following the formula laid out in so many of his novels, Gary now allowed the media to be the primary vehicle for Ajar's amplification—the more the media itself carried out Ajar's construction, the more he infiltrated reality. Reviewers were soon lulled by their own demonstrations of Ajar's legitimacy and began to integrate elements of his biography into their interpretations. Tournier, for instance, noted Ajar's experience as a film technician and thus read *Madame Rosa* as applying cinematic devices to narrative structure (Tournier 337–38). Gary and Pavlowitch could sit back for the moment and watch the legend grow. Pavlowitch recalls, "The whole thing was always quite unplanned. As soon as it became public, it no longer depended on us" (Pavlowitch, *L'homme* 114).

But if Gary and Pavlowitch no longer needed to direct it, it also meant that they could no longer control it. Now that journalists were on Ajar's scent, Gary and Pavlowitch immediately learned the difference between the Parisian literary press and national investigative journalism. With the search for Ajar moving from the literary supplement into the news pages, the media had very different resources at their disposal. Using little more than the Baby article and the materials circulated by Cournot, journalist Jacques Bouzerand from *Le Point* tracked down and confronted Pavlowitch at his home in Caniac-du-Causse (Lot). Here, Gary's luck held out:

the journalist was an old family friend of Pavlowitch's wife and agreed to withhold Pavlowitch's name in exchange for a two-part interview and blurry photos.[9] Coming from a source like *Le Point*, the articles actually worked in Ajar's favor, because even the most skeptical critic became convinced that a *new*, previously unknown writer was hiding behind the name Ajar.

Ajar was not the only phenomenon disrupting the calm and dignity of the Goncourt proceedings. The previous year "Aguigui" had sounded a warning bell (literally) by disrupting the announcement of the winner with a troupe of co-conspirators honking bicycle horns (Caffier 89). In 1975, the protests would escalate considerably. Days prior to the announcement of the laureate, Jean-Édern Hallier began a campaign against the Goncourt, aided by several little-known writers. Tournier was doused with a glass of tomato juice, a photo of which was duly carried by the papers. Days later, an unknown assailant smashed a cream pie in the face of seventy-six-year-old Goncourt Academy member Armand Salacrou. Hallier soon resurfaced as a guest on several television programs announcing the creation of a new prize, an anti-Goncourt. Its unwieldy name, *le prix du Groupe Information Culture Lecture Édition* (Prize of the information culture reading publishing group), produced an equally cumbersome acronym: the *GICLE* (Spurt). Hallier bestowed the award upon Pierre Goldman, whose first novel, *Dim Memories of a Polish Jew Born in France*, had attracted some interest but received little promotion, since Goldman was serving time for the murder of two pharmacists.[10] Goldman issued an abusive refusal from prison, so Hallier imperturbably re-assigned the GICLE to Jack Thieuloy's *La geste de l'employé*—a manuscript that would be published by none other than Hallier himself (Caffier 90). Known for championing cannibalism, Thieuloy happened to be in prison as well, accused of having left a Molotov cocktail on the doorstep of yet another Goncourt jurist, Belgian author and journalist Françoise Mallet-Joris. Thieuloy happily accepted the GICLE, hoping to use it to pay his legal fees—but Hallier's check issued for the fifty thousand francs in prize money bounced.[11]

Events took a more serious turn in the final hours before the fateful decision. Explosive devices were left at the residences of critics Galey and Georges Charensol (Renaudot jury), while another was thrown at a supermarket (a symbolic protest against the commercialization of literature). A bomb caused considerable damage at Éditions Grasset, a fire flared up at Éditions du Seuil, and a terrorist threat was phoned in to Éditions Gallimard. The blue and gray vans of the CRS security forces were summoned to the Goncourt luncheon at Chez Drouant, where Hallier threatened to unleash Thieuloy's pet monkey, Chiro.

In stark contrast with this chaos, Ajar's reticence worked in his favor. Having acquired sufficient credibility in the press's eyes to be considered legitimate, Ajar captured the 1975 Goncourt Prize, edging out Decoin and Patrick Modiano in the eighth round of voting. (Ajar was also the unanimous pick of the Renaudot jury, but this honor took a backseat to the Goncourt.) Gary's principal legal adviser, Fernand Bossat, in on the secret and running out of patience with the charade, was adamant that Gary refuse the prize (Pavlowitch, *L'homme* 161). Gary was rattled enough that he instructed Pavlowitch to issue a letter through Halimi (who soon resigned as Ajar's legal counsel). In it, Ajar announced, "Over the last two days, the attribution of the Goncourt . . . has multiplied the difficulties I've experienced in communicating with the public only through my book" (Bona 347–48). A haughty and annoyed Hervé Bazin responded in the name of the Goncourt Academy: "The Academy votes for a book, not a candidate. The Goncourt Prize cannot be accepted or refused any more than birth or death. Mr. Ajar remains the laureate." [12] His statement was contrary to the very conception of the prize, which was created to help free young authors from material want and thus was intended to be attributed to a particular type of *person* (see Edmond de Goncourt's will, reprinted in Robichon 332). Nonetheless, Bazin's remarks clear the way for the Academy to honor *Madame Rosa* despite Ajar's tardy abstention.

It was an unprecedented second honor (an author may only be crowned once), giving Gary a dramatic demonstration that his writing still merited critical consideration and analysis. The very same Audouard who dubbed Gary "creatively impotent," for instance, classified *Madame Rosa* "the best love story of the season" and was even willing to pardon Ajar's suspicious behavior: "Yes, M. Émile Ajar has a device. In particular, to shroud his residence and origins systematically in mystery. But from a literary point of view, a 'device' that holds up for 270 pages of thirty lines and sixty characters each is not a device, it's talent. Pure talent." [13] A survey of past Goncourt winners allowed Gary an opportunity to pitch in his own two cents: "I liked *Gros-Câlin*, but I haven't read *Madame Rosa* yet. I don't think the author will stay in hiding much longer." [14]

Though this moment would bring Gary his greatest triumph, his real trials were about to begin. After the Goncourt Prize, events would evolve in directions he had never imagined. At each step of this elaborate chess match between Gary and the press, the difficulties of his position would multiply exponentially. The type of rivalry between art and the Powers-that-be that he had been seeking was very much in evidence here, but Gary would be forced to parry each new element at a dizzying pace, trying to spin fictions faster than reality could unravel them.

Pythons and Picaros

> *My vocation was not to put an end to the illusion and provide backup for reality but, on the contrary, to maintain the former in order to enrich the latter.*
> Ench *359*

Spurred by the *Point*'s revelations, the *Dépêche du Midi* also located Pavlo-witch at his home near Cahors, but reporter Martin Malvy and his editor refused to show the same professional courtesy demonstrated by Bou-zerand. The paper identified Pavlowitch by name and revealed his family tie to Romain Gary.

This should have been the end of the episode, particularly given Gary's known affection for pseudonyms and the thematic similarities between Ajar and Gary. One of the few to pursue this angle is the extreme right-wing journal *Minute*, once again unabashedly stooping low in its attacks on Gary. Remarking that the wealthy Gary "has enough studio apart-ments at his disposal to set up a small literary kibbutz," the journal man-aged, with its usual dubious flair, to double an anti-Semitic slur with the insulting reminder that Gary was alleged to rely on ghostwriters.[15] Another journal ruled out Gary's participation, however, arguing that he was too publicity conscious to resist benefiting from the Goncourt.[16]

The terms of the hunt had changed, however. The Ajar novels are strewn with clues tying them to Gary's novels, clues that are too minor to draw attention in and of themselves, but too specific not to be ample proof if analysis reaches the stage of textual comparisons.

Gros-Câlin provides some useful examples. Just as *Madame Rosa* is a deliberate reworking of *Promise at Dawn*, *Gros-Câlin* is in many ways an off-beat parody of the ecological concerns raised in *The Roots of Heaven*, using the Resistance once again as a backdrop. The same humanist themes of man's fraternity with the animal kingdom are present, transferred from the epic scale of Gary's world to the confines of Cousin's strange mental universe. The description in *The Roots of Heaven* of Minna being reassured by the muzzle of an affectionate antelope placed in her hand is repeated word for word in Ajar's description of Cousin with the muzzle of a mouse snuggling in his palm (cf. *RH* 53 and *GC* 26). A similar connection exists between the character of Colonel Babcock, who has a pet jumping bean for company during his reconnaissance flights in *The Roots of Heaven*, and a citation from this episode inserted into a discussion of Cousin's ties to his python (cf. *RH* 242 and *GC* 65).

"Gros-Câlin" is not even the first python in Gary's works. In fact, the re-lation between Cousin and his serpent can be considered the fleshing out of a single paragraph occurring early in *White Dog*. In this semiautobiographical work, Gary has a pet python named Pete the Strangler that he is forced to give up to a kennel because Gary's frequent travels make caring for the snake impossible: "I'd had to give Pete up because my friends refused to take care of him when, seized by one of those claustrophobic fits of someone who suddenly can't stand to be closed up in his own skin, I would take off running from one continent to another, searching for someone or something different" (*WD* 10). These phrases are echoed in *Gros-Câlin* with Cousin running about his two-room apartment, searching for a way out, envious of his snake's molting. A few lines later in *White Dog*, when Gary returns to visit Pete, we come across another passage prefiguring Cousin's relation with his python: "We stared at each other for a long time with boundless stupefaction . . . *Finding oneself in the skin of a python or in that of a man* was such a mind-boggling *metamorphosis* that our mutual fear became a form of true fraternity" (*WD* 11; emphasis added).

Direct Flight to Allah insists awkwardly on its pythons, which suggests that even though it appeared in print first it was in fact written during or after the Ajar novel. *Direct Flight to Allah* is set in the ancient city of Haddan, which is described as encircled by a boa in light of its series of concentric ramparts (*DFA* 387). This observation is made on several occasions without its being particularly clear what it contributes to the narrative (see *DFA* 315). In addition, two of the characters, Ted Henderson and especially Murad the bodyguard, are referred to as boa constrictors, again with an insistence that is otherwise gratuitous (*DFA* 32, 53). Finally, on the last page, a mention of the "boa" surrounding Haddan will be one of the heroine's last phrases (*DFA* 439).

Though many critics were watching Gary carefully now, he realized that the majority of them were so set in their opinion of him that even confronted with unambiguous textual evidence they could not recognize that he was capable of writing Ajar's texts. Pivot's exclamation on *Apostrophes* probably summed up the thoughts of many reviewers: having just summarily dismissed Gary's work, Pivot turned his attention to *Madame Rosa*: "Ah! Ajar! Now that's *real* talent!" (qtd. in *LDEA* 42). After an initial reaction of panic, Gary realized that the mob of journalists blocking the stairs leading up to his rue du Bac apartment were there trying to hunt down *Pavlowitch* and not him. The discovery of the family tie between Gary and Pavlowitch added an unexpected element to the equation. In creating Ajar, Gary wanted to experiment as a writer free from the weight of his own authorial image. He was probably also hoping for some eventual measure of revenge: seeing Ajar's work well received would confirm his suspicion that critics were not reading Gary objectively. Under those circumstances, it would be a *private* satisfaction shared by him and the handful of those close to him. Once the media uncovers the family tie, however, critics explicitly compared the two writers, not so much tex-

tually as in terms of their literary stature and image. Quite unexpectedly, what was a personal battle for Gary passed onto the public stage.
As Gary would later recall, he was hearing the echoes "from fashionable
dinners where people pitied that poor old [Gary] who must be feeling a
bit sad and jealous at his cousin's meteoric rise into the literary heavens,
especially when even Gary had admitted his own decline in *Your Ticket Is
No Longer Valid*" (*LDEA* 43). Though it arguably could have fatal consequences for him, it presented an unhoped-for opportunity to push his
strange literary experiment to another level.

In spite of the textual evidence and rampant speculation, Gary decided
to go even farther out on a limb. He convinced Pavlowitch to play a new
role: Pavlowitch would claim to have been hiding behind a pseudonym
because he wanted to protect his family's privacy and to publish without
giving the appearance of capitalizing on his reactionary relative's celebrity. Gary took charge of disseminating this version of events: "[Paul] is
my cousin's son but he's dead set against me. He doesn't want me to talk
about him and he's never accepted a penny from me" (Bouvard). Amaz-
ingly, this bold maneuver worked perfectly. The discovery of the stand-
offish Pavlowitch hidden away in the Lot satisfied many in the press that
the mystery is solved.

Gary and Pavlowitch henceforth embraced their roles as the picaros
that Gary had promoted throughout his literary career. Pavlowitch now
lived upstairs from Gary in a small studio apartment, which allowed them
to plan out each announcement or provocation. Gary had Pavlowitch
ham it up as a paranoid, volatile person fleeing all public relations activities. What began as playacting immediately took on other proportions,
however. Pavlowitch was chased through the streets of Paris by reporters
on motorscooters until he hid in the changing room of a women's fashion boutique. Later he punched an overly insistent photographer (Jean-
Pierre Tartrat of *L'Aurore*) in order to fight his way through a throng of
onlookers (Pavlowitch 173–74). In this light, Modiano's assertion that he
knew Ajar's paranoia to be disingenuous because it did not correspond
to the reality of a modern author should be questioned.[17]

Gary's new public connection vis-à-vis Ajar-Pavlowitch brought an end
to a period in which Gary was forced to sit in the background while Pavlowitch met with editors and interviewers. Gary could now act as a foil to
help divert attention and to shore up Pavlowitch's credibility. To this end,
Gary used his own productivity during this period to discourage anyone from thinking that he would have the time to write Ajar's books as
well. Tongue firmly in cheek, Gary stated: "I'm not a superhuman genius
capable of writing Paul's books in addition to mine. No, it's time to clear
away all this smoke and take Paul seriously."[18]

In his contacts with the press, Gary affected being paternalistically pleased with his nephew's success, though his very insistence on his lack of jealousy was seen as a sure sign of it. Since Ajar-Pavlowitch was the young upstart of French fiction, Gary exaggerated his role of has-been burdened with a flagging imagination. This is reflected in his choice of novelistic subjects during the Ajar period: *Your Ticket Is No Longer Valid* and *Clair de femme* are the only Gary novels in which the male protagonist is elderly. In contrast to the child narrators of his first novels, he now presents the figure of an aging writer dealing with the problems of maturity: loneliness, *désœuvrement*, sexual impotence, and mourning.[19] Stylistically, he reverts to using the old-fashioned *passé simple* (simple past), whereas he had adopted the *passé composé* (composed past) by the late sixties and was using it for Ajar's novels.[20] Along these same lines, to heighten the contrast between the "reactionary" Gary and the rebellious outsider Pavlowitch, Gary sets these two novels in the upper-middle-class Parisian milieu that had become his own—his only two situated there (McKee 61).

With the few readers who did take the time to discover the parallels between the themes and stylistic habits of Gary and Ajar, Gary, far from rewarding their attentiveness, played it as brazenly as his character Genghis Cohn. When a reporter from *Paris-Match*, Laure Boulay, met with Gary to discuss *Clair de femme*, she also took the opportunity to enumerate citations and thematic similarities found in Gary and Ajar novels. Moved but poker-faced on the outside, Gary responded: "Yes, of course. No one has realized the extent to which Ajar is influenced by me. In the example you so judiciously cite, one could even speak of plagiarism. But he's a young author and I really don't have any intention of raising objections. Generally speaking, the influence that my work exerts is not stressed often enough. I'm pleased that you have noticed" (*LDEA* 36–38).

On another occasion, Gary fired back a brutal personal attack when a friend and admirer, director of the *Journal des gaullistes de gauche* Jean-Michel Royer, persisted in implying that Gary could be Ajar: "Your maneuver consists of cutting the balls off a newcomer by attributing his work to me, all the while protecting yourself with a 'maybe.' Even by Parisian standards, this is truly low. I've denied these rumors . . . You know it full well and so you must be looking for trouble. You'll find it" (qtd. in Pavlowitch, *L'homme* 248). On the few occasions when Gary or Pavlowitch slipped up, Gary was even prepared to perjure himself to continue the charade. The working title for *Madame Rosa* had been *La tendresse des pierres* (The tenderness of stones), which Gary had forgotten was the title he gave to a book written by his character Jess in *Ski Bum* (*SB* 90). Realizing it at the last minute, Gary instructed Pavlowitch to force Mercure de France to change the title, which they begrudgingly did. On November 21, 1975, just four days after the Goncourt, Piatier confronted Gary with this information, asking for his word of honor, in writing, that he had not written Ajar's books. The signed document was published in facsimile by the *Monde* the following week.

Certain people—journalists, lawyers, publishers—would later reproach Gary for this aspect of his conduct. But not only is it consistent with his literary program, it is, as we have seen, announced in nearly every one of his works. These schemes are rehearsed explicitly in *The Colors of the Day*, *Talent Scout*, *The Enchanters*, and *The Guilty Head*. One will recall, for instance, that Cohn's artistry in *The Guilty Head* consists solely in the means he devises to reproduce Gauguin's legend. Pavlowitch would find himself performing as Ajar in exactly the same manner.[21] In his review of *The Guilty Head*, R.-M. Albérès was one of the rare critics to understand the rules of the game for these picaresque figures: "This world is made up of special effects. For some, the art of living becomes the art of cheating. Cheating conscientiously or—I would almost go so far as to say—honestly."[22] Or, as Gary would state, rather less generously, "You cannot be a man of complete integrity and a great writer" (qtd. in Pavlowitch, *L'homme* 202).

Paul Pavlowitch and "Tonton Macoute"

> *One never knows what's what with you. Everything is so scrambled, tangled up, camouflaged, backwards, sideways, underground and hanging lightly headfirst from the ceiling.*
>
> CM *44*

Although the public antics would go a long way toward making Pavlowitch-Ajar credible in the press's eyes, Gary set to work on a third Ajar novel in the days immediately following the Goncourt, a work that is one of Gary's neglected achievements and certainly one of his most outrageous. Written in a frenetic twelve days after the revelation of Pavlowitch's identity, Gary incorporated the new developments surrounding Ajar's adventure, in particular the discovery of the family tie between Pavlowitch and Gary. Entitled *Pseudo*, it was designed to throw everyone off the track with a scandalous parody of Pavlowitch, the press, and Gary himself. Gary pushed for it to be published in the wake of the Goncourt, but, unnerved by the potentially defamatory nature of the text, Simone Gallimard delayed its publication several times. First, she sent what she believed to be Pavlowitch's manuscript to Gary, promising to make any changes that Gary might request. Gary responded: "I refuse to read the manuscript [and] I release Émile Ajar-Pavlowitch and publisher of all liability. I hereby waive all right to file claims against the book for defamation of character. [You] are therefore entirely free to publish it without any fear of legal action on my part" (qtd. in Bona 365–66). When this failed to reassure Mercure de France, Gary had Pavlowitch deliver an ultimatum announcing that Ajar would never write another line unless his manuscript was published. Simone Gallimard finally caved in, and *Pseudo* came out nearly one year after the Goncourt, in December 1976.

Pseudo purports to be *Pavlowitch*'s personal story; it is the autobiography following the Goncourt. *Pseudo*, in other words, is supposed to be to *Madame Rosa* what Gary's *Promise at Dawn* was to *The Roots of Heaven*. Writing as Pavlowitch, Gary draws an unflattering psychological portrait of Pavlowitch. Gary attributes to him everything from a paranoid desire to remain incognito to a strong repugnance for his famous relative, viciously satirized as "Tonton Macoute" (the nickname given to former Haitian president François Duvalier's henchmen). Not content to elaborate his own legend or that of Ajar, Gary now sets about inventing Paul Pavlowitch! Whereas before it was Ajar that was being fabricated, constructed out of the mold of the picaro and *poète maudit* (cursed poet) now Pavlowitch himself is fictionalized, turned into a literary character. Thus, the method would shift from drawing on literary character types like Fosco, Genghis Cohn, and Momo to making use of the concrete material afforded by Pavlowitch's own life. Gary rummaged through Pavlowitch's past, exploiting elements like the interview with Baby, the bungalow near Cahors, and even the death of his mother.[23] Imagining himself as Pavlowitch-Ajar, Gary now inhabited a new, rapidly evolving public and authorial persona that would provide yet another range of parameters for creative inspiration.

The real target here was the Parisian press. Since the hunt for Ajar forced critics to take a position on Ajar's significance and legitimacy, Gary had at his command the ideal resources for focusing public attention on how an author is constructed in and read by the media. Using the clipping files forwarded to Pavlowitch from Mercure de France, Gary sifted through the innuendo and conjecture and sorted out the various images of Ajar produced by critical readings. Identifying critics by name and article, he worked these into Pavlowitch-Ajar's neurotic musings so that all of the positions adopted with respect to Ajar are reproduced within *Pseudo*. To make matters worse for critics, these discussions are cast in a delirious discourse whose exaggeration and blackening of all concerned recall aspects of Céline's *Conversations with Professor Y*.

The result is an immense hall of mirrors, where all of the actors from the Ajar story are present, but their reflections are skewed by Gary's wild parody. We start from what the public knows or imagines it knows about Ajar; Gary then reshapes it to provide a new version of these same events, presented as Pavlowitch's confessions; but all the while Gary is taking advantage of the confusion to tell *his own story* under the cover of his irony! By having "Ajar" turn all of the accusations leveled against him inside out, Gary pokes fun at both his critics and Pavlowitch's. Gary masterfully juggles a number of concurrent scenarios, where often a single sentence can be turned in several different directions, depending on what the reader believes of Ajar-Pavlowitch's story.

Gary begins by giving some precision to Pavlowitch's supposed problems with identity, though these are in fact Gary's own themes translated into the voice of May 1968 disaffection, that of Pavlowitch's generation. The concept of identity is fairly traditional (despite Ajar's roundabout formulations), conceived of as the product of biological and social attributes escaping his control: "I did not create myself," Gary has Pavlowitch say. "There's the mom and pop heredity, with alcoholism, cerebral sclerosis and, a bit further back, tuberculosis and diabetes" (*P* 13). To exist is to have been engendered by others at all levels, and from there onward one cannot help being placed accordingly within various social structures: "There is no beginning. I was conceived—we each get our turn—and ever since I've 'belonged.' I've tried everything possible to get out of it but no one has ever succeeded. We're all a bunch of sums" (*P* 9). In the course of Pavlowitch's meandering reflections, race, nationality, and social situation are named as contributing traits, added in with one's genetic makeup. These identities are thus necessarily alienating, since one's persona is determined in one's absence. This vision of an ensemble of predefined elements weighing upon the individual is a reformulation of Gary's notion of the Powers-that-be and Malraux's destiny.

One's choices with respect to identity are therefore extremely limited, since the two poles—self-invention and anonymity—appear equally impossible to achieve. The only recourse is to simulate accepting one's role: "There was a plumber, an accountant, a civil servant. Of course, they weren't really plumbers, accountants, or civil servants. They were each something else altogether. But nobody suspects anything. They simulate, act pseudo-pseudo eight hours a day and people leave them the hell alone. They live hidden on the inside and only come out at night" (*P* 21). The use of the pseudonym Ajar and the reclusive attitude that accompanies it are Pavlowitch's version of this strategy, which he names "the Ajar Defense," patterned after chess terminology. In this sense as well, then, Pavlowitch's approach mirrors that of Gary, who resorts to clandestine tactics or simulates his own capitulation in order to divert attention from himself.

Given these thematics and the language employed, *Pseudo* casts Pavlowitch much more in the image of *Gros-Câlin* than *Madame Rosa*, a neurotic loner rather than a disenfranchised minority. The narrator's choice of metaphors repeatedly links Cousin's lack of social adaptation to Pavlowitch's recourse to a pseudonym, and Pavlowitch only seems to be sinking deeper into his difficulties with personal and authorial identity. The experience of winning the Goncourt and having been tracked all over Europe for two years has apparently shattered his fragile equilibrium. In this scene, for instance, using pythonesque images lifted from *Gros-Câlin*, Pavlowitch is shown interned in a clinic where he practices his authorial signature:

> After having signed my name several hundred times, to the point that the carpet of my digs was covered with white pages and my pseudo who was crawling all over the place, I suddenly was gripped by a terrible fear: the signature was becoming more and more set [and] identical . . . *It* was there. Someone, an identity, a trap for life, a presence of absence, an infirmity, a deformity, a mutilation. It was taking possession and becoming me. *Émile Ajar*.
>
> I had incarnated myself.
>
> I was set, fixed, immobilized, caught and cornered. (*P* 76)

One can hear echoes of the dilemma I evoked in the Introduction, Jean Carrière's sense of having been dispossessed of his own signature following his Goncourt Prize in 1972. The language used by Ajar-Pavlowitch would appear to indicate that we have the opposite form here—he speaks of "possession," where Carrière experienced dispossession—but on further examination it is apparent that this experience of "incarnation" is just as alienating as what Carrière underwent. Gary's old struggle to escape the fixity of his image, his hostility toward succumbing to one's celebrity, is now placed on Pavlowitch's shoulders, who is portrayed as trapped within the authorial identity of Émile Ajar, one that he is supposed to have created himself but that now has taken on a life and consistency of its own. At the same time, however, Gary, speaking through Pavlowitch, would become victim of an even greater dispossession as he watched another be celebrated in the press at his expense.

Having established the justifications for Pavlowitch's themes and reclusiveness, Gary turns to the press's treatment of Pavlowitch. Pavlowitch is presented as hurt and disoriented by the media's persistent denials of his existence. From his perspective, it is not just Ajar who has been accused of not existing but Pavlowitch himself: "I set up an answering machine . . . whose message announced that I don't exist, that there is no Pavlowitch and that I am a mystification, a hoax . . . Obviously, I show certain exterior signs of existing but it's all just literature" (*P* 24). The press finds itself under scrutiny, being laughed at for ever having doubted that Pavlowitch wrote these texts. At the same time, of course, Gary is in fact telling the truth: Pavlowitch, *as presented to the public*, is a mystification, a prank, a pure product of literature.

Ajar's supporters do not escape Gary's burlesque treatment either. In the more laudatory reviews, Ajar's actions were frequently endowed by critics with intentions that were pure projection on their part. Françoise Ducout's piece is typical of the assurance with which reviewers would speak for the timorous Ajar. Just prior to the Goncourt, she would write: "One has only to read his first two novels to sense that Émile Ajar lives in marked opposition to our lifestyle. For example, he refuses the life of today's writers (the interviews, television). He refuses out of a fear that these obligations would compromise his work" (Ducout 10).

Caught between those who believe he does not exist and those who confer meaning even down to his silences, Pavlowitch-Ajar argues that he has been dispossessed of any possibility of self-definition: "You have no idea how difficult my situation is. Apparently I could cease writing or publishing . . . and this would still be seen as a poem . . . They'd see romanticism, gesticulation, sensitivity and aspiration—typical literary attitudes and poses. When it comes to bookishness and braying lyricism, you can't go any further as a mode of expression and an act of faith than refusing to write as a statement of principle and dignity, as a conscientious objection" (*P* 40). Just as Rimbaud's fugue in North Africa as an arms trafficker has in time become a *literary* gesture for those promoting a legend, Ajar's eventual refusal to continue as a writer would be interpreted as further proof of his writerly temperament. Using the allusion to Rimbaud (mentioned explicitly in other passages), Ajar argues that any withdrawal from the rites of literary fame can and will be recuperated by the institutions that stage those ceremonies. One does not escape the press: a refusal to acknowledge it is itself material for speculation and helps define one's image. By placing Ajar in the context of other reclusive writers—in interviews Pavlowitch would list anti-institutional writers such as Henri Michaux, Julien Gracq, Monique Wittig, and Thomas Pynchon as his chief influences—Pavlowitch reminds us that celebrated authors struggle to keep the press at bay and to maintain a separation between their life and work.

In keeping with the critics' regard for Ajar's work (or perhaps with the element of uncertainty, which would lead some of them to read him more carefully), reviewers would address questions in *Pseudo* that they had generally refused to recognize in Gary's work. Though an untiring adversary of Gary's "commercialism," Audouard went overboard in his endorsement of Ajar's literary merit: "What really matters in this work is that rarely has an author ever ventured so far into the mysteries of literary creation."[24] Dominique Autrand asked the questions that Gary's works in the sixties and seventies failed to elicit from critics: "How does one constitute an identity through writing? What is the meaning of this abstract incarnation of a man in a book? Where does one situate the truth of the person who writes?"[25] Just as satisfying for Gary were the issues Ajar's ad-

ventures raised among his peers. Having won the Goncourt the year before Ajar, Pascal Lainé reacted to Pavlowitch's declaration that Ajar would
not give interviews, sign books, or appear on television: "I wasted a year
of writing playing that game, so I admit that Émile Ajar annoys me a bit
[with this decision]. He's getting off too easy! A writer signs books, answers when spoken to and politely accepts when offered a free meal . . .
But what if one doesn't like playing the clown? I can't say that Ajar has
got it wrong. Authors and readers are at the mercy of fashions and advertising . . . I have nothing against literary prizes—so far no one's come
up with anything better. But why do we have to pull up to the trough
in this manner?"[26] Gary's credibility was too severely undermined in the
mid-seventies—owing to his conservative politics, his past role in Gallimard's advertising campaigns, and his healthy bank accounts—for this
critique to be accepted coming from him. Yet the elaborate staging of
Ajar combined with the content of the texts themselves made the message
hit home.

For Gary's attack upon Parisian literary institutions to be effective, it
was therefore essential that he continue to steer discussion toward envi-
sioning a writer who is trying to *avoid* having a legend. Only then could
Gary divert critics and realize his project surreptitiously with Pavlowitch-
Ajar. To keep the press off balance, Gary anticipated the complaints of
the more cynical journalists. *Pseudo* has one of Pavlowitch's friends accuse Ajar of being a publicity machine: "Turning down [the Goncourt]
was very impressive, old boy. It's going to generate tremendous publicity.
Bingo for the Goncourt, bingo for the refusal. Bravo" (*P* 185). This effectively unsettled those who suspected Ajar for those very reasons. Unbeknownst to readers, what is being said of Pavlowitch was in reality being
held over Gary's head. At one juncture, for instance, Pavlowitch's lawyer is
portrayed as cautioning: "Try not to lay it on too thick, Pavlowitch. You've
already pulled off your stunt. No photo of your face, just the eyes to bol-
ster the secret. No biography. You let people call you a Lebanese terrorist,
an abortionist, an occasional pimp and a wanted felon in France. You've
given rendez-vous in Copenhagen. It's perfect. There's no better legend
for a writer than mystery" (*P* 177). Not only does this passage outline in
naked detail Gary's strategy, but judging from Pavlowitch's own account
in *L'homme que l'on croyait,* Gary heard these same words from Bossat, his
powerful but disapproving lawyer charged with charting a course around
potential legal land mines (Pavlowitch, *L'homme* 161).

Gary had so shuffled the cards that critics no longer dared challenge
Ajar's irony. By casting Pavlowitch as an insecure writer struggling with
his pseudonymous creation, Émile Ajar, Gary could even recount to a
certain extent his own adventure with Ajar without anyone being any the
wiser. In the words of another character from *Pseudo,* we learn that "[the

truth] has been buried by lies under a pseudo-pseudo hodge-podge composed from its own ruins. So now you can really go to it. The more sincere you'll be, the more people will acclaim you as bogus. The more you tell the truth, the better you'll hide it. Go to it. Write. Publish. There's little risk that they'll find you out" (*P* 61). Bringing to mind the late stages of *L'homme à la colombe* or *The Guilty Head* for the boldness of its scam, the advice is addressed to Pavlowitch but applies just as easily to Gary. In writing *Pseudo* and performing the public gestures to back it up, Gary would become a sort of puppet master, manipulating several images at once: his own, Ajar's, and Pavlowitch's. It would allow him to coordinate many different sides of the equation, invisible to any other commentator. It was a desperate but concerted attempt to retake control of a process that had largely escaped his means ever since Pavlowitch entered onto the scene.

Yet one of the most striking features of this text remains the way it takes aim at Gary himself. This facet of *Pseudo* is cast as Pavlowitch's settling of personal accounts with Gary. Speaking through Pavlowitch-Ajar's voice, for instance, Gary in essence acknowledges that the elements that made up Gary's early legend are now often seen in a very different light by a generation that has rejected de Gaulle and a "heroic" French Resistance: "I've got an uncle that I call 'Tonton Macoute' because during the war he was an aviator and massacred civilian populations from way up high" (*P* 26). In addition to allegedly spending a good deal of time in detox clinics, Gary is shown as driven to exploit social causes by a desire for money and fame: "I was thinking about Tonton Macoute, a notorious writer who always knew how to extract a nice literary capital from suffering and horror" (*P* 17). Even Gary's Goncourt for *The Roots of Heaven* comes in for some ribbing: Pavlowitch-Ajar describes his uncle as lounging about at home in "a blue bathrobe with elephants on it to publicize one of his books. A trademark" (*P* 167).

The strained relationship between Pavlowitch and Gary is depicted as a necessary outgrowth of these ideological differences. In reviews of *Gros-Câlin*, Ajar had already been singled out as the alternative hope of French fiction: antiestablishment, antitradition, and anti-Academy. Arnothy wrote, for instance, "Ajar marks the revolt against the literature of our daddies; Ajar is the anti-cliché combatant" (Arnothy, "Un amour de python," 3). Gary, in contrast, with his allegiance to de Gaulle, Clark Gable mustache, and London-tailored suits, was clearly the paradigmatic representative of "daddy's literature." Catonné recalls the public's pleasure at the discovery of Pavlowitch behind Ajar: "What a pleasant surprise to discover hidden in the shadow of Romain Gary, that fading, out-of-date official writer, a nephew with genius, an absolute marginal, an outsider from the very first, with the look of a gypsy" (Catonné, *Romain Gary*

92). This opposition was reinforced by their respective literary heroes. Since Gary had always claimed Malraux as his model, Henri Michaux would be Pavlowitch's: "There's Michaux and then the rest. I think he's the greatest prose writer going. He does what he wishes with words."[27] Malraux, Michaux: they are conveniently connected by their assonance, yet diametrically opposed in their literary and professional images. Playing on the perceived incompatibility between Pavlowitch and Gary in a post-1968 Paris divided along generational lines, *Pseudo* exploits what the public desires to find before slipping its hidden narratives in behind it.

Like Willie Bauché in *The Colors of the Day* using ever more scandalous lies about himself to stave off revelations about his failing marriage, *Pseudo* is the willing sacrifice of Gary's own name and image in order to shield that of Ajar. The decision was a double-edged sword, however, regardless of—or *because* of—its effectiveness. Previously, Ajar's rapid rise had been to some extent at the expense of other young writers. Symbolic in this respect is a follow-up article on the 1976 Goncourt winner, Patrick Grainville's dizzying, beautiful, and perverse *Les flamboyants*: it slipped below the fold of *Le Monde*'s literary pages to make room for a review of Ajar's *Pseudo*, the headline stretching across all columns (*Le Monde* December 12, 1976: 31). But in using *Pseudo* to focus attention on an Ajar/Gary opposition, Gary invited having his own work further disparaged. In so doing, he strengthened prevailing opinions concerning the value of his work (until, in theory, the day when the secret would be uncovered). However much Gary may have enjoyed the irony of these unflattering comparisons, he probably also pondered what posterity might hold for his earlier writings.

A repercussion of this strange situation is that Gary became obsessed with the question of the paternity of Ajar's works. In a strictly literal sense, this concern was perhaps justified, for Gary realized that if he were to die unexpectedly, Pavlowitch could then claim to have been Ajar all along! As Gary's typist recalls, Gary decided to "scatter key-phrases throughout Ajar to have one more proof [of his authorship]. He was afraid that Paul might steal his identity."[28] The literary manifestations of this preoccupation with Ajar's paternity are present throughout *Pseudo*, and here again Gary contrived a mischievous way to slip a grain of truth into these tangled proceedings. The text of *Pseudo* grew out of the attempt to represent Gary's own circumstances masked behind Pavlowitch's, with Gary's characteristic double discourse being at once diversionary and exploratory. To this end, Pavlowitch is shown relishing his uncle's fear of being overlooked and forgotten. In the following dialogue, for instance, Pavlowitch reports Gary's irritation at the press's failure to name him as a possible mastermind of the Ajar mystery:

"It is really is amazing how little consideration I receive in France," said [Tonton Macoute]. "They've suspected Queneau and Aragon but not me, despite the fact that we're so close."

"I could call them and ask them to add your name to the list."

"No thanks. I could care less. If they're not capable of figuring out who the great writers today in France are all by themselves, too bad for France."

I acquiesced. It's a word that's no longer in fashion either. (*P* 178)

Completely reversing their situations, Pavlowitch-Ajar even accuses Gary of trying to lead the press to think that Gary has been the ghostwriter of Pavlowitch's works: "[Tonton Macoute] started shouting, denying, protesting, just to insinuate by the excess of his objections that he had in fact helped me a lot, that he had touched up my texts a bit" (*P* 69).

Gary pushes the limits of decency, however, when he extends these ambiguities into much more personal matters. Since Pavlowitch was an illegitimate child like Gary himself, Gary links the questions of genealogy and literary paternity. Playing on his father-figure status for the younger Pavlowitch-Ajar, Gary insinuates that Pavlowitch might actually be his *biological* son, the result of a brief tryst with his cousin Dinah: "[Tonton Macoute] takes himself for my father and imagines that I feel filial resentment toward him . . . Tonton Macoute never hid from me that he had loved my mother very much, despite the blood ties that connected them. I'm pretty much certain that they slept together" (*P* 26–27). Such tactics understandably strained his relationship with Pavlowitch and threatened to bring an end to their already deteriorating collaboration. But, at the same time, they allowed Gary to announce in a concrete though deceptive way that he is in fact Ajar's father, his "author."

Later in the same passage, however, Pavlowitch-Ajar realizes that his suspicions concerning Gary's role in his past change very little for him. Even if Gary is his father, his absence and neglect have already left an indelible mark: "That would also explain why I resemble Tonton Macoute a little bit—not physically . . . but morally. I too am devoured by such a need for an Author because I'm the son of a man who left me in a state of want for my entire life. One shouldn't forget that when Tonton Macoute was younger, he got himself killed in the war, but afterwards he worked it all out" (*P* 27–28). The last line of this passage seems merely a malicious barb mocking Gary's conversion of his war record into a literary and diplomatic career, an opposition of Gary's social stature to Pavlowitch-Ajar's precarious isolation. In fact, however, it is an allusion to Gary's decision during the Resistance to exchange his patronym for a pseudonym, a figurative slaying of the thin identity left to him by Lebja Kacew, the man who may have been his father. This is the situation in which Pavlowitch-Ajar finds himself, for having irretrievably lost the trace of the man who "authored" him, any familial identity he constructs for himself is invented and potentially undermined by doubt. Gary and Pavlowitch both are left with provisional identities of their own making.

Through a completely different discourse, we are brought back to the objectives of *Promise at Dawn*. In it, the urgency behind Gary's quest to reinvent himself stems in part from his missing father. Speaking of the disappointing succession of professors hired for his upbringing, for instance, the narrator notes, "A father would have done the trick much better" (*PD* 74). In taking a pseudonym, he did what his father was supposed to do for himself: bestow a name upon him.[29] *Pseudo* stages a scene, minus the innocence of Gary's *Promise at Dawn*, in which Pavlowitch-Ajar realizes what he has accomplished with his pseudonym and Goncourt Prize:

> "I'm Émile Ajar!" I yelled, pounding my chest. "The one and only! I'm the son of my works and the father of the same! I'm my own son and my own father! I don't owe anything to anyone! I'm my own author and I'm proud of it! I'm authentic! I'm not a hoax! I'm not pseudo-pseudo—"
> [Tonton Macoute] prepared a needle and administered my medication. (*P* 192–93)

Pavlowitch's self-creation is articulated in the same terms as Gary's but is immediately deflated by a satirical voice unable to share Gary's prior faith in France and the future. The discussion of these issues is handled in such a way as to provide the press with a biographically and thematically consistent author in Pavlowitch-Ajar, while discreetly extending reflections that date back to *Promise at Dawn*.

With the publication of *Pseudo*, speculation about Ajar died down. The decision to target "Tonton Macoute" was indisputably one of the most effective elements of Gary's evasive tactics, for after passages like the preceding ones critics no longer believed that the image-conscious Gary could be hiding behind Ajar. The case was closed, the dogs called off, the hunt abandoned. Those critics particularly predisposed to disliking Gary's work could henceforth give vent to their disdain without any fear of being embarrassed. When *Clair de femme* came out in 1977, just a few months after *Pseudo*, they set upon Gary's tale of geriatic love with open jubilation. Recalling that Rainier had already been struggling with impotence in *Your Ticket Is No Longer Valid*, Audouard would write: "At more than sixty years of age, the author of *Your Ticket* . . . persists in writing belated love stories. He still gets it up but he's a bit lacking in new ideas. Facing the onset of (literary) impotence, . . . he should pay more attention to his style. Or choose better ghostwriters".[30] In a critical reception reminiscent of the Surrealists' attack on Anatole France (*Un Cadavre*, issued in 1924), the press enacted a sort of public burial of Romain Gary the writer. Galey, hostile toward Gary's work since the late fifties, offered his services as undertaker: "One more novel, Mr. Executioner, it will be the last." [31] Even Jacqueline Piatier, a longtime supporter of Gary's writing and Ajar's most ardent admirer, turned in a smarmy and belittling review.[32]

Pavlowitch would henceforth be openly recognized as Ajar. He took a job working at Mercure de France as a literary adviser, where he lived up to his role of eccentric but able literary craftsman. One of the young authors sent to work with him, Valérie Schlumberger, remembers appreciating his editorial eye but notes, "[Pavlowitch] drops little tidbits about himself here and there that don't add up: he lives in the country, he likes Barbès and the main thoroughfares. He doesn't sleep, he gets up early, he has two daughters and a donkey, he has an apartment in the Marais." [33] Jacques Chirac, then mayor of Paris, invited Pavlowitch as guest of honor for a municipal book fair, while the Socialist Party tried to recruit his participation for a Leftist think-tank. True to his reputation, Ajar declined both invitations (Pavlowitch, *L'homme* 154).

The Final Steps: Rehearsals of Death

Pseudo would mark the peak of the Ajar saga, and the French literary scene would turn to other preoccupations. In 1977 and 1978, Decoin and Modiano would win the Goncourt Prizes that Ajar "stole" from them, while elsewhere a new round of *fait divers* would pass fleetingly through the newspapers. Though in reverse, one such example foreshadowed the end of the Ajar episode: a roundtable lecture in 1978 in honor of the "recently deceased" Mathieu Bénézet, author of *Imitation de Mathieu Bénézet: Mélodrame, dits, et récits du mortel*, drew a small crowd of curious well-wishers, not the least of whom was Bénézet himself, very much among the living.

Gary continued to forge ahead. For this last flurry of activity, he cleared out his files of revised definitive editions (*The Roots of Heaven* and Sinibaldi's *L'homme à la colombe*), a French translation of *The Gasp* (*Charge d'âme*, 1978), a theatrical adaptation of *The Company of Men* (*La bonne moitié*, 1978), and an extensive rewrite of *The Colors of the Day* (*Les clowns lyriques*, 1979). Lastly, he published two final original works, one as Émile Ajar (*King Solomon* in 1979) and one as Gary (*Les cerfs-volants* in 1980).

King Solomon tells the story of a friendship between a young taxi driver (Jeannot) and an elderly Jewish man (Solomon Rubinstein). These protagonists are fashioned in the respective images of Ajar and Gary, analogous to *Your Ticket Is No Longer Valid* with its opposition of Ruiz to Rainier. Jeannot's thuglike appearance belies an idealist's soul, while Rubinstein uses his philanthropy to distract himself from his own loneliness. The novel's conclusion, in which Jeannot helps Rubinstein reunite with a former girlfriend, constitutes a solution to the romantic impasse encountered in Gary's work (the strange triangle of Rainier/Laura/Ruiz). In this instance, the elderly hero reconciles himself to his age and thus is able to imagine a future for himself. Once again it is as if Ajar's input makes it possible to resolve a psychological dilemma, and the link to *Your Ticket Is No Longer Valid* would appear to be intentional: Jeannot's father, after all, turns out to have been a *ticket puncher* for the Parisian metro!

As usual, Gary wove in a number of links to his own work, but now the citations are more explicit. Not only is Rubinstein's physical appearance cast in Gary's image, but the references used to describe him—"Mister Solomon has the face of a Spanish grandee in the 'Burial of Count Orgaz' or that of José-Maria de Heredia in 'The Conquistadors'"—reappear almost verbatim in Gary's novels from the same period.[34] Jeannot completes the parallels, for in his physical appearance he resembles Pavlowitch and his problems with language accurately reproduce Ajar's stylistic tics. Comments one of Jeannot's friends, "You have a strange way of expressing yourself, Jeannot. It's as if you were always saying something other than what you said" (*KS* 240). Not only did Gary seem to be testing his readers, but by multiplying these points of contact he continued to develop the connection between his two principal authorial personae, in order to see for himself what their differences and similarities are.

The tone in *King Solomon* is much more traditional than in the other three Ajar works. Also, the narrative is directed by nostalgia and a pervasive anxiety about death that are germane to Gary's fiction from this period. Similar in respects to Gary's *Ski Bum* or *Clair de femme*, *King Solomon* would have been more appropriately published under Gary's own name. In fact, parts of it *had been published under Gary's name*: material previously serialized in 1971 by Gary for *France-Soir* was worked into *King Solomon* without anyone remarking it (*LDEA* 33–36). This is precisely the experiment Gary had in mind. *King Solomon* can be read as deliberately placed at a crossroads between Gary and Ajar—as a future demonstration that Ajar did in fact grow out of Gary, that Gary is in fact the author of Ajar. Having used *Pseudo* to regain control of Pavlowitch, Gary now maneuvered to reaffirm his grip on Ajar, so that posterity would see Ajar as an offshoot or derivative of Gary, rather than as an independent voice casting a shadow upon him.

The revision of *The Colors of the Day* in the form of *Les clowns lyriques* moves in the same direction, for it is an important proof that the thinking that led to the theatricalization of Ajar had always been at the center of Gary's writing aesthetic.[35] Despite its early date—in 1952 *The Colors of the Day* was Gary's fourth novel—it must be considered one of the most complete statements of his literary credo. Its republication was a calculated risk, insofar as it spells out in astonishing detail the strategies and motivations behind the production of a figure like Émile Ajar. Finally, it is an eerie work, too, anticipating several of the darker elements of Gary's final years, when the processes of self-invention would slide into ones of self-destruction. This pattern is found, of course, in other Gary novels such as *Talent Scout* or *Ski Bum*, but here the trajectory of the protagonist's life is particularly relevant to the Ajar episode. So taken is Bauché by this fight for self-definition that even in planning out a suicide attempt he remains obsessed with the desire to make his death an artistic creation whose representation is entirely orchestrated. In *The Colors of the Day*, for instance, Bauché rejects one method on the grounds that "it didn't bear [Willie Bauché's] stamp sufficiently . . . [He needed to find] an improved scenario" (*CD* 233). Bauché leaves behind a letter for his wife, which his father-in-law destroys, judging it mediocre and thus detrimental to Bauché's legend. In the rewritten version of this passage that appears in *Les clowns lyriques*, the concern shifts slightly: "[Willie] wondered what they would do with his corpse. He had invented hundreds and hundreds of analogous scenes, back when he was just a smalltime scriptwriter under contract in Hollywood. Willie absolutely had to know what they would do with his corpse. Without that, it was if he were leaving without knowing the end of the movie . . . Fortunately, he had made his arrangements" (*CL* 252). The preoccupation with one's funeral is linked to a concern over how one will be perceived in one's absence. Bauché is just one in a long list of Gary's characters whose last gestures are dedicated toward the arrangement of their final mask.[36]

Gary himself was no exception, having made arrangements to restore his own damaged image with *Les cerfs-volants*. Whereas *Les clowns lyriques* features characters attempting to hide from the past at all costs, *Les cerfs-volants* is dedicated to memory. Lyrical and serene, stripped of cynicism and bitterness, it tells the story of Ludo and his uncle, a kitemaker whose fragile vessels are designed in shapes representing different ideals of France and the Resistance. With its tribute to all variety of heroes from World War II pitched in an older, fablelike prose, this work reaffirms the legends under siege throughout France in the seventies. In a sense, *Les cerfs-volants* is an appeased response to *A European Education* at thirty-five years' distance, a reflection on a few heroic acts indeed worthy of commemoration and of the legacy left by the individuals who performed them. It is an emphatic statement on Gary's part that he stands by his original work, values, and image as a novelist of the French Resistance. Moreover, it is clear that this is ultimately the image Gary wished to preserve of himself. In these same years, he turned down the invitation to be a candidate for Joseph Kessel's vacant chair in the French Academy (Catonné, *Romain Gary* 240) and refused the academy's Paul Morand Prize (owing to Morand's behavior during the war; Bona 383–84), but he did take the time to make detailed arrangements in anticipation of his funeral: state honors surrounded by his surviving comrades from the Free

French forces and the Companions of the Liberation, to be celebrated in the most hallowed halls of the French military, the Hôtel des Invalides.

Having made these final adjustments to the portraits of Ajar and Gary, and without unveiling Ajar's identity, Gary took his life on December 2, 1980, with a gunshot to the head.

Conclusion

Having seen five masks and five costumes prepared for a ballet, yet seeing only one dancer, a barbarian asked who would play the other characters. When he learned that the one dancer would perform by himself, he thought: "It must be the case then that in a single body there are several souls."

Antoine Coypel

On the day of his death, Gary mailed legal arrangements dating from August 1980 to Robert Gallimard, with whom Gary had just shared lunch. In his apartment, Gary left letters where his companion, Leïla Chellabi, would find them: some were addressed to those closest to him, and one was a communiqué for the press. As for Pavlowitch, he was bound by prior agreement to preserve Ajar's secret even after Gary's death. It was evident that Gary's suicide was long-premeditated.

For Pavlowitch, however, remaining hostage to his role as Ajar was an untenable personal and professional situation. Like the trained poodle in *Clair de femme* that continues its routine while its trainer succumbs to a stroke backstage (*CF* 154), Pavlowitch found himself in the role of a puppet obliged to dance in the absence of the puppeteer. After seven difficult months, he decided that he could not go on with the charade any longer. On July 3, 1981, in order to reclaim his life for himself and his family, Pavlowitch broke his promise and revealed the truth about Ajar on an episode of *Apostrophes* that had been announced as the nephew's tribute to his deceased uncle. This disclosure was accompanied by the publication of Pavlowitch's book *L'homme que l'on croyait.* The press, wary and thoroughly confused, wondered whether Gary could possibly be responsible for this text as well. Caught off guard, Gallimard soon riposted, issuing a pamphlet left by Gary for posthumous publication that explained the author's version of events.

Already completed by March 1979, *Life and Death of Émile Ajar* presents the unique instance of an autobiographical text written by a writer who no longer exists (the deceased Gary) correcting the autobiography of a writer (Pavlowitch) who did not write the works of a writer (Ajar) who never existed in the first place. To further impress upon readers that *Life and Death of Émile Ajar* is a posthumous address to the public, Gary engages in some fairly lugubrious humor. On his refusal to enter into greater detail concerning Ajar's creation, for example, Gary comments wryly, "[Days] and days after my death, I have other fish to fry" (*LDEA* 39–40). In a chilling imitation of the *dybbuk* who plagues ex-SS officer Schatz in *The Dance of Genghis Cohn*, Gary sets out to haunt the critics who assumed that with Gary's passing his voice would be extinguished as well.

Accordingly, the most immediate result of this postmortem revelation was that Gary was now recognized as being responsible for the invention of authors "Romain Gary," "Fosco Sinibaldi," "Shatan Bogat," "Émile Ajar," and "Paul Pavlowitch" (insofar as *Pseudo* purported to be Pavlowitch's autobiography). In total, there were five masks designed for an elaborate ballet that spanned a forty-five-year career and produced two films, countless articles, thirty-two books, and two Goncourt prizes.

In 1981, reassessments of Gary's career and talent were thus in order. One is reminded of the first drawing produced by the narrator of *The Little Prince* in which, to the child's disgust, adults see only a hat where in fact they are supposed to see an elephant swallowed by a large snake (Saint-Exupéry 7–8). Indeed, critics had failed to see the elephant of Gary's *The Roots of Heaven* tucked inside the belly of the boa that was Ajar's *Gros-Câlin*. Embarrassed readers wondered how it was that such a "predictable, over-the-hill writer" could have been mistaken for a brilliant young innovator, or how an unrepentant Gaullist could have seduced a generation hostile to the pre-1968 status quo. While Gallimard and Mercure de France hashed out the thorny legal issues (Gary was under exclusive contract with Gallimard), critics for their part faced the Borgesian quandary of how to reconcile Gary's authorial identities. Are his pseudonymous creations episodic, picaresque permutations of the *same* writer—five souls in one body, as our "barbarian" would say? Or are they a collection of siblings all on separate but equal footing, authors distinct and independent of one another? I will approach these issues via three avenues of inquiry: How should we situate "Ajar" with respect to "Gary" once we learn that Gary was responsible for both of them? In what ways did Gary remain a victim of the functioning of his authorial identities, despite his attempts to control them? In what ways did Gary's critique of the press's conception of authorial identity succeed in its aims?

Two Goncourt Authors or One Laureate Twice Decorated?

Gary's consecration in 1956 for *The Roots of Heaven* was marred by attacks unleashed by conservative sectors of the press. While praised in prominent mainstream columns for his humanist themes and exotic adventures, right-wing critics heckled Gary mercilessly, claiming that his writing was crippled by grammatical and idiomatic mistakes. As mentioned in Chapter 2, Kléber Haedens led the charge: "[Gary's] biographers inform us that he knows seven languages. I am assuming that it would never occur to anyone to include French among these."[1] Following up on Haedens's opening volley, a handful of critics regaled their readers with citations taken from *The Roots of Heaven*. The weekly journal *Arts* was especially persistent. First, René Georgin noted: "I find it particularly regrettable that Romain Cary [*sic*] uses the famous cliché *sur une grande échelle*: 'Did [Mina] know that ivory smuggling was still practiced *on a large scale*?' "[2] Georgin's misuse of the term cliché is probably a greater offense against the French language than Gary's repetitions of the phrase in question, but the next issue of *Arts* pursued its campaign of derision undeterred. Here, at least, it did produce some amusing examples, as in the following awkward phrasing: "He had taken a bullet in the arm, but had felt nothing in his enthusiasm."[3] Another paper claimed to be deluged with letters chronicling Gary's stylistic *faux pas* and pleaded with its "readers to keep these pearls for themselves. [We] have run out of room in our filing system."[4] Even some of the Goncourt Academy members joined the fray. Jean Giono voiced his appreciation of the sentiments promoted by *The Roots of Heaven* but regretted "that Gary doesn't always write in French."[5]

These attacks on Gary's reputation gained momentum once the accusation made the rounds—from unnamed sources—that Gary's stylistic infelicities were so pervasive that his publishers were obliged to enlist ghostwriters for each manuscript. The authorship of two of Gary's most acclaimed novels was called into doubt: it was reported that Calmann-Lévy had arranged an extensive rewriting for *A European Education*, whereas Camus and Jacques Lemarchand were said to have helped with *The Roots of Heaven*.[6]

As a result, Gary was challenged to defend his professional honor at the very moment when he should have been savoring his laurels. He counterattacked in a round of promotional interviews with Paul Guth (*Le Figaro littéraire*), Roger Grenier (*France-Soir*), Gabriel d'Aubarède (*Les Nouvelles littéraires*), and Claude Le Roux (*Paris-Presse*), citing the material obstacles created by his distant obligations in Hollywood and La Paz as the primary reason for the imperfectly proofed galleys. The damage was done, however, and the label of imperfect stylist would dog him. A few years later, for example, during a televised panel discussion on contemporary writers, Gary's then-recent triumph with *Promise at Dawn* was mentioned. Respected *Figaro* critic Robert Kanters blurted out, "Romain Gary is an interesting writer, but he writes in Moldo-Wallachian." When the live audience protested, Kanters amended his remark, assuring spectators that it was not his intention to insult anyone—an apology clearly directed toward Rumanians and not Gary.[7]

Despite the official recognition brought by the Prix des Critiques and the Goncourt Prize, Gary's stature as a *French* author was thus contested. He would remain known chiefly for what he represented—a successful Francophile immigrant, Gaullist war hero, diplomat, and humanist—without receiving acknowledgment for the complex formal experiments that distinguished some of his writings in the sixties.

The shadow cast over Gary's first Goncourt remained an affront to Gary's pride. In *Pour Sganarelle*, for instance, he spends several pages taking personal jabs at Haedens and Georgin (*PS* 371–73), as he in fact had already done more briefly in 1957 ("Le moment de la vérité" 4). Thus, when the project to create Émile Ajar took shape in the early seventies, this episode constituted a matter of unfinished business for Gary. If, as some critics had argued, *The Roots of Heaven* was all content and no form, then Ajar would offer a novel whose merit lay in the verve and originality of its expression.

Indeed, while no one ever did manage to explain what *Gros-Câlin* is about, most critics were nonetheless enchanted by its clever and disarmingly moving voice. The striking tone is in large part the result of specific turns of phrase employed by Ajar. To help render his protagonists' detachment from contemporary urban society, Ajar created narrators whose difficulties in self-expression manifest themselves through a variety of "accidental" abuses of the French language. *Gros-Câlin*'s narrator, Cousin, candidly admits to these troubles from the outset of his report on pythons: "[I] must apologize for the mutilations, misuses, carp's leaps, sprains, acts of disobedience, crabisms, strabisms and unregulated immigrations in my language, syntax and vocabulary."[8] As this passage shows, the problems consist of metaphors taken literally and euphemisms and clichés turned inside out, along with other conceptual and idiomatic malapropisms. In most instances, however, these botched phrases are employed in such a way as to give them a poetic turn. For instance, although the metaphor (carp's leap), medical term (strabismus), and social euphemism (unregulated immigration) are improperly employed, one nonetheless can imagine how they could describe Cousin's verbal contortions and distortions: a carp's leap is a gymnastic maneuver where one lies down with one's back arched and then springs to one's feet, while strabismus is an eye defect marked by crossed or wandering eyes. Later in the same passage, we encounter interference between (at least) three idiomatic phrases created through the repetition of related cognates: "It would be an ordeal for me if I was asked through official summons to use words and forms that had already circulated widely without finding a loophole, but I don't mean to be circuitous."[9] This tangle of terms ultimately illustrates its own claim in that the semantic disarray is attributed to the fact that the words have already run in circles.

Since these catchy stylings would become Ajar's trademark (known in the press as "Ajarisms"), Gary would receive indirect recognition for his prowess as a French prose writer. While previously Gary's Russian heritage was cited as an impediment to his literary development, Ajar's foreign birth was seen as marking a relative distance from the French language that thereby enabled him to act upon it. One example of this opinion is the praise from a member of the French Academy (which regulates linguistic use in France), Belgian-born writer Félicien Marceau. Marceau congratulated Ajar on his linguistic liberties in the following terms: "I was struck by this sort of parallel language which could be a variety of Francophone expression."[10] So strong was the focus on Ajar's technique that Gary could even indulge himself in a private triumph, playing off of compliments addressed to Ajar by critics disdainful of Gary's work. In *King Solomon*, Jeannot employs a description lifted from Galey's review of *Gros-Câlin*: "Chuck says that I'm the Douanier Rousseau of vocabulary. It's true that I rummage through words like a customs officer [*douanier*] to see if they are hiding anything" (*KS* 204).[11] Gary appreciates the analogy linking Ajar to Henri "le Douanier" Rousseau, a self-taught Naïve painter whose exotic, dreamlike landscapes caught the attention of avant-garde artists at the turn of the century. Cousin's innocent, befuddled speech patterns can be considered a sort of *art brut* rendered syntactically, but Gary extends the comparison with the pun on *douanier* to make it clear that Ajar is undertaking a deliberate examination of the literary possibilities of the French language. Moreover, in so doing, Gary also adds a sly allusion to Ajar's clandestine situation, since customs officers verify identities more commonly than semantics.

The Ajarisms tend to be composed from bits of discourse taken by the narrators from a heterogeneous ensemble of sources: various civic authorities, coworkers, neighbors, ethnic groups, and other loners like themselves. In discussing his situation, for instance, Momo recognizes the relevant terms to employ but does not yet fully master their meanings. He often confuses contexts or reverses their significance. When M. Hamil hesitates to answer Momo's questions about love, Momo remarks, "[M. Hamil] must have been thinking that I was still *forbidden to minors* and that there are things I'm not supposed to know" (*MR* 11; emphasis added). Though Momo has used the phrase improperly, we understand immediately what he means. Moreover, the very fact that he knows the phrase "forbidden to minors" is a reminder that, raised in a milieu of prostitution, sex shows, con artists, racism, domestic violence, and drugs, this minor has already seen and heard a great many things that are indeed inappropriate for his age. Struggling with the many cryptic terms used by the people frequenting Madame Rosa, Momo can only piece together a garbled understanding of the issues facing prostitutes and their off-spring. Thus, birth control is presented as "the legal pill for the *protection* of childhood" (*MR* 80; emphasis added) and Madame Rosa's wards as "just a bunch of kids who weren't able to get themselves aborted in time" (*MR* 19). Ajar's insight is to divert common expressions in ways that end up reflecting more accurately the reality of his characters' existence than the proper formulation would. For example, in attributing responsibility for their plight to the children themselves, Momo unwittingly reveals one of the tragedies of these foster children's situation: the belief that they are somehow to blame for being unwanted. Where Momo has not understood the precise definition of many of these terms, his mistaken application of them usually signals in the text that he has stumbled onto a more important truth hiding behind them (Day 81).

Like Cousin before him, Momo's quirky non sequiturs also voice pointed social truths that show the extent to which these characters unknowingly incorporate the preconceptions and prejudices surrounding them. This often manifests itself in clever confusions of causal links. "For a long time, I didn't know I was Arab because nobody was insulting me," recalls Momo. "I only learned it when I went to school" (*MR* 12). Momo's naive communication of this fact shows that he implicitly accepts the negative connotations attached to his ethnic identity by the surrounding Caucasian community. Véronique Anglard's artful description can pass as a good summary of the Ajarisms in general: "[Momo's] remark imposes itself [on the reader] as the consequence of a syllogism that Momo has rendered more economic: Arabs receive insults and thus, when you do not, you are not conscious of your condition" (Anglard 338). A second, more complicated illustration is Momo's reference to "the Orleans rumor."[12] In the company of Madame Rosa in 1970, Momo could have heard this incident mentioned many times, but again its full dimensions escape him: "The Orleans rumors were when the Jews working in ready-to-wear weren't drugging white women and sending them off to work in whorehouses and so everybody would get mad at them. Jews always draw attention to themselves for no reason at all" (*MR* 29). Momo recognizes that these rumors are the expression of racist beliefs among a portion of the population but only vaguely grasps the nature of the accusations. In inverting the claims (the Jews *weren't* drugging women and *weren't* selling them into forced prostitution), Momo completely misconstrues the content of the racist stereotype. This is precisely what makes Ajar's twist so effective. On the one hand, in his innocence, Momo in fact gets right what the anti-Semites have gotten wrong: there is no Jewish conspiracy and no cause whatsoever to be preoccupied with the Jewish population of

France. On the other, in highlighting Momo's confusion, Ajar also parodies how rumors take shape and are rescripted or amplified.

Finally, Ajar's distinctive, economic style also exposes in a seductive way how institutional and colloquial formulas reflect the values of those exerting control over certain categories of individual. They remind us that these aspects of our daily vocabulary are the linguistic equivalent and material vehicle of institutional prejudice. The child narrator's misapplication of these "grown-up" words or administrative euphemisms reveals exactly what these phrases were originally intended to mask. Ajar's wordplay demonstrates how this language objectifies, defines or holds its human subjects at a distance.

The critical recognition of Ajar as an innovative stylist in the French idiom was sweet revenge for Gary. Ajar's literary renown was due to traits that are the opposite of those that brought Gary his fame. Yet, in a sense, the linguistic device that makes Ajar's characters endearing is based on the very thing that caused Gary such grief at the time of his first Goncourt: an imperfect mastery of the nuances of French colloquialisms and grammatical rules.

What can we conclude, then, about this juxtaposition of Gary and Ajar? Are they one and the same writer, as their common onomastic origin implies, or contraries, as their critical reception and biographical portraits suggest?

Based on my discussion here, "Ajar" appears to have produced texts that "Gary" could not or, at least, did not write. Thus, the former cannot be reduced to the latter. Yet in signing *Life and Death of Émile Ajar* with the name Romain Gary, Gary was plainly claiming paternity and proprietorship of Ajar. In fact, Gary went much farther. Arguing that Ajar-like phrasings are found throughout his own fiction, he asserts that professional readers should have been able to recognize the common source behind the two: "It would have sufficed to read *The Dance of Genghis Cohn* to discover immediately the identity of *Madame Rosa*'s author" (*LDEA* 18). Gary thus dismisses the notion that his multiplication of authorial selves leads to a corresponding fracturing of voices, stating that an essential resemblance between Gary and Ajar is inescapable: "I don't believe that a 'doubling' is possible. The roots of a work are too deep and their apparent divergences, even when seemingly quite significant, would not resist a thorough study—what was formerly known as 'textual analysis'" (*LDEA* 34). Doubtless this is what he was suggesting in a veiled manner when Cousin notes in *Gros-Câlin* that his snake always remained the same in spite of its repeated sloughs.

These remarks made in his final years go against the grain of many suggestions found elsewhere in his work. Gary even claims that *Gros-Câlin* was *written as Romain Gary*, with the invention of Ajar coming after the novel's completion (*LDEA* 23). In other words, Ajar is a mask employed by the writer Romain Gary, to be placed on the same footing as Bogat and Sinibaldi, and a remarkably original work like *Gros-Câlin* is just one more novel in Gary's extensive production. Were this true, it would invalidate Gary's hypothesis of a reciprocal relation between author and work, whereby the author is produced with each new work but the work itself grows through the discovery and development of the nascent authorial persona.

We can, I believe, safely discredit Gary's claim that he devised the author-character Émile Ajar after he wrote *Gros-Câlin*. Pavlowitch, for example, states that they were devised together: "At the end of 1972, Romain Gary told me that he was planning to write 'something completely different under a completely different name,' because, he insisted, '[he] no longer had the necessary freedom [to write as he wished]'" (Pavlowitch, *L'homme* 7). The numerous comparisons in *La nuit sera calme* between Gary's own youth and that of an Algerian immigrant imply that Gary indeed was already focused on the Ajar persona early in 1973, whereas the manuscript for *Gros-Câlin* was not completed until December of that year.

Just as importantly, the textual analysis Gary calls for also works against his argument. A first point to be made on this subject is that a number of the examples of stylistic resemblance identified by Gary in *Life and Death of Émile Ajar* are little more than brief citations from Gary's earlier novels discreetly inserted into Ajar's (see *LDEA* 36–37). The reappearance in *Gros-Câlin* of a phrase like "I grow attached very easily," fourteen years after *Promise at Dawn*, does not prove that Gary's writing voice operates according to the same linguistic mechanisms as Ajar's. Gary's objective in these examples is more analogous to that of the medieval troubadours who wove hidden signatures into their songs, proof of their presence in otherwise authorless works (see Dragonetti 9–12).

Nevertheless, it is true that Gary's writing changed from the fifties to the sixties. Much of this is mirrored in a transformation of how he expressed his sociopolitical views. During his years as a diplomat, Gary often affected a deliberately outdated moralist discourse as a rhetorical device to mark his rejection of certain facets of modernity. No doubt partly influenced by de Gaulle in this respect, Gary was willing to pass for an old-fashioned liberal humanist (in the eyes of some) or even as a reactionary idealist (in the eyes of others). After his marriage to Jean Seberg, however, Gary presented a different face. Most of the causes that motivated him remained the same, but he was now in contact with a younger generation. Despite his denigration of Hollywood civil rights activists in *White Dog*, for instance, Gary shared Seberg's fervent opposition to racism in all its forms. He weighed in with extremely progressive arguments on a number of France's social issues (e.g., abortion, consumerism, delinquency) and resigned from the Ministry of Information out of solidarity with the students during May 1968.

Accordingly, Gary's writing style evolved as well. There are a number of occasions in Gary's novels from the sixties where euphemisms, clichés, and catch phrases are intentionally diverted from their usual context. In *Ski Bum*, for instance, the narrator speaks of ski fanatics who by hook or by crook find "at least three days a week of clean snow *unspoiled by demographics*" (*SB* 20; emphasis added). Ajar, as we have seen, used this type of formula quite effectively.[13] However, while Gary demonstrated an unerring knack for selecting timely topics for his novels (from the complexities of racial conflict in the United States and socioeconomic development in the former French colonies to ecology and sexual dysfunction), his experiments with spoken language are among the least convincing aspects of his writing. In the late sixties, these generally took place in his "American comedy" trilogy, novels that were written initially in American English and only later loosely translated into French by Gary himself. The narrators employ folksy phrasings derived from contemporary speech patterns and slang. As Dominique Rosse notes, Gary's use of quotation marks within the text at times signals a parodic intention (97), but the overall result remains an approximate imitation of how disaffected American youth are perceived to speak, and it has not dated well. In the following passage from *Ski Bum*, the narrator speaks first of men who try to impress women with fast cars or big boats and then digresses onto other subjects:

It's like those dudes who need a fast car or a Riva motor boat with two engines and forty horse-power instead of what nature should have given them. You take a girl out on the water in a Riva and the girl opens right up all by herself. Bug Moran was right when he said that we're living in a civilization of dildos and other nasty stuff against nature that substitutes and pretends: cars, Communism, home and country, Mao, Castro . . . It's all just dildos. [Chicks] made love with a girl who was using a diaphragm distributed by Connecticut Democrats. It had "I am for Kennedy" marked on it. There's no hole left to hide in. (*SB* 14)

While one detects a few distant premonitions of Cousin's alienated musings, stylistically Gary's attempt at a casual, populist tone grates as awkward and affected.[14] It clashes with the arguments and references offered, failing ultimately to jell as a persuasive literary voice. The tone is simply not a compelling vehicle for voicing Gary's distrust of ideology and various forms of chauvinism. Moreover, trying to provoke his readers but somewhat out of his element, Gary treads a thin line. As in *Your Ticket Is No Longer Valid*, his critique of phallic compensation bears echoes of the very thing it sets out to deflate: modern expressions of reactionary machismo.

If we reverse the comparison and look at those passages where Ajar's favorite themes can be traced back to Gary's work, we again see that the earlier formulations lack the linguistic turns employed by Ajar. From Gary's pen, many of the stylized passages bog down in the self-conscious irony and sarcasm that typify his less successful works. Sticking with *Ski Bum*, one reads at another juncture: "*Hobos* avoid learning languages in general so that they won't get snared by all the things that go with vocabulary. Vocabulary always comes from others—it's a sort of inheritance that falls in your lap. We're always speaking the language of others, you know? It's not our fault. Nothing in it belongs to us. Words are just counterfeit coins that people pass off on us" (*SB* 22). In 1969, neither the themes nor the language used to convey them were novel any longer. On the contrary, *hobo* (in English in the French edition as well) was a slang term already out of fashion by the late sixties and its usage here is arguably incorrect. (Did Gary confuse it with "hippie"? Did he believe it to be derived from the French *hobereau*, meaning "country squire"?) In many respects, the linguistic concerns in these passages are closer to Gide's *The Counterfeiters* than to Ajar's *Gros-Câlin*.[15]

Gary's novels simply do not measure up to Ajar's in their quest to develop a voice for expressing social marginality. In fact, Gary's most successful works from this period (*White Dog* and *Your Ticket Is No Longer Valid*) are largely free of stylistic experimentation and adopt realist narrative approaches to convey their social critiques. Ultimately, in works like *The Dance of Genghis Cohn* and *Ski Bum*, Gary was *seeking* to do something along the lines of what Ajar would later accomplish, but at that point his narrative voice tended to break down in its flippant and world-weary self-consciousness. Gary's characters have understood too much about life's disappointments, while Ajar's characters stumble upon fresh forms of expression owing to the gap between what the world throws at them and what their limited experience allows them to comprehend. It is in this shift from a jaded, cynical attitude to an ever-hopeful, offbeat voice that Gary would find the stride that suited him. Consistent in every detail with their sense of alienation, Ajar's characters' apprehension of the world is perfectly contained within their manner of expression. It constitutes the very tissue of the narrators' being. This change in narrative voice is possible only having donned the persona of Émile Ajar: slightly neurotic, bewildered by the world's commotion, heart on his sleeve, still tragically hopeful for human kindness. The Ajar episode is remarkable for this very reason: the change of identity did enable Gary to tap into another literary vein and bring to fruition a long-harbored but previously unsuccessful aesthetic project. Had there not been a significant transformation, Jacques Brenner notes, Gary would never have experienced the "rebirth" described in "The Life and Death of Émile Ajar" (Brenner 193).

Thus, while many of the thematic similarities between Gary's and Ajar's novels are undeniable and, as we saw in Chapter 5, deliberate, their discourses cannot be said to be comparable. Moreover, Gary may have intended *The Roots of Heaven* to convey the same notions as *Gros-Câlin*, but, as Öostman argues (166), their dissimilar genres and narrative voices ultimately transformed the message. Thus, I cannot agree with Gary when he states that all of Ajar was already contained in his own novels; more accurately, one can say that the theoretical, thematic, and literary steps leading directly to Ajar are evident throughout Gary's fiction.

This is not to say that Gary was an *inferior* writer; Gary and Ajar, in a sense, were not competing on the same terrain. They emerged as entirely different writers whose distinct identities were grounded in the stylistic and thematic traits specific to their body of work. Just as the linguistic flair of the Ajarisms is missing from Gary's texts, the humanistic, historical vision that gives Gary's finest works their timeliness, dignity, and epic breadth is absent from Ajar's more modest, claustrophobic literary universe. *Gros-Câlin* by Romain Gary violates the spirit of that work and seems every bit as inappropriate as reprinting *A European Education* under the name of Émile Ajar.

Stereotype and Archetype

Chapter 3 examined the ways in which the narrative frames of Gary's writing unknowingly contributed to the lack of resilience in Gary's authorial image. In theory, these problems should have been resolved once Gary resorted to the strategy of producing new pseudonymous personae. That is, the discovery of Gary's development as Ajar should have sufficed to demonstrate that Gary had been greatly underestimated by many of his professional peers. As we have seen in the Introduction, however, critics did not necessarily alter their opinions of Gary's talent after the revelation of Ajar's identity; on the contrary, some even altered their opinion of *Ajar's* talent. *We cannot, in other words, fully account for Gary's dilemma if we restrict ourselves to textual analysis.* Part of the problem lies in institutional issues and is inherent in the dynamics of celebrity, and particularly that of literary fame in France. To explore this facet of Gary's case, I will discuss the roles of myth and stereotype in the dissemination of French authorial images.

Starting from the principle that "nothing great or lasting can be created without a myth as its grounding" (*GH* 211), Gary organized his literary practice around directives inspired by the examples of de Gaulle and

Malraux. Masters at the art of projecting themselves as symbolic figures in the service of a cause, de Gaulle and Malraux produced legends with very few original elements, drawing their components intentionally from France's cultural canon. The fact that the traits composing de Gaulle's portrait preexisted him actually served de Gaulle's purposes, because he was seeking a simple, recognizable image to be legitimized by its rootedness in France's past. His goal, after all, was to unite the people of France. In the first stage of his writing, Gary devised protagonists like Nadejda and Morel in the mold of such legends but neglected to tailor his own image in a coherent manner. When his quest for the 1945 and 1956 Goncourt Prizes was threatened by speculation about his identity, however, he discovered the pitfalls of not properly anticipating public perception. Henceforth, Gary would carry out his attempts to embody certain values by plotting his authorial image in the mold of media myths, creating legends in miniature by drawing on the issues he judged to be present in the public's mind.

That Gary's success is owed to these tactics is equally true for Ajar *and* Gary. From the end of the war until de Gaulle's return to power, Gary's public persona fulfilled a social function, providing a positive image of the French war effort and of France's status as a haven for European political, economic, and ethnic exiles. With *Promise at Dawn*, other easily identifiable character types were worked into his portrait: the young immigrant driven to achieve in order to redeem his abandoned mother, the cosmopolitan diplomat, the lone wolf, the movie star's husband, and so forth. These were Gary's responses to the necessity of continually adding new episodes to the legend, but the predominant feature remained those reflecting a heroic French Resistance. When the sociopolitical climate swung after May 1968 to the opposite extreme, Ajar arrived on the scene as the ideal antidote to Gaullist authoritarianism. Employing relatively few details, Gary endowed Ajar with the quintessential traits of the artist as colorful and uncompromising misfit: a Bohemian beset by run-ins with the law, a thorn in the side of the political and literary cliques, socially ill adapted, neurotic, and vaguely menacing, a marginal artist flirting with permanent exile. It is the Rimbaud myth updated for a seventies audience seeking an antiestablishment figure to counter the graybeards of the French Academy and to poke fun at what it saw as moth-eaten fables of the Resistance. "Gary" and "Ajar" were both compilations of time-worn scenarios and topically useful character types.

Thus, if Gary found himself stuck within stereotyped images, he was once again partly to blame for his troubles. He readily recognized his responsibility in this respect, commenting in his final piece: "Perhaps, unconsciously, I lent myself to the process. It was easier: the image was already completely prepared and all I had to do was settle in" (*LDEA* 29).

Gary's point that the image *preceded* him is significant. Gary can be said to have orchestrated his images, to have manipulated them, even embellished them creatively, but he did not really *invent* them. The character types were there waiting for him; he merely identified and enacted them, as much in the instance of "Gary" as with "Bogat," "Ajar," or "Pavlowitch." Such myths do not create social beliefs; they actualize existing ones.

The root of Gary's problems lies here. Where his authorial activity was effective is in the ways it evoked the outline of these character types, leading readers to recognize the figure in question and flesh out the details on their own. As Jean-François Jeandillou notes, "Thus the imaginary biography is usually based on an accumulation of stereotypes: the belated revelation of an 'unknown' genius, the reconstitution of his 'life' according to 'sources' characterized by their scarcity and unreliability" (*Supercheries* 479). With a keen sense of how public opinion and the media function, Gary accurately predicted his readers' responses. But this only worked because the use of stereotypical topoi plugged Gary into scenarios whose narrative elements were already familiar, consciously or unconsciously, to the public. In other words, he could trigger a process that would channel readings along predictable paths, but that does not mean that he had the ability *to redirect those paths.* The stereotypes that allowed Gary as a relative unknown to replace a former identity with one of his own invention would ultimately lock him into a caricatural image that he would be powerless to dismiss later. In a sense, Gary's dilemma was similar to that of Genghis Cohn in *The Guilty Head,* who thinks he has managed to escape his identity by donning that of the Tahitian reprobate, only to find himself an accidental pawn in a larger plot (the secret service mistakes him for a nuclear scientist).

Having exploited these features, Gary also became their victim. He could suggest identities that corresponded to preexisting narratives, but he could not directly modify the stereotypes that make up these narratives, because the media processes that perpetuate myths are highly economic, based on assimilation and recuperation. The schematization involved in the promotion of these authorial images in the daily papers, on television, and on the radio erases all possibility of nuance and renewal. As Amossy writes, "anyone who [has been] the incarnation of a stereotype with a mythical value [remains] prisoner to it forever. Its recurrent and fixed pattern is characterized by the immutability of its 'form-meaning': it allows neither change nor development" ("Stéréotypie" 179). In other words, the very weight of the mass diffusion that propagated the contours of his image in the first place worked against him when he sought to redirect or reinvent his legend. The image produced by Gary would soon be out of his hands: "[From] the moment the fixed collective pattern becomes the receptacle [of a] value, the myth will depend upon the society

that produced it . . . As a collective image, [the myth] is henceforth subject only to changes in public opinion or fashions" (Amossy, *Idées reçues*
113). Gary's success in riding his identification as a Resistance hero or an
Algerian misfit to public prominence is proof of how deeply rooted the
public's belief in such character types is. The *valorization* and *importance*
of that image will inevitably change, according to variations in its social
utility, but the content itself remains fixed.

Two different forms of image construction come into direct competition, with the literary mode serving as a point of departure for
the popular construction but finding itself pushed increasingly into the
background, unable to rein in the effects of the media's culturally pro-
grammed readings. The public image of the author is thus ultimately
drawn according to the desires of the institutions and public concerned,
and only minimally by those of the writer.

Writers who participate in this process find themselves trapped in a
downward spiral. Since the public is fascinated by figures that express and
confirm its beliefs, the pressure placed upon celebrities to embody and
pantomime their own images is substantial. In an article signed by Jean
Seberg but ostensibly written at least in part by Gary, a conjunction between movie star and popular author is quite apparent: "Perhaps, the day
arrives when what [the actor] has to offer is à la mode—the little-boy lost
quality of James Dean, Van Johnson's freckles, the soft-hearted gangster
face of Bogart. What happens? The audience identifies him with this special personal quality, and the movie moguls capitalize and produce it for
a mass market. [The actor] suddenly has no self to sell anymore; *he has
only the carefully mimicked imitation of himself as he once was.* And finally the
public will feel this, too" (qtd. in Richards 105).

For Gary, this process began with the self-reflexive elements of *Promise at Dawn*, which effectively turned what little he possessed of his past
into an ironic myth. This transformation into self-parody is an eventual
dead end that degrades both the image and the actor/author: "Once [the
stereotype] settles upon a chosen being and embodies itself in him or
her, the work of destruction begins. The prefabricated image seizes reality
and remodels it imperiously. It erases the rich multiplicity [of reality] in
order to present itself in its purest form . . . The person in question is
conscious of the fact that reality attains mythical status only by yielding
to its violence (Amossy, "Stéréotypie" 173).

As Gary was well aware, the public figure backed into such a corner pays
a heavy price. The mythical image subsumes and devours its embodiment.
It is an *Horla*-like struggle in which celebrities are alienated from themselves in a vampirical relation. They come to incarnate their image in the
most tragic of ways. Early in the seventies, Gary would write: "Whether
you be a Lana Turner, an Ava Gardner or a Marilyn Monroe, when you

have been made into a 'myth,' you are always faced with a tremendous amount of irreality. And if this tremendous amount of irreality enters into conflict with the small amount of your remaining physiological and psychical reality, you become Marilyn Monroe entirely and forever more by committing suicide" (*NSC* 248). Dispossessed by his own myth, Gary ended up in the same dilemma as the Hollywood actresses he analyzed years earlier. Once he realized that he had played into the trap, despite all his efforts to the contrary, Gary chose to take his own life when he felt he no longer possessed the means to transform it.

Gary's Tactics Against Institutional Reading Practices

With twenty books in French, German, and Danish dedicated to his work in the two decades since his death, Gary can nonetheless be said to have won his battle for recognition. Even more favorably, these critical works are now moving from Gary's impressive biography to the equally rich books he produced. Thus, while the toll paid in Gary's personal life was extraordinarily high, the literary strategies adopted in the second half of his career have won him a new generation of readers.

In looking at these last, most resourceful stages of Gary's career, we are reminded that the writer has weapons at his or her disposal that the movie star does not, insofar as the textual medium allows writers better opportunities to script their own roles. That is to say, in an era when image means increasingly just that—a largely pictorial promotion through photography, television, and cinema—the rules of production for these figures are nonetheless still fundamentally based on textual means. The superficiality of the mass media changes nothing; the dissemination of public image is rooted in rewriting, reinterpretation, and (con)textualization. Proof can be found in that Gary produced his authors simply by adapting a series of narrative techniques (the very same techniques used to construct his fictions) to different media domains. Let us turn our attention, then, to the means Gary devised for attacking the reading habits of his colleagues in the press.

In order to situate Gary's choices within their specific domain, I will briefly examine how his responses fit with respect to other writers from the same period of French literature. At the extremes, one discovers two principal branches. One response comes from the handful of writers who do not owe their acclaim to intrigue and who took an uncompromising stance that it is up to the writer to abstain from these media rites. Of an admittedly different rank from Gary in the hierarchy of French letters, these writers and their demeanor are viewed as most in keeping with the dignity of literature as a "high" art form. In the cases of Samuel Beckett and Maurice Blanchot, for instance, the categorical refusal to deal with the press or public was consistent with their aesthetic and philosophical positions.[16] On more institutional grounds, de Beauvoir's snubbing of the Goncourt ceremonies in 1954 and Sartre's refusal of the Nobel Prize in 1964 were critiques of an award system in literature. Similarly, for others such as Henri Michaux or Julien Gracq, the issue was also one of personal discretion and a certain notion of what constitutes literature (seen as incompatible with glorification of the author).

At the opposite end of the spectrum is a brand of writer that thrives on the acrobatics of celebrity. These are professional provocateurs and eccentrics who claim to be persecuted by the establishment but curiously enough have frequent access to television, radio, journals and publishers. During the sixties and seventies, Sollers, Gabriel Matzneff, and Jean-Édern Hallier became seasoned professionals of the Parisian circuit of self-promotion. Hallier, for instance, made his name largely by staging his own kidnapping from La Closerie des Lilas in Paris at the publication of his first novel. While Sollers established a reputation in academia through his decades-long involvement in literary theory, his chameleon-like posturing and willingness to shock exposed him to an entirely different public through television appearances on programs such as Thierry Ardisson's eighties variety show *Les Bains-Douches*. For Matzneff, the titillation and scandal of his thinly veiled pedophilia kept him in the limelight as an ostensibly iconoclastic literary figure. In comparison with these figures, one is forced to admit that Gary's fake driver's license for Pavlowitch is somewhat tepid.

Where should we situate Gary's invention of pseudonymous alter egos in relation to these other positions? Do we place Gary on the side of Hallier, whose literary theatrics "[grow out of] the traditions of Punch 'n' Judy and bumper cars"?[17] Or did Gary's orchestration of authorial identities go beyond ludic or vindictive motivations to address these institutional dilemmas constructively?

The question of Gary's resemblance to the literary pranksters can be dispatched fairly quickly. While Gary might have appreciated a certain anarchic element introduced by his stunts, Hallier's impostures nonetheless took root in what was in fact a perfectly stable and predictable literary identity. Hallier and Matzneff could exist only if these institutions existed; they lived off of these institutions and certainly did not threaten them in any real way. Gary, on the other hand, was seeking a *mobile* identity, a means of escaping the institutional grasp.

In the other direction, though, how should we evaluate Gary's choices with respect to the writers who withheld their participation from these promotional rituals? Were Gary's difficulties his just desserts for having entered the arena in the first place? What did his adventure contribute toward destabilizing these rituals? Without claiming that Gary is an author of the same caliber as a Beckett or a Michaux, I think it is possible to demonstrate that his approach enacted an institutional critique from which the writers of "passive resistance"—Beckett, Blanchot, Michaux—cut themselves off. A brief comparison will clarify what I mean.

In his 1949 pamphlet critiquing the commercialization of French literature, Gracq, like Gary, casts the press as principal culprit: "One gets the impression that in France critics only agree to read . . . a writer once: the second time around, the writer is already established, embalmed in the *Textbook of Contemporary Literature* that public opinion and reviewers rack their brains to keep up-to-date" (Gracq 43). For each new book, Gracq argues, critics seek only to confirm the presence of a sort of permanent essence underlying surface variations. Writers are constantly brought back to their initial definitions, rather than being allowed to evolve with the works. Gary and Gracq, in other words, end up more or less on the same page, even down to characterizing the promotional rituals as a theatricalization of authorship: listing all the different types of public appearance imposed upon the writer, Gracq remarks that they are designed so that "the writer's talent [will triumph] in the public's eye through the range and dimensions of his performance, like a chess champion who gives simultaneous match demonstrations" (Gracq 68).

In this respect, the difference between Gary and Gracq boils down to their widely divergent decisions on *how to react.* For Gracq, the writer should not be a performer, nor even a dramaturge; image is irrelevant to the reception of one's work. Gary, however, recognized the process of fabricating authorial identities as inevitable in our current literary institutions. Beckett, Blanchot, and Gracq did not cease to be *represented* in the press, despite their reclusive uncooperativeness. On the contrary, their nonconformity only piqued the public's curiosity and was inevitably incorporated into critics' portraits of these writers.[18] When one pores over the intense production of journalistic and academic materials concerning Blanchot or Beckett, one realizes that they were turned into stereotypical figures every bit as much as Gary and Ajar.

Rather than trying to escape these institutions, Gary countered, focusing attention precisely on how they function and what their effects are. The early political satires (*Tulipe*, *L'homme à la colombe* and *Johnnie Cœur*) feature characters who exploit institutions capable of imposing or bestowing identity (the press, popular opinion, governmental agencies, etc.). The protagonists' strategies are deliberate attempts to wrest control of their images from these institutions. Yet, after an initial period in which these characters find it easy to determine the contours of a self-invented persona, all of them ultimately fail because they stay *within* the frame established by those conferring identity upon them. Gary's quandary was much the same. What could a Goncourt author do to undermine this experience of being turned into a stereotyped figure imposed by his or her own success?

In withdrawing behind a pseudonym, Gary put in his place puppet figures of his own design (Sinibaldi, Bogat, and Ajar), prefabricated fictions tailor-made for the workings of the literary press. Rather than attacking from the front, in other words, he attempted to subvert from within. The susceptibility of the critical press to this type of maneuver is shown by the successful staging of several other fictitious writers in this same period. Claude Bonnefoy compiled a volume in 1978 for Éditions du Seuil's *Écrivains de toujours* series on nonexistent poet Marc Ronceraille. In 1976, Frédérick Tristan published the diary and poetry of a supposed German poetess who was believed to have thrown herself under a train in the Gare de Lyon at the age of 17.[19] The fact that this motif became commercialized in 1979—Éditions Jean-Claude Lattès published a work entitled *L'âge d'amour* and announced a contest to uncover which famous writer was hiding behind its author's pseudonym of "Michael Sanders"—suggests that the public was largely aware of the artifice propping up authorial convention.[20] The chaos created by Gary drew out into the open what many already suspected, be it consciously or unconsciously.

How exactly did this work? For Ajar or Pavlowitch to be believable, their staging first had to correspond to a plausible image of an author. Gary had to anticipate accurately the reactions of the press and public—or, rather, their preconceptions, their expectations. The trick then as now was to trust that *the public would inevitably find what it desired all along to believe*: "[The mystification must be] in harmony with the state of mind of the milieu in which it occurs. Through its tastes and tendencies, its preoccupations or aspirations, the public's psychology must be prepared to receive and believe it . . . Without these aspects, the most finely-turned prank will remain confined to the circle of connoisseurs of whom some are dupes and the others amused at the formers' expense" (Picard 213). Given its success, the portrait of Ajar clearly corresponded to a mapping out of a given readership's desires. The critics' assertions about Ajar reveal more about the critics themselves than they do the unknown writer.

By running this puppet figure through the critical gauntlet, Gary exposed all the actors in this production without showing his own hand. This is the genius of a properly executed prank: the operators of social rites reveal the incoherence of their own methods. "Pranksters slip clandestinely into the play of rituals, customs and social habits of their victims. The victims are unaware that they are playing, that they are observing abstract rules. Even down to their language, they reproduce the ritual gestures whose vanity has been decrypted by the pranksters . . . All the pranksters need to do . . . is introduce new rules—false ones—that perturb the game without the victim suspecting the change" (Caradec 108–9).[21] They become the tool of their own undoing. In having taken his falsification of identity several steps farther than what the conventions of the pseudonym normally allow and what critics could reasonably suspect, Gary sheds light not just on the conditions under which fiction is produced but on how these institutions produce reality as well—for example, how publishers and newspapers create authors for the literary market. What is put on display are the blind spots of a generation of literary journalism whose activity rarely engages in analytical or epistemological concerns, even in the banalized form of information. Their biographical portraits in particular obey the peculiar rules of literary truth (suspension of disbelief), which demand verisimilitude, not veracity. In other words, one of the things revealed by Gary is that a function of the literary press is *to believe in these fictions* as well. In this respect, the legends set in motion by Gary meet up with my earlier discussion of stereotypes as preprogrammed readings, for these critical assessments amount to little more than self-fulfilling prophecies.

Here we see the larger stakes in Gary's quarrel with the press. Gary's desire for a fair reading in the press is one thing, but his concern with questions of identity, and in particular with how stereotypes prevent individuals from determining their own identities, runs even deeper still. Gary may well have lost some of his battles against stereotyping, but I believe that he won several others.

In *Declining the Stereotype*, Mireille Rosello argues that while it is the content of a stereotype that offends or wounds, contesting that content is not necessarily an effective approach to defeating a stereotype. "The desire to oppose stereotypes as meaningful statements is a self-defeating attempt. To declare them wrong, false, to attack them as untruths that [we can] replace by a better or more accurate description of the stereotyped community, will never work. As tempting as the correcting reaction may be, it is often a misguided effort that fails to analyze the structure of stereotypical statements . . . and the specific form of social harm they can do" (13). As evidence, Rosello notes that certain stereotypes thrive on being denounced, regardless of how convincing or rational the argument that disputes them. Opposing stereotypes head-on can backfire, for it reinforces consensus on the content of the stereotype, even where one wishes to discredit it. The strategy that Rosello proposes is intriguing: "Stereotypes are more usefully confronted as a contestable way of speaking, of using language, as an objectionable style, rather than as an opinion whose content we disagree with" (16). In other words, a more promising tactic is to attack the stereotype as a *form* of expression, a particular linguistic and conceptual structure given to (mis)information and representations.

One method open to writers therefore is to employ language in ways that disrupt the structure of the stereotype and thereby disarticulate its content as well. For instance, one can seek to break down the stereotype's memorability, the boundaries it establishes, its rigid and univocal nature. Ajar's *Madame Rosa* is one of the texts Rosello selects for her demonstration, and she focuses very adeptly on the linguistic and semantic facets of the Ajarisms that I discussed earlier (see Rosello 128–49). Ajar's distortions of causal links, the unexpected turn given to familiar euphemisms, and the misuse of ideologically charged terms emerge as so many different ways of rattling the very form of stereotypical expression without ever directly contesting its content.[22] The specificity of Ajarisms lies in this feature. Rosello reminds us that these phrases are the product of a complex and personal transformation operating within the language and not the result of the introduction of a certain number of external elements: "We are not invited to discover non-Parisian Francophone languages, nor do we find a sustained reproduction of a certain jargon, of regional cultures or of a given social class" (131). In this light, we understand better why Gary's earlier attempts at linguistic experimentation are not effective. Though he is seeking a nonconformist use of language in *Ski Bum*, Gary looks for it in the form of a populist, pseudo-hippie discourse that he does his best to imitate. But these slang terms and the accompanying syntax are foreign to Gary, and his use of them smells of artifice. In the end, it fails because Gary's own performance falls victim to stereotypes of how disaffected American youth speak.

With Ajar, however, familiar phrases are hijacked so that their old meaning is implicitly acknowledged but undermined simultaneously by a new, ironic one. Based on this gap between what we expect to hear and what arrives in its place, Rosello refers to this kind of subversion of the stereotype as a discursive doubling, "an impossible hybrid, an improbable stereopoetic language" (130).

Using Rosello's formulation of this strategy, we can identify a number of other instances in Gary's work where the struggle against the univocal drive of stereotyped identities takes pluralist paths like this. In fact, the role of this technique is considerable in Gary's work and operates on a number of textual levels, both in Ajar's novels and in Gary's.

This description of a stereopoetic language seems perfectly apt, for instance, to characterize the hidden narratives designed for *Your Ticket Is No Longer Valid* and the Ajar novels. One will recall that in *Your Ticket Is No Longer Valid* the primary narrative offered is the story of an aging man's reliance on the image of a young thief to maintain his sexual virility. The dissimulated threads are multiple. On the one hand, this plot is a figurative recounting of Gary's decision to adopt the identity of Émile Ajar. On the other hand, the portraits given of the old man and the young thug are traps set by Gary, since these represent contrast between the stereotyped images of Gary in 1975 and Kacew in 1935.

Gary developed this technique over a number of novels, and it reached its apogee with *Pseudo*. *Direct Flight to Allah* and *The Gasp* are the product of a similar technique, where the use of popular genres like espionage novels and science fiction is a diversionary tactic whereby he hides personal projects underneath the apparent superficiality of commercial fiction.[23] Carried to this level, however, the tactic is quite risky, for the effect depends on the delayed unveiling of the press's faulty reading habits. First, without the benefit of knowing the author's identity, the press commits to a certain reading; then, once Ajar's identity is disclosed and new readings appear, lazy or biased interpretive practices will in theory be exposed.

Gary also plays out this strategic attack on stereotypes in much less perilous ways, however. One of the most effective techniques is Gary's use of another type of hybrid figure. Somewhat like the bewildered Kadir faced with the prospect of a Jewish son in *Madame Rosa*, critics are not sure what to make of an Algerian author whose python is Jewish (*GC* 181) or who brings up the specter of Captain Dreyfus's incarceration on Devil's Island by playing on the name of the narrator's black coworker from Guyana, Mlle Dreyfus (*GC* 45). Similarly, the prevalence of Jewish and Islamic cultural references in *Madame Rosa* creates a fundamental ambiguity within the novel. For example, Jeffrey Mehlman sees the confrontation between Kadir and Madame Rosa as a parody of the judgment of Solomon (1 Kings 3) in which Solomon, to resolve a dispute between would-be parents (one of whom, like Madame Rosa, is a prostitute), uses the ploy of agreeing to cut a child in half to determine the identity of his rightful parent (Mehlman 229). In this same direction, Madame Rosa, of course, is a Polish survivor of Auschwitz. In a very different direction, the epigraph is a citation from an ancient Arab poem, and in the course of the novel Momo evokes four of the five fundamental obligations of practicing Muslims (Thérien 180).

Critics wanted the novel to be either pro-Jewish or pro-Islamic, and they resorted to the author's identity in order to eliminate their uncertainty. In resonance, however, the name "Émile Ajar" is neither definitively Jewish nor North African. Acting on an assumed imperative that the question must be resolved in one direction or another, they would betray themselves with some frankly myopic readings. Poet and critic Claude Michel Cluny, for instance, was led into making extremely serious (and irresponsible) accusations: "I would advise Mr. Ajar to read [Édouard] Drumont or [Lucien] Rebatet . . . [*Madame Rosa* is] a book that arrives too late: under the good old government of Vichy, people would have been falling over themselves to give it an award."[24] These sentiments would find echoes in reviews appearing in *L'Express* and *Arts* as well.[25] In playing on a confusion of identities deemed by some to be irreconcilably opposed, Gary induced precisely the kind of misdirection that Genghis Cohn favors in *The Guilty Head*. Victim of his foreign birth yet a hero of the French Resistance, victim of his Jewish heritage yet rejected by some prominent Jewish institutions at the time of *The Dance of Genghis Cohn* for being a "hybrid," Gary now found himself taxed with being a Vichyist anti-Semite!

This apparent undecidability of Ajar's and Momo's identities confounded critics' desire to resolve what they saw (consciously or unconsciously) as irreducible differences between Arab and Jew, Émile and Ajar, Mohammed and Moïsché. These figures composed from amalgamations of identities deemed mutually exclusive are a repetition of a device used previously in Gary's work, where Genghis Khan and Moïsché Cohn find themselves united within the single name of Genghis Cohn. For Gary, this is not merely a literary conundrum posed to tease critics. It reproduces an internal division stemming from Gary's ancestry, a feature that he considers fundamental to his sense of self and identity as a European. As Gary states in an interview, "My mother was a Russian Jew and my father a Tatar—in other words, I'm born of a man whose race had a bothersome specialization in pogroms. In the end, I am Genghis *and* Cohn." [26] For him, it is impossible to reconcile the two sides because identity is not an "either/or" question. One cannot identify him as "simply" Jewish or "simply" Mongol; he embraces both, entirely: "I have no idea what 'half-Jewish' means. 'Half-Jewish' is like half an umbrella. It's a notion employed by maniacal racists in Israel" (*NSC* 235). This balancing act between Gary's Jewish and Tatar origins would later be translated with Ajar into the image mentioned above of a sort of Jewish-Arab coexistence.

Seen in the light of Gary's global production, we see that these couples of irreconcilable opposites are a staple in his writing. In *The Dance of Genghis Cohn*, the hero exists as the Jewish *dybbuk* living in the skin of the ex-Nazi Schatz and producing a double-speech that is intended to address the psychic trauma of post-Holocaust Europe. Similarly, America's racial conflicts are figured in *White Dog* by the schizophrenic dog, trained first by white southerners to attack blacks, then by an equally racist African American animal expert to attack Caucasians.

Stereotypes posit identities as innate, as natural. By positing his characters as the repository of mutually exclusive stereotypes, Gary forces a recognition of these identities as matters of subjective perception, trained behavior, and the products of particular modes of representation. The reversals of attributed identity in *White Dog* and *Madame Rosa* hollow out their stereotypes, rendering their content meaningless. Gary thus challenges the normative function of stereotyping which works toward maintaining strict boundaries between univocal identities.

If Ajar struck a chord with the reading public, one must remember that a great part of his persona was made up of post-1968 paranoia concerning how society imposes ill-suited identities upon individuals. The literary establishment may have been the most immediate target, but Gary was also tweaking the nose of the media in general. That there was a public receptive to this message was demonstrated by the sales figures for *Madame Rosa*, which remained the fourth highest ever for a Goncourt as the prize approached its centenary (Caffier 100). The orchestration of Ajar thus did not merely renew the age-old antagonism between critics and artists; Gary's staging carried out a critique of certain literary and journalistic institutions that was more *effective* than Gracq's pamphlet. For regardless of however insightful Gracq's polemics may have been, the circus surrounding the Goncourt Prize survived Gracq's attack unblemished. The proof is that one year after Gracq's pamphlet scathingly dissected the functioning of France's literary prize system, the Academy Goncourt awarded him—the Goncourt Prize! That Gracq refused the prize changed nothing. As juror Dorgelès commented laconically: "With the Goncourt Prize, we make a writer famous. Oh, well! Gracq will now be famous in spite of himself" (qtd. in Caffier 78). Moreover, Gracq became wealthier in spite of himself, too, since he did not refuse the royalties that blossomed substantially due to the Goncourt publicity (Caffier 83).

The End of an Era

In the preceding section, I have argued that Gary's authorial and aesthetic strategies effectively critiqued media and racial stereotypes. Does this mean that Gary's literary exploit brought about change in French letters? With the revelation of Gary's role in the creation of Ajar, Gérard Dupuy wrote in *Libération*: "Your final gift is a cruel inheritance for your admirers! More than ever now, the dirty business of French letters lies agonizing in the public square. You have imposed a rudimentary and salubrious lesson upon the pastry chefs of culture and their tea parlor patrons: everything in the publishing world is rigged."[27]

It is clear that the Goncourt lost some of its luster, too. Juror Bernard Clavel resigned his position in 1979, voicing similar sentiments: "I don't know if it's all rigged. If the word bothers you, find another one. After all, literature depends on that very exercise. But what is sad is to see the extent to which the other books are ignored . . . This typically French phenomenon strikes me as impossible to purify" (qtd. in Caffier 92). Clavel perhaps took a better measure of the dilemma in his remarks, although doubtless no one writer could single-handedly redirect the trends of mass media culture. Accordingly, I would be overstating my case if I claimed that Gary's actions provoked a new era of institutional practices and thinking. More accurately perhaps, I can say that Gary exposed the shortcomings of an era of French literary journalism that had outlived its time. In effect, by the end of the seventies, the conditions that had produced the pressures exerted upon Gary and that later made the Ajar adventure possible no longer existed in comparable form.

Substantial changes would occur in at least three important areas: France's political landscape, the French media, and the Parisian literary scene.

Following on the heels of de Gaulle's passing, the end of the cold war sparked the gradual dissolution of the great ideological divide operative within French politics and culture since World War II. As a result, the political map was redrawn. The election in 1974 of Valéry Giscard d'Estaing confirmed that Gaullism proper would not survive its founder. For the first time since World War II, the general's followers did not dominate the terms of debate on the French political Right. And, while it is true today that the French Republic boasts a president eager to claim his place as heir of the Gaullist tradition, Jacques Chirac and the other prominent Gaullists (Philippe Séguin and Nicolas Sarkozy) are more preoccupied with economic prosperity than ideology. Moreover, the reappearance of political parties on the extreme Right (Jean-Marie Le Pen's National Front, Bruno Mégret's splinter group National Republican Movement, and Vendéean Philippe de Villier's Movement for France) has attracted the ire of concerned citizens on the Left. Similarly, the rise to power of the Socialist Party in 1981 under François Mitterrand further cemented the bystander status of the PCF. Three consecutive terms of governmental cohabitation—the kind of circumstance that ever since the 1800s has toppled French Republics—demonstrate that the philosophical differences between Right and Left in France today express themselves largely through campaign politics and policy decisions, not revolutionary opposition.

There has been a corresponding realignment in the press. The reign of the great populist newspapers like *France-Soir* and *Le Petit Parisien* has passed, with only *Le Parisien* continuing among the top five (Charon 126–27). Even more marked has been the precipitous drop since the late sixties in the French phenomenon of "opinion" papers. As Jean-Marie Charon notes, beginning with the fall of the Second Empire, every important political or ideological movement in France had its own publication and these tended to be fairly influential, even authoritative, in expressing and shaping public opinion (129–32). Today, however, *Paris-Turf* (the French *Racing Form*) easily outdraws *L'Humanité* and the Catholic vehicle *La Croix*.[28] The rest have been condemned to paltry numbers or have ceased operation altogether.

In place of the populist and opinion papers, a new crop of publications has flourished, heralding a more modern, professional approach to journalism. Founded in 1973 by May 1968 veteran Serge July, the leftist newcomer *Libération* has grown quickly to form a triumvirate with the *Monde* and the *Figaro* (moderate to conservative Right but rarely courting extreme elements). *Libération* has mellowed considerably since the Socialist Party rose to prominence, and, in parallel fashion, the *Figaro*, under ex-*Nouvel Observateur* director Franz-Olivier Giesbert, has eased its strident anti-Socialism beginning with Mitterrand's second term (Thogmartin 240). Thus flanked, the *Monde* has been squeezed toward the Center. Among ideological critics, the intellectuals active in today's media —Régis Debray or Bernard Henri-Lévy—owe more to Malraux than to Sartre or Aragon. At present, personality plays a more divisive role than ideology, with only elder journalists like Jean-François Revel still unforgiving in their anti-Gaullist grudges. The Gaullist heritage itself is more likely to be represented by a figure like Count Jean d'Ormesson, who, though born into a powerful political family and a former director of the *Figaro*, embodies a *Belles-Lettres* version of Gaullism with his twenty-three appearances on Pivot and his passion for Chateaubriand.

In the specifically literary trade market, the economic malaise of the seventies served to accelerate a crisis that was already brewing in French newspaper publishing. One of the most immediate victims was the *Figaro littéraire*, eliminated in 1971 and incorporated into the *Figaro* as a weekly supplement. Similarly, Aragon's *Lettres françaises* folded in 1972 and the *Nouvelles littéraires* was jettisoned by Larousse in 1971 (Albert 155). In their stead, a changing of the guard occurred. At the same time that these black-and-white papers were disappearing, for instance, the new monthly magazine *Lire* outgrew its initial modest format and reemerged as today's glossy color production.

Moreover, it is probably not by chance that *Lire* claims Pivot as its first director (since replaced by Pierre Assouline), for things have evolved substantially in the television market as well. Pierre Lepape notes the stakes implied by the passage from the first television program wholly dedicated to books, *Lectures pour tous*, to the show that would redefine the concept:

Between *Lectures pour tous* by Pierre Dumayet and Pierre Desgraupes and *Apostrophes* by Bernard Pivot, there are not just ten years (1964–74) of changes in television but there is also a slippage from a literature of writers to a literature of authors. In the first case, what counted in the interview was a rhetoric of uncertainty, silence and re-creation . . . Pivot's program, in part because it brings together five or six people, is on the contrary produced as a dramatic encounter in which each one plays a role, the effectiveness [of the program] being gauged by the power of seduction that the authors exert during their allotted speaking time. (Lepape 2274)

Pivot himself would not quarrel with this language, referring to his own program as "a kind of spontaneous theatrical performance" on the part of the writers (qtd. in Heath 1054). At its best, the Friday night ritual of *Apostrophes* could match and even exceed the ratings produced by shows like *Dynasty* dubbed into French (Heath 1055).

The shift in emphasis toward more garrulous guests would entail a corresponding shift in the position occupied by literature, a trend that was all the more pronounced in Pivot's following program, *Bouillon de culture*. Literary fiction slides toward the background to become just one more book product among those available to Pivot's audience. For instance, on a recent visit *chez* Pivot (January 14, 2000) to discuss his *Le jour de la fin du monde, une femme me cache* (The day of the end of the world, a woman hid me), Grainville was surrounded by Pascal Sevran (entertainer and Merv Griffin-like variety-show host), Patrick Poivre d'Arvor (a nightly news anchor), and a hostile Michel Polac (a television polemicist and talk-show host). Placed among seasoned professionals of the small screen, familiar with the peculiar rhythm and tension of live television, it takes an exceptional figure like Grainville to be able to impose a literary presence on such a program.[29] The small handful of other literary writers to fare well in the current climate have been distinguished by their capacity to combine decent sales with critical consideration. The generous but shy Le Clézio has evolved into a sort of passive complicity with the promotion of literature. Enjoying extremely strong support from Gallimard, the handsome and seemingly ageless Le Clézio routinely wins popular readers' polls in France—probably not solely on the merits of his considerable literary talent (Jollin 735–37). Along the same lines, capable of satisfying the juries of both the Prix Relais H du Roman d'Évasion (the equivalent of a Hallmark stationer's award) and the Grand Prize of the French Academy, Patrick Modiano is comfortably installed as one of France's most acclaimed writers but has lost a considerable amount of the venom and risktaking that made his feisty debut with *La Place de l'Étoile* in 1968 so remarkable.[30]

With the disappearance of the cold war divide, the ideological issues driving French letters has relocated to other geopolitical and social domains. In the image of the nation's changing economic status, French literature no longer commands the same prestige as it did in the fifties, with critics and editors alike increasingly drawn to foreign writers in their considerations. Thus, though the publishers are still centered in the capital, the Parisian male clique has lost some of its cultural hegemony in the literary world. The Goncourt Prize can be taken as a barometer of this trend. Under Bazin's tutelage, the jury has been rejuvenated and has somewhat diversified its laureates. In the seventy-one years prior to Ajar's

Goncourt, for instance, only one non-European Francophone author had been crowned, and that back in 1921 (René Maran, born in Martinique but educated in Bordeaux and Gabon). Since 1975, a number of Canadian and Maghrebin writers have been recognized (Antonine Maillet, Tahar Ben Jelloun, Patrick Chamoiseau, and Amin Maalouf). The three women recipients (Marguerite Duras, Pascale Roze, and Paule Constant) over the last two decades nearly equals the total for the preceding eighty years. This improved diversity has been mirrored by an effort, in Bazin's words, to "de-Parisianize" the Goncourt. The 1974 deliberations were held in Montreal, while in 1975 the jury retired to the peace and quiet of the Haute-Marne (birthplace of the Goncourt brothers) for some of their meetings. Later sessions would take them to Senegal, Switzerland, and Russia (Caffier 98–99). Thus, the ideological battlegrounds have filled up with new causes as writers grapple with the challenges posed to "French" culture by postcolonial nations and the Americas.

In a curious sense, Gary's writing announced this reconfiguration. A rare instance of a polyglot author publishing in France and the United States, Gary always conceived of his literary production in a more global context. And with respect to the French context itself, he also realized in the seventies that one of the principal stories not being told in French fiction was that of its immigrants and former colonial subjects. It is not by chance, for instance, that Calixthe Beyala would take *Madame Rosa* as one of the points of departure for her *Little Prince of Belleville*. Thus, Gary's experimentation and deceit went far beyond questions of personal revenge, for in the end it was the public that was treated to a dramatization of literary and sociopolitical concerns: "If a prank makes someone laugh, it is usually not the victim or the prankster but an observer . . . For a brief moment, we see the laughter of the carnival reborn" (Caradec 51). This book has sought to encourage other readers to share in that laughter as well as better understand the tragedy it accompanied.

Notes

1. This remark appears in a preface written by Von Chamisso in 1837, which is omitted from the Rodale Press translation. See Von Chamisso, *Peter Schlemihl* 97.

2. Myriam Anissimov is currently writing the first authoritative scholarly biography of Gary for Éditions Gallimard. The project has been authorized and assisted by Gary's only child, Diego.

Introduction

1. Gary thus achieved this ranking without the benefit of the initial runs of *A European Education, The Roots of Heaven,* or *Promise at Dawn* (Todd 189 n. 5).

2. Pivot, "Romain Gary réincarné avant de mourir," *Lire* May 1987: 11.

3. Queneau's 1968 novel recounts how a writer returns to his manuscript one afternoon to discover that Icarus, his protagonist, has flown the coop, sneaking off the page to run about in the real world. The novelist combs the cafés searching for his truant offspring, who is understandably ill prepared for modern-day Parisian life.

4. Among similar postwar fabrications, Gary's antics created the biggest literary scandal since *I Shall Spit on Your Graves,* by "Vernon Sullivan" (Boris Vian, 1946), and *The Story of O,* by "Pauline Réage" (Dominique Aury, 1954).

5. Priscilla Parkhurst Clark's *Literary France* takes a broader, sociohistorical approach to these questions, tracing century by century France's cultural investment in literature.

6. Studies of authorial self-representation frequently focus more narrowly on philosophical issues or poetics, debating the nature of the subject or the origins of the autobiographical act. The study of the institutions that impact reading and writing slips through the cracks or else draws on a sociological discourse that lacks the tools to discuss the aesthetic forms in question. A hallmark study that reconciles these divisions is Alain Viala's *La naissance de l'écrivain*; it analyzes shifts in ideas, social groups, legal statutes, and publishing practices in the classical age.

7. For an excellent account of the publicity campaign for *The Devil in the Flesh,* consult Gabriel Boillat.

8. Though the plan fell through when the sponsor went bankrupt, the tale entered Simenon's legend as having occurred (Assouline, *Simenon* 78ff.).

9. The analysis of these issues thus could also be articulated in a larger cultural frame: in the case of Colette, for instance, the tension between her commodification (a line of perfumes, garters, dolls in her likeness) and her innovative use of autobiographical fictions would help plot out the curious evolution of her literary stature. On the role and dynamics of movie stars' images, Richard Dyer's work is useful in the approaches it proposes for treating them as textual productions (see *Stars* and *Heavenly Bodies*).

10. The cultural significations of the introduction of pocket paperbacks, for instance, are difficult to appreciate in the United States, but the polemics over the book's transformation from luxury item into object of consumption were fierce. One has only to read André Gouillou or Antoine Spire and Jean-Pierre Viala to get a sense of the importance given to these issues. Head of public relations for the French department store giant FNAC, Gouillou attacked the conception of the publishing industry as a noneconomic entity, using the argument that subventions encourage fiscal irresponsibility. Spire and Viala presented the French Communist Party's position, questioning the Giscard d'Estaing government's favoritism toward the giant publishers.

11. Pingaud, "La non-fonction de l'écrivain" 77–78. While one should not overlook other television programs dedicated to books (e.g., *Cercle de nuit, Ex-Libris*, and *Caractères*), Pivot's now-discontinued *Apostrophes* remains the best-known example (see Chiaselotti). Since his return to television, Pivot has reformatted the series as *Bouillon de Culture*.

12. Jacques Dubois stresses the extent to which the Goncourt competition draws attention to the existence of these institutions without ever displaying the rules of their mysterious functioning (Dubois 97).

13. The fictional work *Le prix Goncourt*, signed by a certain "St. Lorges," is a catty roman à clef targeting contemporary authors, critics, and publishers to show how the makeup of a jury largely predetermines which books have the potential to win the award. It invents as its premise François Nourissier's resignation from the jury, which triggers skirmishes in Parisian literary circles among those seeking to draw personal benefit from the new appointment.

14. *Guide des prix littéraires*, 5th ed. This figure quintuples the number of first-time novelists published in most years.

15. Arland, "L'une des plus belles figures d'aujourd'hui," rpt. in Gaillard 25. Note that the emphasis is not on writing but on behavior and biography, i.e., persona.

16. Gary responds: "Money is not the real problem; it is what we have to do to earn it that is intolerable . . . The authors are the advertisers and the booksellers the distributors. In our system, a book has three months to establish itself—otherwise, it gets scrapped" (Quiquéré, "Romain Gary: À bas l'intellect dominateur," *Le Matin de Paris* March 11, 1977: 24).

17. Charged with providing promotional copy for Gallimard but lacking time to familiarize himself with Deguy's approach, Jean Dutourd fell back on the comparison to France's Nobel Prize-winning poet. Perse's verse is considerably more traditional in form and has a predilection for epic grandiloquence that his more arcane successor would reject.

18. See the Céline Archives held at the Institut Mémoires de l'Édition Contemporaine (IMEC), Paris, France.

19. Pivot, "Jean-Louis Bory s'explique," *Lire* June 1977: 30.

20. Schwarz-Bart's life is perhaps one of the unavowed inspirations for the bur-

lesque character of Genghis Cohn in Gary's *The Guilty Head* (1968), in which a former Auschwitz prisoner become famous flees to Tahiti, where he takes up with a local girl.

21. The apocryphal Rimbaud prose poem "discovered" in 1949, *La chasse spiri-tuelle*, is a prime example of such a project. Actress Akakia-Viala and director Nicolas Bataille wrote and published the work after their theatrical production of *A Season in Hell* was derided by critics (see Lacassin 1183–84).

22. Rouart is citing from the first lines of Jean-Jacques Rousseau's *Confessions* (Rouart, "Songe et mensonge," *Le Quotidien de Paris* July 7, 1981: 2).

23. Qtd. in "Faut-il écrire masqué?" *Le Figaro littéraire* March 23, 1987: v.

24. In juxtaposing the works and biographical portraits of these "authors," Jeandillou recognizes that their invention obeys the same literary principles and that the writing process feeds off of both elements in a dialogic relation.

25. Gary's self-styled genealogy of charlatan artists has no pretense to historical accuracy. On the contrary, it intentionally doubles the protagonists' deceptions with those of the author. In *Lady L.* and *The Enchanters*, for example, Gary fabri-cates his bibliographies, inventing the works of M. Dulac (*Charlatans, parasites et picaros du XVIIIᵉ siècle*), Van der Meer (*Art et charlatanisme*), Giuseppe H. Varari (*Magicien du verbe et du vin*), and M. de Serre (*Histoire du charlatanisme depuis ses origines*). This bogus erudition duped a few critics, including one of Gary's most belligerent foes, Matthieu Galey: "Drawing on numerous documents, Mr. Romain Gary indulged himself in the reconstitution of the romanesque and wild world of the late nineteenth-century anarchists" (Galey, "Deux romans pour passer le temps: Romain Gary *Lady L* et Maurice Toesca *Les passions déchaînées*," *Arts, Lettres, Spectacle, Musique* April 17–23, 1963: 4).

Chapter 1. The Invention of Romain Gary

1. Bonnard would become minister of education under Vichy and be con-demned to death in absentia after the Liberation, while Mussolini met a bloody death at the hands of Italian partisans. Henriot would become an active promoter of collaborationist politics, be appointed state secretary in the Vichy Ministry of Information, and be executed shortly after the Allied victory. French author Drieu La Rochelle embraced fascism in the prewar years, would side with extrem-ist elements throughout the Occupation, and would commit suicide March 15, 1945, to avoid being brought to trial.

2. On the one hand, he claims that his mother had kicked him out the door "the day he took it into his head to write for a right-wing paper [*Gringoire*]," thus acknowledging that they knew it to be a vehicle of the far Right (qtd. in Jean Be-noît, "Des prix et des hommes . . . Aujourd'hui: Le Goncourt et le Renaudot," *Combat* December 3, 1956: 3). On the other hand, however, 1960's *Promise at Dawn*, which Gary was already writing at the time of the preceding interview, represents his mother as being ecstatic at his publication in *Gringoire*, brandishing the issue for all the neighbors to see. No reference is made to its ideological orientation (*PD* 212).

3. See "Dessins et légendes de G. Pavis," *Gringoire* February 15, 1935: 9.

4. "Romain Gary," n.d., Calmann-Lévy Publishers' Archives.

5. Gary, for example, was recruited to host a televised tribute on the fifth anni-versary of the general's death (*De Gaulle première* November 9, 1975, TF1).

6. Gary later acknowledged these dates as accurate (Bona 62; *PD* 300). See also Charles-Louis Foulon, "Les médias et la France Libre," in Institut Charles de Gaulle, *De Gaulle et les médias* 19.

7. De Gaulle's first volume (*The Call to Honor*) was published in 1954, the second (*Unity*) in 1956, while the final volume (*Salvation*) would come out in 1959. On de Gaulle's interpretation of the events of World War II, see Rousso, "La Seconde Guerre mondiale." Gary's articles are collected in *OH*.

8. The Polish government was among those that refused to collaborate with Germany. Its government in exile formed in France until the French defeat forced it to fall back on England. The Polish army, however, had also reformed in France and was in contact with the British Secret Services by late 1939. Many of these Polish soldiers were among the first to help organize armed resistance within France after the armistice in June 1940 (Garliński 47–59, 76–97; Noguères 72–73).

9. At one juncture, for instance, a child asks another what the word "fascism" means and receives the answer, "It's a form of hatred" (*EE* 1945: 71). The novel concludes with an affirmation of its humanist message, albeit embittered by the war's carnage: "Nothing important ever dies . . . Just people" (176).

10. It was rejected by his publisher; see Letter from Romain Gary to Robert Calmann-Lévy, n.d., prior to June 1945: 3, Calmann-Lévy Publishers' Archives.

11. The Battle of Stalingrad took place in the winter of 1942–43, with the Germans capitulating in February 1943. Concentrating first on the Far East and then North Africa, American forces would not really enter the European theater of operations until their July 1943 landing in Sicily. Gary's novel by then was nearly completed.

12. *FA* 38. In all French editions, the Polish anthem is replaced with "La Marseillaise."

13. Budberg was part of a coterie of cosmopolitan exiles who gravitated to Aron's journal (Colquhoun 221).

14. The Ministry of Foreign Affairs is commonly known as (because located on) the "Quay d'Orsay" in Paris, while the French Academy of immortal authors sits on the Quay Conti.

15. Queneau, "La Vie des Livres: Pologne," *Le Front national* September 8, 1945: 4.

16. Sartre 199; Romain Gary to Pierre Calmann-Lévy, August 28, 1945, Calmann-Lévy Publishers' Archives.

17. See [Pierre?] Calmann-Lévy to Romain Gary, October 11, [1945], Calmann-Lévy Publishers' Archives.

18. Steered by René Benjamin, who showed his colors in 1942 by writing *Le Maréchal et son peuple*, and other right-wing writers like Léon Daudet and Roland Dorgelès, the wartime Goncourt Academy honored Henri Pourrat's *Vent de mars* (1941), a paean to French peasant life ambiguously close to the propaganda of the Pétainist "national revolution" in its terminology and themes. To restore the Goncourt's integrity, Lucien Descaves, still cantankerous and uncompromising at eighty-four, was named to preside over the jury.

19. Pierre Calmann-Lévy to Romain Gary, August 8, 1945, Calmann-Lévy Publishers' Archives.

20. Les Alguazils, "Déjà le Prix Goncourt," *Le Figaro* October 6, 1945: 2. Earlier in the year, the academy retrospectively awarded the 1944 Goncourt to Triolet's collection of short stories, *A Fine of Two Hundred Francs*.

21. Calmann-Lévy's choice of words is unambiguous: "We are sending you . . .

the latest reviews to appear of your book. You will also find a little note published in the *Figaro* of last Saturday that crystalizes a *rumor* your rivals are spreading. We think that it would be a good idea to send a note of *rectification*. Would you please be kind enough to put together a short press release to this effect that we can pass on to the media?" Pierre Calmann-Lévy to Romain Gary, October 11, 1945, Calmann-Lévy Publishers' Archives; emphasis added.

22. Romain Gary to Pierre Calmann-Lévy, October 27, 1945, Calmann-Lévy Publishers' Archives.

23. Blanch would maintain this position into the fifties: "My husband was not born in Russia, contrary to what people say; the truth is that he was born in Nice" (qtd. in Janine Auscher, "Chronique radiophonique," December 1956).

24. The biographical information from the Calmann-Lévy Publishers' Archives is undated. One can reject with certainty the claim that Gary was born in France and can probably discount the assertions that he was born in Poland. Though it appears no longer possible to prove where he was born, Russia would appear to be the correct country of origin (see Larat 12–22). In addition to Larat's detailed arguments, the fact that Kacew's two principal pseudonyms are taken from Russian, not Polish—*gari* means "to burn" and *agar* is "embers"—further argues for Russia.

25. Gary met with Henriot of the Critiques jury to inform him of his desire to withdraw from consideration owing to paper rationing, while Calmann-Lévy enlisted Aron to contact Gabriel Marcel, also of the jury, for a tactful resolution (see Romain Gary to [Robert?] Calmann-Lévy, October 27, [1945]; [Robert?] Calmann-Lévy to Romain Gary, October 16, 1945, Calmann-Lévy Publishers' Archives).

26. Gary would later suggest on several occasions that Russian silent movie star Ivan Mosjoukine was his biological father (see Sciascia 40–42).

27. Romain Gary to Pierre Calmann-Lévy, October 27, 1945, Calmann-Lévy Publishers' Archives.

28. Romain Gary to Pierre Calmann-Lévy, n.d. [May 30, 1945], Calmann-Lévy Publishers' Archives.

29. One of Gary's first literary heroes, Mickiewicz (1798–1835) was exiled for an anti-Russian conspiracy while studying at Wilno University. He later settled in Paris, where he furthered the cause of Polish nationalism and was considered Poland's greatest romantic poet.

30. Nadeau, "*Tulipe* et cœur brisé," *Combat* July 5, 1946: 2; Kemp, "Trois livres à surprises," *Les Nouvelles littéraires* September 5, 1946: 3.

31. See Romain Gary to Robert Calmann-Lévy, August 2, 1956, Calmann-Lévy Publishers' Archives.

32. Henriot, "Mœurs et caractères du jour," *Le Monde* March 16, 1949: 3.

33. For Thiébaut, Gary's recent failure was due to his interest in American literature, which adversely affected Gary's choice of subjects and techniques (Thiébaut, "Paul Guth, Jean Dutourd et Romain Gary," *La Revue de Paris* [December 1952]: 161). It should be noted, though, that Thiébaut had been literary director at Calmann-Lévy, the publishing house Gary had abandoned (LeSage and Yon 208).

34. Claudel, "Un poème de Saint-John Perse," *La Revue de Paris* (November 1949): 3–15; for Martin du Gard, see his letter cited in Bona 164.

35. Romain Gary to Pierre Calmann-Lévy, n.d. [July?] 1947, Calmann-Lévy Publishers' Archives. As moving as this letter is, some of its content might be subject to caution: Gary, for instance, is reputed to have been a nondrinker.

Chapter 2. The Consecration of Romain Gary

1. François Brigneau, "Voici les nouveautés du Salon de la littérature," *Paris-Presse L'Intransigeant* September 9–10, 1956: 8. Reviewers, of course, had advance copies.

2. Henriot, " 'Les Racines du ciel' de Romain Gary," *Le Monde* October 24, 1956: 7; Billy, "Pitié pour les éléphants . . . et pour les hommes!" *Le Figaro* October 17, 1956: 15; Bauër, "Un romancier s'affirme dans un grand livre," *Journal d'Alger* November 17, 1956; Arnoux, "A qui le Goncourt?" *Les Nouvelles littéraires* November 22, 1956: 1, 6.

3. Corniglion-Molinier, "*Les Racines du ciel* de Romain Gary," *Paris-Presse L'Intransigeant* October 6, 1956: 2.

4. Berchet, "Gary: L'écrivain à suivre sinon à primer," *Tribune de Lausanne* November 4, 1956.

5. Clouard, "Les Racines du ciel," *Beaux Arts* November 9, 1956.

6. Amouroux, "Attention aux éléphants," *Sud-Ouest* October 22, 1956.

7. Rousseaux, "Des éléphants et des tortues," *Le Figaro littéraire* October 20, 1956. On Rousseaux, see Sapiro 325.

8. Jean-François Devay, "Le torchon brûle chez les Goncourt," *Paris-Presse L'Intransigeant* November 27, 1956: 2.

9. Haedens, "Faut-il tuer les chasseurs d'éléphants?" *France Dimanche* November 30-December 6, 1956: 2. The insinuation is that Gary uses ghostwriters; see the Conclusion.

10. Hecquet, "La marge," *Bulletin de Paris* October 18, 1956.

11. Wurmser, "Un éléphant, ça trompe, ça trompe," *Les Lettres françaises* December 6–12, 1956: 1–2. René Bergeron of *L'Humanité* adopts a similar tone, arguing that Gary's novel is not "poorly constructed, it's not constructed at all" and attacking the Goncourt jury as a bourgeois institution ("Les Racines du ciel," *L'Humanité* December 4, 1956).

12. In a chapter on the formation of de Gaulle's RPF, Wurmser follows the lead of PCF chief Maurice Thorez in classifying de Gaulle as a fascist and compares him to Hitler and Mussolini (*De Gaulle et les siens* 245–46).

13. Grenier, "Romain Gary: 'Avant le Goncourt j'avais déjà eu sept prix de français au lycée de Nice,' " *France-Soir* December 15, 1956: 10.

14. Claude Le Roux, "Romain Gary: 'Je ne massacre ni la syntaxe ni les éléphants,' " *Paris-Presse L'Intransigeant* December 15, 1956: 7.

15. Gilbert Ganne, "Diplomate, ancien aviateur de l'escadrille 'Lorraine' Romain Gary méprise l'argent et les succès," *Les Nouvelles littéraires* December 6, 1956: 4.

16. See Jean-Paul Raynaut, "Voici peut-être le prochain Goncourt: 'Les Racines du ciel' de Raymond Gary," *Dimanche Matin* November 11, 1956; "Le Prix Goncourt à Romain Gary pour 'les Racines du ciel,' " *La Dépêche: La Liberté* December 4, 1956: 1, 16.

17. "Les Racines du ciel," *La Croix Nord et du Pas de Calais* December 9, 1956; Henriot, "Les Racines du ciel," 7.

18. "Romain Gary," *Le Parisien libéré* December 4, 1956: 6.

19. In addition to the place changes we have seen above, Gary received his French citizenship under his given name, Roman Kacew, in 1935. In 1944, he used his Resistance pseudonym, Romain Gari de Kacew, for his marriage license with Lesley Blanch. On November 20 of that same year, he received the Croix de la Libération as Romain Gary, which became his legal name in 1951. His passport,

however, shows him as born on May 21, not May 8 (respectively, Bona 41, 104, 87–88, 143; Larat 12).

20. Gary qtd. in Georgette Elgey, "L'un des cinq survivants de la bataille d'Angleterre: C'est au cri de 'Sauvez les éléphants!' que Romain Gary a gagné le Prix Goncourt," *Paris-Presse L'Intransigeant* December 5, 1956: 2.

21. Jean Benoît, "Des prix et des hommes . . . Aujourd'hui: Le Goncourt et le Renaudot," *Combat* December 3, 1956: 3.

22. Respectively, Francis Dumont, "*Les Racines du ciel* de Romain Gary ou le mariage du romanesque et du politique," radio broadcast, November 30, 1956; "Les Racines du ciel," *La Croix du Nord et du Pas de Calais*; Elgey 2.

23. Jean Prasteau, "Romain Gary: *Prix Goncourt*. André Perrin: *Prix Renaudot*," *Le Figaro* December 4, 1956: 14.

24. Chadourne, "Romain Gary Raconte . . . ," *Quatre et Trois* July 25, 1946: 6.

25. "Un Tour de Scrutin a suffi pour donner Le Prix Goncourt à Romain Gary," *Le Parisien libéré* December 4, 1956.

26. "This African epic comes quite close to being a very important book, worthy of *The Plague* or *Man's Fate*. It needs a finer sense of resources and proportions, a less anarchic structure, and a clearer style" (Boisdeffre, "Le Prix Goncourt attribué aujourd'hui aux 'Racines du ciel' de Romain Gary?" *Combat* December 3, 1956: 1). The references to Malraux are frequent; see Jacques Cathelin, "Les éléphants et 'l'affaire homme,'" *Demain* October 18, 1956; and Dominique Aury, "Le démon de la justice," *La Nouvelle Revue française* December 1, 1956: 1067–68.

27. Rocher, "Histoire d'éléphants," *L'Espoir de Nice* November 15, 1956: 2; Juin, "'Les Racines du ciel' et le Prix Goncourt," *Combat* November 22, 1956: 7.

28. Lalou, "'Les Racines du Ciel' par Romain Gary," *Les Nouvelles littéraires* November 1, 1956: 3.

29. Jean Bouret, "Un Goncourt Olympique," *Franc-Tireur* December 4, 1956: 6.

30. "Interrogé à la Paz Gary déclare," *Les Nouvelles littéraires* December 6, 1956: 4. The mention of 1936 is another allusion to his supposed participation in the Spanish Civil War.

31. Larat gives January 26, 1944, as the date of the incident (45).

32. "Romain Gary (Prix Goncourt) préféré à Clark Gable," *France Dimanche* December 7–13, 1956: 5.

33. Qtd. in Paul Guth, "Les Portraits-Interviews de Paul Guth," *Le Figaro littéraire* December 22, 1956: 4.

34. "The story is completely true," Gary promised one critic (Gabriel d'Aubarède, "Rencontre avec Romain Gary," *Les Nouvelles littéraires* December 27, 1956: 2).

35. Charles C. Lehrmann, for instance, takes *Promise at Dawn* as truthful, calling it "the book that furnishes the key to an understanding of *The Roots of Heaven*" (278).

36. For instance, *Promise at Dawn* satisfies the criteria of the "autobiographical pact" as defined by Philippe Lejeune in *On Autobiography*.

37. Barthes shows that the transformation of history into "nature," into inevitability, is an essential function of myth (129–31).

38. Fiche from *La Revue Bibliographique* July-August 1960.

39. In an essay on the protagonists of *Dangerous Liaisons*, Malraux writes: "The mythical image influences the living image, which then becomes its model in action, confronted with life, incarnated. Works of art benefit both from the method necessary for this incarnated image to realize its actions and the durable prestige of the mythical image" ("Laclos" 382).

40. Malraux, *Anti-Memoirs* 4 (I prefer my translation). De Gaulle's Saint-Cyr writings predict the inadequacies of French military strategy prior to World War II and the failings of the Fourth Republic's Constitution, while a short story, written by de Gaulle at age seventeen, imagines a "General de Gaulle" who saves France during a war with Germany (Pierre Lefranc, "De Gaulle: Tentative pour un portrait," in Institut Charles de Gaulle, *De Gaulle et Malraux* 23).

41. Jean Blanzat, "La Promesse de l'aube," *Le Figaro littéraire* May 7, 1960: 15.

42. A reviewer hostile to *The Roots of Heaven* writes: "The author's design clearly is to raise Morel's adventure and his dear elephants to the level of myth. But not everyone can reach that level. You must have a capacity for poetic transfiguration or, lacking that, a lyrical voice that transports the reader to another land and raises the adventure well above the status of simple anecdote. This is what can confer an exemplary—if not legendary—meaning upon it" (Henri Hell, "Chroniques: Les Romans," *La Table ronde* February 1957: 205). Where Gary possibly fails with Morel, he succeeds in *Promise at Dawn*.

43. One of the rare reviews to mention the other novels is entirely erroneous concerning both *Tulipe* and *The Company of Men*; it would appear that the reviewer had read neither (Georges Guilleminault, "Huit rescapés pour les prix," *Paris-Presse L'Intransigeant* November 24, 1956: 6).

44. Gautier, "Aux lundis de la Michodière: 'Johnnie Cœur' de Romain Gary," *Le Figaro* September 19, 1962: 22.

45. Philippe Dasnoy, "Johnnie Cœur," *Beaux Arts* October 13, 1961.

46. One of the only critics to endorse *Johnnie Cœur* was also one of the most significant: Catholic existentialist Marcel ("L'Escroc et la politique," *Les Nouvelles littéraires* September 27, 1962: 12).

47. The narrative of *Tulipe*'s life is punctuated by mock-historical footnotes, as if it were a question of an ancient religious manuscript being annotated, authenticated, and amended.

48. *T* 15–16 n. The internationally renowned French hotel and travel book is mistakenly referred to as *The Mussolini Guide*.

49. Though Gary proudly identified himself with the Resistance effort throughout his career, one area that he did not embellish was his role in it, avoiding any pretension to dramatic exploits. In *The Company of Men*, he suggests caution toward claims of French wartime heroics: "[We] have to look at that legend very carefully: filter it, sift through it, decant it" (15).

50. It is at least in part for this reason that Gary would use a pseudonym (Fosco Sinibaldi) for *L'homme à la colombe*, just as three years later Jean-Pierre Angrémy, also with Foreign Affairs, would find himself obliged to use one (Pierre-Jean Rémy) for a novel on Algeria (Boncenne 29–30). Once Gary had resigned from the diplomatic corps, he launched several attacks against the UN in his own name (Gary, "L'ONU n'existe pas . . ." 4; and, in the same year, *Johnnie Cœur*).

51. *Paris-Match* February 29, 1957: 52–53.

52. "All that remained for us to do was find a pseudonym worthy of the masterpieces the world was expecting" (*PD* 31–32). Johnnie settles on "the Man with the Dove," while in *Tulipe* the protagonist chooses the "White Mahatma of Harlem."

53. Prior to the French presidential elections in 1974, Gary wrote, "I will vote against all candidates presenting themselves as relics of General de Gaulle. If there's one thing that Charles de Gaulle's memory seems to demand, it's originality. And that means the end of the reliquary" (Gary, "Carnet d'un électeur" 4). On the second point, I believe for this reason that Huston overstates the case

in arguing that Gary's obsession is to incarnate Christ (see Huston, *Tombeau de Romain Gary* 98–100).

54. In this same period, Gary deflates the Sartrean insistence on authenticity in a philosophical fable from *Hissing Tales* entitled "The Fake."

55. Romain Gary to Pierre Calmann-Lévy, June 13, 1946, Calmann-Lévy Publishers' Archives.

56. We see it with Morel in *The Roots of Heaven* (he targets governments, poaching rings, hunting and tourism associations, journalists), the Polish partisans of *A European Education* (their use of wartime propaganda to influence fellow Poles and the German army), and *Tulipe*, *L'homme à la colombe*, and *Johnnie Cœur* (who exploit the credulity of the American public, the diplomatic community, and the press corps).

Chapter 3. Strategies of Mobile Identity

1. "La Promesse de l'aube," *Le Méridional* September 25, 1960.

2. As Krull sets off to Lisbon to assume the identity of the Marquis de Venosta, he reflects, "I was struck . . . by the fact that in this change of existence there was not simply delightful refreshment but also a sort of emptying out of my inmost being—that is, I had to banish from my soul all memories that belonged to my no longer valid past . . . It was no loss whatever that they were no longer mine. Only it was not altogether easy to put others, to which I was now entitled, in their place with any degree of precision . . . I became aware that I knew nothing about myself [i.e. his new persona]" (Mann 252).

3. Sganarelle appears in *Sganarelle or the Imaginary Cuckold*, *The School for Husbands*, *Don Juan or the Feast of the Statue*, *Love Is the Best Doctor*, and *The Reluctant Doctor*.

4. *Frère Océan* is a group of works conceived as the description of his literary project (*Pour Sganarelle*) and two novels demonstrating it (*The Dance of Genghis Cohn* and *The Guilty Head*).

5. Qtd. in André Weber, "Le Goncourt à Romain Gary pour 'les Racines du ciel,'" *Le Courrier de Limoges* December 4, 1956: 1.

6. "[Picaros] were cheerful profiteers, without faith or scruples, parasites living off of all the various forms of the Powers-that-be: kings, lords, the Church, the police or the army. Cohn dreamed of equaling them, of rediscovering that invigorating good luck, healthy carefree nature and mocking laugh" (*GH* 9). Gary's language establishes a link with Tulipe, which was the nickname for happy, carefree soldiers during the absolute monarchy (see Öostman 160).

7. Gary uses Gauguin's correspondence and journal in his preparation of *The Guilty Head*; the following passage in which Gauguin discusses his future caught Gary's eye: "And the day will come when people will believe that I'm a myth or just an invention of the press" (Gauguin, "Lettre XXVII" [October 1897]: 113).

8. Gary, "Ode to the Man Who Was France" 42c; *De Gaulle, première*, TF1.

9. Colonna's unpublished thesis was the first full-length study to provide an overview of what has become one of the most prevalent forms among modern French writers. His Genettean vocabulary is sorely tested in his attempt to define the genre's formal characteristics, but the extensive range of texts selected from across the twentieth century gives a clear sense of the genre's importance and diversity.

10. Frédéric Sauser's Promethean pseudonym, *Blaise Cendrars*, is composed

from *braise* (embers), *cendres* (ashes), and *ars* (arts in Latin). In *Promise at Dawn* (175), Gary adds a circumflex accent to Stendhal's autobiographical alter ego, Henry Brulard, changing it to *Brûlard* (also from *brûler*, to burn).

11. Gary, interview with Paule Neuvéglise, "Romain Gary avec 'Chien blanc': 'J'ai fait sans le vouloir, dans ce livre où tout est authentique, une anatomie de la haine,'" *France-Soir* April 3, 1970: 4.

12. Indeed, scholarly work over the last fifteen years has discovered Gary as a "Jewish writer," shifting the focus away from the Ajar incident: see books and articles by Bellos, Horn, Kauffmann, Mehlman, Rosenmary, Sungolowsky, Wardi, and Yogev in the Bibliography.

13. The persistence of anti-Semitism in postwar France is striking: Bona lists the other names legally changed on the same day as Gary's, and all but one or two (Maurice Cocu, for instance) are Jewish in resonance (Bona 143).

14. Gary anchors the novel in a rewriting of the Yiddish legend of the *dybbuk*, which can be a spirit haunting those responsible for wrongful deaths or an evil presence that latches onto and inhabits an otherwise innocent person. (I wish to thank Jerome Charyn for his helpful clarifications on this point.)

15. As Claude Nachin remarks (62–63), these are prevalent at the end of Gary's career, too: there is Ludo's teepee in *Les cerfs-volants* and the basement shelter at the end of Ajar's *Madame Rosa*.

16. In *The Company of Men* the former Vichy collaborationists and black marketeers are driven into hiding (including the protagonist, Luc Martin, a.k.a. "Étienne Roger"). The anarchist circles of *Lady L.* include real and fictional pseudonyms, while in *The Colors of the Day*, the mafiosi, Hollywood stars, and war veterans all use invented names. In the spy intrigue of *The Guilty Head*, no one's identity is ever known with any certainty.

17. Perhaps in this respect *Promise at Dawn* does do more than just *mythologize* Gary's past, insofar as it provides the autobiographical narrative that connects these two primary figures. It is important to note that, contrary to those who fail to live out their inventions (Vanderputte, Willie Bauché, or José Almayo in *Talent Scout*), those who succeed in doing so also reconcile themselves with their past. In each instance, this is done *through writing*, through an acknowledgment of one's origins: Janek completes Dobranski's manuscript (*A European Education*); the narrator of *Promise at Dawn* recounts his life as the narrative of his debts; Lady L. dictates her biography to Sir Percy; Fosco tells his father's story (*The Enchanters*); and Ludo is the heart of a novel dedicated "to memory" (*Les cerfs-volants*).

18. This identity is of course unverifiable, and there remain indications suggesting that Cohn is someone else entirely (*GH* 248). Whatever the case may be, Cohn's identity is essentially taken over by that of a character from another novel: Marc Mathieu, the inventor in Gary's science fiction spy thriller *The Gasp*. The CIA and other forces that pursue him are to be seen as the action novel's version of the "powers-that-be."

19. The theme of the clandestine tenant is used in various ways in *Lady L.*, *The Dance of Genghis Cohn* (with the dybbuk), and Ajar's *Gros-Câlin*; it is an excellent figure for the author in Gary's writing, a sort of textual stowaway.

20. These latter are among his only novels not commonly issued in Gallimard pocketbook (Folio) editions, yet again their American translations were favorably received.

21. An Israeli journalist supposedly asked Gary during a press conference whether he was circumcised. Recalls Gary, "It was the first time the press took an interest in my penis, and on live radio at that!" (*WD* 164).

22. Gary borrowed Malraux's phrasings in *The Metamorphosis of the Gods*, where there is a similar ambiguity in whether art's contestation consists in its independence from reality or in its infiltration of it.

23. His formulations of an aggressive, creative relation to reality are far removed from those identified by Charles Lalo in his curious presentation of a *littérature dégagée* ("uncommitted" literature, as opposed to committed literature, *littérature engagée*). Lalo argued (in 1947!) for a movement that strives for a total divorce from reality in art as a means of evasion into an ideal world of form and style.

Chapter 4. The Invention of Émile Ajar

1. Arnothy, " 'Les Têtes de Stéphanie' de Shatan Bogat," *Cosmopolitan* (France) August 1974.

2. Amette, "Humour: Drôles d'espions," *Le Point* July 1, 1974: 78.

3. Pierre Canavaggio, "Les Policiers du dimanche: 'Les Têtes de Stéphanie' par Shatan Bogat," *Le Quotidien de Paris* June 15–16, 1974: 11.

4. "Livre nouveau," *La Nouvelle République du Centre-Ouest* September 9, 1974: g.

5. Marc Michel, "Les Têtes de Stéphanie," *Nostradamus: L'hebdomadaire de l'actualité mystérieuse* June 6, 1974: 2.

6. P.-H. Liardon, "Les Têtes de Stéphanie," *Vingt-Quatre Heures* (Lausanne) July 15, 1974.

7. Collard, "Romans policiers: Les Têtes de Stéphanie," *France-Soir* June 3, 1974: 19.

8. Zylberstein, "Les Têtes de Stéphanie par Shatan Bogat," *Le Nouvel Observateur* July 8–14, 1974: 12. Bogat's biography provided some elements that could have traced the prank back to Gary. While Bogat "was awarded the Dakkan Prize for his coverage of international gold and weapons traffickers," the opening of *Les trésors de la mer Rouge* stated that it would not be about "black market gold smuggled . . . toward the safes of Indian traffickers" (3).

9. Queneau published texts such as *We Always Treat Women Too Well* under the guise of an apocryphal Irish actress and writer, Sally Mara.

10. Decoin, "Chronique: Gros-Câlin," *Les Nouvelles littéraires* November 4–10, 1974. See also M. G. [Michel Grisolia], "Gros-Câlin," *Magazine littéraire* 98 (November 1974): 8; Michel Mohrt, "Mythe et python," *Le Figaro* August 28, 1974: 13; Piatier, "Quand les pythons servent à l'humour: Une fameuse découverte," *Le Monde* September 27, 1974: 13–14.

11. Galey, "Python mon amour," *L'Express* September 23–29, 1974: 36; Amette, "Love Story," *Le Point* September 30, 1974: 107; Jean Freustié, "Gros-Câlin," *Le Nouvel Observateur* September 20, 1974: 91. It is interesting to note that Amette, enthusiastic supporter of Bogat's literary qualities, found them lacking in Ajar!

12. Two of the most legendary heroes of the French Resistance, Moulin and Brossolette both died at the hands of the Gestapo. Taken prisoner in 1943 at a meeting in the Lyons suburbs, Moulin succumbed to injuries inflicted by his Nazi torturer, Klaus Barbie. To avoid the risk of betraying his comrades under torture, Brossolette committed suicide while in captivity in occupied Paris by throwing himself out of a fifth-story window on Avenue Foch in 1944.

13. Anne-Charlotte Öostman notes that Brossolette and Moulin played the same role for this narrator as Nadejda did for Janek (155).

14. André Bourin, "Un python pour un apologue: 'Gros-Câlin' par Émile Ajar," *La Nouvelle République* November 6, 1974: d.

15. The slide into delusional substitution is even more pronounced in the original (as yet unpublished) ending to the novel, a synopsis of which is provided in Öostman 92–93. Cousin's collapse into gentle delirium harks back to one of Gary's very first texts, "Citoyen pigeon," in which the narrator, unable to recover from the shock of having met a talking pigeon, ends his account believing that his best friend has also become a bird (*Cadran* 18: 30). One finds similar endings in *Tulipe, The Colors of the Day, The Dance of Genghis Cohn*, and *Europa*: the story comes to a halt when the protagonists "pass to the other side of the mirror," as Gary calls it, that is, slip into a psychotic state in which they can no longer distinguish themselves from others, real or imagined.

16. The press release Gary quotes later urges, "Do not forget Nazi medical practices!" ("Un avortement de convenance ne devrait pas être opéré par un médecin, estime le conseil de l'ordre," *Le Monde* April 8–9, 1973: 24). Gary had already attacked these positions under his own name in *La nuit sera calme*, published just one year prior to *Gros-Câlin*: "When you condemn abortion with a lofty 'morality,' as does, for instance, the French Medical Association, knowing all the while that a million poor women will continue to subject themselves to torture each year for underground treatments — well, I say that you cannot get much lower than those 'high morals'" (14–15).

17. Head of the Roman Catholic Church in France, Cardinal Marty issued a statement on June 1, 1973, reiterating the Church's opposition to abortion.

18. Despite being the cousin of Gallimard director Claude Gallimard and the brother of its founder, Gaston, Robert Gallimard promised not to interfere again. He kept his word, despite the extremely delicate position it placed him in with respect to his relatives and colleagues in the publishing world (Pavlowitch, *L'homme* 58–59). Ironically, the Renaudot is considered "the journalists' Goncourt," with the award being named for Théophraste Renaudot, founder of France's first newspaper in 1631.

19. Arnothy, "Gros-Câlin (L'impuissance et la gloire)," *Le Parisien libéré* October 29, 1974: 6.

20. Arnothy, "Un amour de python," *Parispoche* November 14–19, 1974: 3. Was Arnothy in on the secret? She reviewed both Bogat and Ajar with insightful, enthusiastic readings. Gary spent time in Budapest in 1966, the year of Arnothy's first review of a Gary novel, and her husband, Claude Bellanger, was a Resistance hero faithful to de Gaulle who later served as director of *Le Parisien libéré*.

21. During the latter program, Gary's ill humor at the circuslike proceedings was evident; he maintained a gruff distance from most of the discussion ("La sexualité masculine," *Apostrophes*, June 13, 1975 [Antenne 2], Archives of the Institut National de l'Audiovisuel [INA], Paris, France).

22. Poirot-Delpech, "Retours d'âge," *Le Monde* May 9, 1975: 9.

23. Oster, "Éros voyage sans ticket," *Les Nouvelles littéraires* July 28, 1975: 4.

24. This is typical of the misunderstanding surrounding Gary's image, for this assessment of Rainier's character conveniently ignores central features of Gary's fictional identity. Gary undertakes a systematic mutilation of his heroic image that should in principle cause one to question Rainier as an emblem of masculine force: in *The Colors of the Day*, Rainier is an amputee; in "Birds in Peru," he is impotent; and in *Your Ticket Is No Longer Valid* he again confronts sexual inadequacy.

25. G. B. [Georges Bratschi?], "Aujourd'hui ce livre," *Tribune de Genève* July 21, 1975: 2.

26. Rosset, "Le Nouveau roman de Romain Gary: Le glas de la phallocratie blanche," *Le Quotidien de Paris* June 17, 1975: 13. Published in a radical Left news-

paper, Rosset's reading neglects the fact that Gary explicitly addresses these problematic implications in his protagonist's choice (*YT* 162).

27. Tolstoy's moralizing *Kreutzer Sonata* (1890) is named on several occasions as a betrayal of literature, precisely because the novel seems to fail owing to Tolstoy's inability to envisage a creative resolution to his *personal* troubles. For Gary, it marks a failure of imagination confronted with the challenges of the real, the victory of "destiny" over art.

28. During Kadir's internment in a psychiatric ward, the receipt stayed with his brother-in-law who lived, as it turns out, in Brazil (*MR* 190).

29. Romain Gary to Joseph Barnes, September 8, 1950, Joseph Barnes Manuscript Collection, Columbia University.

30. This pattern is fairly widespread in Gary's novels: in *A European Education,* Janek sees Adam's book through to publication, while in *Lady L.* the street urchin-cum-English aristocrat dictates her memoirs to Sir Percy Rodiner.

31. French and English editions of the novel were published, both presented as translations but with different authorial signatures (Bogat and Deville)!

32. Romain Gary to Joseph Barnes, April 25, 1955, Joseph Barnes Manuscript Collection, Columbia University. "Jack" is also a name for the devil.

33. Gary, unable to resist the temptation to sprinkle some clues as to Ajar's real identity, occasionally scrambles the boundaries between Gary and Ajar. A few of the examples are noteworthy: for instance, Momo walks around whistling "En passant par la Lorraine" (Passing through the Lorraine), which is incongruous for a fourteen-year-old in Belleville but less so for an ex-member of the French Air Force squadron *Lorraine* (*MR* 108). David Bellos also notes that the taxi ride with the Zaoum brothers takes Momo and Madame Rosa along the banks of the Marne River, a discreet allusion to the legendary "taxis of the Marne" (62).

Chapter 5. The Consecration of Émile Ajar

1. Piatier, "La tendresse des 'paumés': Le second exploit d'Ajar," *Le Monde* September 17, 1975: 1; Fouchet, "La Vie devant soi," *Le Point* October 6, 1975.

2. Freustié, "Ajar: La Vie devant soi," *Le Nouvel Observateur* October 1975.

3. "Michel Cournot, Jacques Lanzmann et Pierre Bénichou: 'Ajar c'est pas nous,'" *France-Soir* November 21, 1975: 18; Pavlowitch, *L'homme* 58; Pivot qtd. in Yrène Jan, "L'amour froid," *L'Aurore* October 29, 1974; Philippe Bouvard, "La Vie devant soi d'Émile Ajar," *France-Soir* November 22, 1975.

4. "Ce Renaudot qui était aussi l'effet du Ajar," *Minute* December 3, 1974: 31.

5. Ironically, the narrator of *Gros-Câlin* was Michel *Cousin.* Did Gary have Pavlowitch in mind from the start?

6. Baby, "La maison d'Ajar," *Le Monde,* October 10, 1975: 20. A follow-up article appeared weeks later: Baby, "La voix d'Ajar," *Le Monde* November 22, 1975: 30. One wonders whether it is a coincidence that a few short years later Baby's first novel would be published by Mercure de France.

7. Ducout, "Emile Ajar, le mystérieux," *Elle* November 1975: 10.

8. Hubert Damisch offers a useful distinction between mask and disguise. A mask, usually presenting a type, is a representation of a face, which no one confuses with a real face. The disguise, however, not only hides one's identity but dissimulates the fact that it is a disguise (130–31).

9. Bouzerand, "Qui est Ajar?" *Le Point* November 10, 1975: 64; "Émile Ajar parle," *Le Point* November 17, 1975: 174–76.

10. Goldman eventually wins his release from prison but is promptly assassinated.

11. *Dernières nouvelles d'Alsace* November 18, 1975: 3.

12. "Ajar refuse le Goncourt," *Le Monde* November 22, 1975: 1, 30.

13. Audouard, "Les enfants de pute et les enfants du bon Dieu," *Le Canard Enchaîné* October 1, 1975: 7.

14. Qtd. in Françoise de Comberousse, "Le nouveau lauréat jugé par les anciens Goncourt," *France-Soir* November 19, 1975: 14.

15. "Un travail de Romain," *Minute* December 3–9 1975: 31.

16. " 'De Paris à Lyon': Les prix littéraires de fin d'année," *Le Tout Lyon* January 1, 1976.

17. "Émile Ajar's attitude around the time of the Goncourt immediately struck me as strange because he was fleeing nonexistent pressures" (qtd. in Payot 47).

18. "Émile Ajar retrouvé à Paris," *Le Monde* November 23–24, 1975: 11. While it is true that Gary was remarkably prolific in these years, he also masked his activity by periodically issuing translations or reeditions where possible (see Chapter 5).

19. *Clair de femme* even borders on the pathetic, its narrator summarizing his dilemma in the following manner: "Never had I found myself in such a needy state" (*CF* 11).

20. An older, written form of the past perfect, the simple past was used exclusively in French literature until Camus' *The Stranger* in 1942 adopted the spoken form of the composed past. Contemporary writers tend to use the latter.

21. Gary even establishes a link between the two, since Gary's "illegitimate offspring," Émile Ajar, owes his first name to Gauguin's illegitimate son—presented, moreover, as Cohn's rival in *The Guilty Head* (see Pavlowitch, *L'homme* 19).

22. R.-M. Albérès, "Intimisme et exotisme," *Les Nouvelles littéraires* May 2, 1968: 5.

23. On the brink of publication, Gary hesitated, asking Pavlowitch if he objected: "I only used [you] to maximize and make people see the fiction of the fiction. It is a *literary genre.* I'm offering to not turn in this manuscript. I'll redo it with an *I* that is even more nonexistent" (qtd. in Pavlowitch, *L'homme* 241). *Pseudo* is thus imagined as being the same kind of autofiction as Gary's earlier projects of passing through a historical but fictionalized first-person narrator who is to be "burned up" in the process. In this case, however, it is Gary putting himself in Pavlowitch's skin.

24. Audouard, "La méthode à Émile," *Le Canard Enchaîné* December 8, 1976.

25. Autrand, "Pour Ajar l'écriture c'est le règne du 'pseudo,' " *La Quinzaine littéraire* January 15, 1977.

26. Lainé, "D'un Goncourt accepté à un Goncourt refusé," *Le Monde* November 28, 1975: 18.

27. Pavlowitch-Ajar, qtd. in Bouzerand, "Émile Ajar parle" 175. These allusions clearly came from Gary, who discreetly expressed admiration for Michaux elsewhere, citing the same unidentified phrase in *The Company of Men* (246), *The Guilty Head* (286), and *The Enchanters* (20). Taken from a short piece called "Voices," which Michaux wrote during the war years, it no doubt struck Gary for its depiction of a humanist vision of humankind: "He that a pebble caused to stumble had been walking already for two thousand years when he heard voices of hate and menace that had the presumption to try to frighten him" (Michaux 36).

28. Martine Carré, "Dix ans avec Romain Gary," interview with Gilles Martin-Chauffier, *Paris-Match* November 6, 1981: 24. Another precaution taken by Gary

was to recopy each of the Ajar manuscripts in notebooks and place them in a bank vault in Geneva.

29. Moreover, Gary did not choose just any name: Gari, as it turns out, was his mother's stage name during her career as an actress (Pavlowitch, *L'homme* 19). When the father failed him, Gary's genealogy would become matrilineal. Rooted in Russian and tied to his mother, his pseudonym *did not* mark a break with the past as supposed by Dominique de Gasquet (66). Rather, it reattached his identity to the only part of his past of which he could be certain.

30. Audouard, "La voie aux chapitres: 'Clair de femme' par Romain Gary," *Le Canard Enchaîné* February 16, 1977: 7.

31. Galey, "Romain Gary: Un nouveau voyage sentimental," *L'Express* February 14–20, 1977: 31–32.

32. Piatier, "Les paradoxes de Romain Gary," *Le Monde* March 4, 1977.

33. Schlumberger, "Émile Ajar directeur littéraire," *Le Quotidien de Paris* July 2, 1981: 31. Barbès-Rochechouart is a busy boulevard separating the northern working-class districts (IX and XVIII), while the Marais is now a fashionable neighborhood in central Paris.

34. *KS* 104; compare with *CV* 62. For de Heredia's poem, compare the repeated citations, *KS* 331 and *CV* 32. Gary's almost fetishistic references to El Greco's painting are no doubt due to the fact the figures in its foreground bear a truly striking resemblance to Gary.

35. Gary once again received confirmation that few readers were paying attention. Following Gary's notes in the preface (*CL* 9), reviewers reported that the novel was adapted from a screenplay, "The Man Who Understood Women," without recognizing that it was in fact a reworking of a prior novel.

36. A number of Gary's novels present such situations: *Tulipe, L'homme à la colombe, The Colors of the Day, Talent Scout* (Radetzky, Diaz with Almayo), *The Guilty Head* ("Victor Turkassi"), *Europa* (Malwyna), and *The Roots of Heaven* (Morel).

Conclusion

1. Qtd. in Pol Walheer, "Les Prix," *La Nation belge* December 11, 1956.

2. Georgin, "Comment ils écrivent: Romain Gary, Hervé Bazin, F.-R. Bastide, J.-C. Pichon, Michel Déon," *Arts* December 5–11, 1956: 4.

3. "Gary a besoin d'être récrit," *Arts* December 12–18, 1956: 1.

4. "Les Racines du ciel," *Beaux-Arts* December 20, 1956.

5. Qtd. in "Un éléphant sur mesure . . . ," *Bulletin de Paris* December 6, 1956.

6. Jean Bouret, "Un Goncourt Olympique," *Franc-Tireur* December 4, 1956: 6. Camus and Lemarchand sent an incendiary letter to *France-Soir* refuting the claim on every point (Carmen Tessier, "Les Potins de la commère," *France-Soir* December 7, 1956).

7. Qtd. in Le Mauvais Œil, "Plumes et paons," *Rivarol: Hebdomadaire de l'Opposition Nationale* June 16, 1960: 4.

8. Given the narrator's unconventional discourse, the original French text is helpful: "Je dois . . . m'excuser de certaines mutilations, mal-emplois, sauts de carpe, entorses, refus d'obéissance, crabismes, strabismes et immigrations sauvages du langage, syntaxe et vocabulaire" (*GC* 9).

9. An English equivalent cannot be easily rendered without substituting a different cognate. The original French plays on variants of *courir* ("to run," but also

"current" in the present participle): "Il me serait très pénible si on me deman-
dait avec sommation d'employer des mots et des formes qui ont déjà beaucoup
couru, dans le sens courant, sans trouver de sortie" (*GC* 9).

10. Qtd. in Françoise de Comberousse, "Le Nouveau lauréat jugé par les anciens Goncourt," *France-Soir* November 19, 1975: 14.

11. Cf. Galey, "Python mon amour," *L'Express* September 23–29, 1974: 36.

12. In 1969, a rumor spread throughout France that Jewish shopkeepers in the
city of Orleans were kidnapping young girls and forcing them into white slavery
(see Morin).

13. A related phrase even appears in *Gros-Câlin*: "My python was on the verge of
starving to death. I finally bought a *cochon d'Inde* ["Indian pig" is the French term
for "Guinea pig"], because India is more demographic. But this one too found a
way immediately to strike up a friendship with me" (*GC* 12).

14. For instance, *les gars* (dudes); *godemichés* (dildos); *sales trucs* (nasty stuff); *tout
ça c'est* . . . (it's all just . . .); the double entendre with *il n'y plus où se fourrer* (there's
no hole left to hide in); and the names Chicks and Bug.

15. Though Gide's name was almost never mentioned by Gary, echoes of the
former can be found throughout the latter's work. Of particular relevance in *The
Counterfeiters* are young Boris's difficulties with language (part 2, chapter 2), the
themes of linguistic and sentimental exchanges "counterfeited" by social conventions, the Protean notion of identity sought by Gide's different narrators, and the
grounding of a literary aesthetic in a rivalry between reality and our representations of it (see 2: 5). Moreover, the gang of young thieves in *Ski Bum* is smuggling
counterfeit gold in Switzerland, much like the youths in *The Counterfeiters*.

16. With Beckett, the entirety of his work struggles with the impossibility of
locating where the "authority" in speech or writing resides, whereas Blanchot en-
visions writing as a process that dismisses the writer from the text. The figure of
the author, in other words, is nullified.

17. Rouart, "Songe et mensonge," *Le Quotidien de Paris* July 7, 1981: 2.

18. *Lire* created a small scandal when it published the only known recent photograph of Blanchot, a paparazzi-like shot taken by Gilles Cahoreau in a grocery
store parking lot (Alain Jaubert, "Enquête: Les écrivains pour ou contre la pho-
tographie," *Lire* June 1985: 46). In a more dignified but related direction, James
Knowlson is reported to have received an astronomical advance for his biography of Samuel Beckett, ironically (in this instance) titled *Damned to Fame: The Life
of Samuel Beckett*.

19. The *Monde* fell victim to the hoax and unsuspectingly reviewed the works
("Le Monde des Livres," *Le Monde* June 11, 1976).

20. Gary was the first accused but turned it into an opportunity to brace up
Pavlowitch's charade. Brenner reports, "[Gary] gave me his 'word of honor' that
he didn't have anything to do with this novel and that, in his opinion, his 'nephew'
Émile Ajar didn't either. 'It's more likely,' said Gary, 'the doing of a Pierre-Jean
Rémy or a Lanzmann'" (Brenner, "Des livres pour l'été," *Le Provençal-Dimanche*
May 20, 1979: 8). Gary was the only writer or member of the press to identify
correctly Jacques Lanzmann, and this without having seen the book!

21. This is why there was such resentment following the discovery that Gary
was responsible for Ajar: "Victims object to pranksters having falsified the rules
unbeknownst to them—and for having made these unknowing players the object
of their own game" (Caradec 109).

22. As Rosello notes, the child narrator, Momo, relies in all innocence on

stereotypes throughout his account, and the adult "Ajar" never intervenes to reject the racist nature of these remarks (143–45).

23. The project for *Direct Flight to Allah* is discussed in Chapter 4. *The Gasp*, written the same year but in English, tells the story of an inventor who creates a machine that sucks up the souls of others, allowing the inventor to live off the energy of their minds. It is, in other words, another figuration of Gary's transformation into Émile Ajar.

24. Cluny, "Les romans de la rentrée: *La vie devant soi*," *Magazine littéraire* (November 1975): 106. Drumont politicized anti-Semitism in France with the publication of diatribes like *Le testament d'un antisémite* (1891), while Rebatet's *Les décombres* (1942) was a bestseller promoting fascistic, violently anti-Semitic positions during the Occupation.

25. Alexandre Sorel, "Vous avez dit Ajar?" *L'Express* December 1–7, 1975; Jean Vigneaux, "Le système en cause: 'La vie devant soi,' " *Arts / Pourquoi Pas?* November 27, 1975: 172–80.

26. Qtd. in Claudine Jardin, "Au fil des lettres," *Le Figaro littéraire* July 4, 1967; see also *WD* 163.

27. Dupuy, "Lettre ouverte à Romain Gary," *Libération* July 1, 1981: 19.

28. From 1975 to 1985, *L'Humanité* lost 30 percent of its sales and by 1997 was running at only fifty-eight thousand daily copies (Albert 120–23).

29. Jacqueline Piatier calls Grainville "the rare writer who has not been unsettled by the Goncourt Prize" (Piatier, "Le nouvel avatar de Patrick Grainville," *Le Monde* January 29, 1988). Armed with a Sorbonne degree and a spell in the CNRS research system, Grainville can speak with a scholar's knowledge of French letters; yet, trained by many years in the classroom, he also has a personality that communicates his considerable passion for words and the imaginary. And when the Parisian knives come out—for instance, Polac's televised attack on his style—Grainville's agile intelligence can quickly gain the upper hand.

30. Modiano has been consecrated with an impressive array of awards: in addition to the Academy and Relais Prizes, he has won the Fénéon Prize, the Roger Nimier Prize, the Diamond Feather Prize, the Booksellers' Prize, the Pierre of Monaco Prize, and the Goncourt (Morris 1).

Bibliography

WORKS BY ROMAIN GARY

(Where no author is given, Romain Gary is the name used for publication.)

NOVELS WRITTEN IN FRENCH

1945. *Éducation européenne.* Paris: Calmann-Lévy. Definitive edition, Éditions Gallimard, 1956.

1947. *Tulipe.* Paris: Calmann-Lévy. Definitive edition, Éditions Gallimard, 1970.

1948. *Le grand vestiaire.* Paris: Éditions Gallimard.

1952. *Les couleurs du jour.* Paris: Éditions Gallimard.

1956. *Les racines du ciel.* Paris: Éditions Gallimard.

1958. Fosco Sinibaldi. *L'homme à la colombe.* Paris: Éditions Gallimard. Definitive edition, 1984.

1960. *La promesse de l'aube.* Paris: Éditions Gallimard.

1961. *Johnnie Cœur.* Paris: Éditions Gallimard.

1962. *Gloire à nos illustres pionniers.* Paris: Éditions Gallimard.

1965. *Pour Sganarelle (Frère Océan I).* Paris: Éditions Gallimard.

1967. *La danse de Gengis Cohn (Frère Océan II).* Paris: Éditions Gallimard.

1968. *La tête coupable (Frère Océan III).* Paris: Éditions Gallimard.

1971. *Les trésors de la mer Rouge.* Paris: Éditions Gallimard.

1972. *Europa.* Paris: Éditions Gallimard.

1973. *Les enchanteurs.* Paris: Éditions Gallimard.

1974. With François Bondy. *La nuit sera calme.* Paris: Éditions Gallimard.

———. Shatan Bogat. *Les têtes de Stéphanie.* Paris: Éditions Gallimard.

———. Émile Ajar. *Gros-Câlin.* Paris: Mercure de France.

1975. *Au-delà de cette limite votre ticket n'est plus valable.* Paris: Éditions Gallimard.

———. Émile Ajar. *La vie devant soi.* Paris: Mercure de France.

1976. Émile Ajar. *Pseudo.* Paris: Mercure de France.

1977. *Clair de femme.* Paris: Éditions Gallimard.

1978. *La bonne moitié.* Paris: Éditions Gallimard.

1979. *Les clowns lyriques.* Paris: Éditions Gallimard.

———. Émile Ajar. *L'angoisse du roi Salomon.* Paris: Mercure de France.

1980. *Les cerfs-volants.* Paris: Éditions Gallimard.

1981. *Vie et mort d'Émile Ajar*. Paris: Éditions Gallimard.
1997. *Ode à l'homme qui fut la France suivi de Malraux, conquérant de l'impossible*. Ed. and trans. Paul Audi. Paris: Calmann-Lévy.

NOVELS WRITTEN IN ENGLISH

1958. *Lady L.* New York: Simon & Schuster.
1961. *Talent Scout (American Comedy I)*. New York: Harper & Row.
1965. *Ski Bum (American Comedy II)*. New York: Harper & Row.
1968. *White Dog*. Serial publication in *Life*; New York: New American Library, 1970.
1973. *The Gasp (American Comedy III)*. New York: Pocket Books.

NOVELS TRANSLATED INTO FRENCH

(All French translations by Gary.)
1964. *Lady L.* Trans. of *Lady L.* Paris: Éditions Gallimard.
1966. *Les mangeurs d'étoiles*. Trans. of *Talent Scout*. Paris: Éditions Gallimard.
1969. *Adieu Gary Cooper*. Trans. of *Ski Bum*. Paris: Éditions Gallimard.
1970. *Chien blanc*. Trans. of *White Dog*. Paris: Éditions Gallimard.
1978. *Charge d'âme*. Trans. of *The Gasp*. Paris: Éditions Gallimard.

NOVELS TRANSLATED INTO ENGLISH

1944. *Forest of Anger*. Trans. of *Éducation européenne* by Viola Gerard Garvin. London: Cresset P. Reprinted as *Nothing Important Ever Dies* and *A European Education*, 1960.
1950. *The Company of Men*. Trans. of *Le grand vestiaire* by Joseph Barnes. New York: Simon & Schuster.
1953. *The Colors of the Day*. Trans. of *Les couleurs du jour* by Stephen Becker. New York: Simon & Schuster.
1958. *The Roots of Heaven*. Trans. of *Les Racines du ciel* by Jonathan Swift. New York: Simon & Schuster.
1961. *Promise at Dawn: A Memoir*. Trans. of *La Promesse de l'aube* by John Markham Beach. New York: New Directions.
1964. *Hissing Tales*. Trans. of *Gloire à nos illustres pionniers* by Richard Howard. New York: Harper & Row.
1968. *The Dance of Genghis Cohn*. Trans. of *La danse de Gengis Cohn* by Romain Gary with Camilla Sykes. New York: New American Library.
1969. *The Guilty Head*. Trans. of *La tête coupable* by Romain Gary. New York: New American Library.
1975. René Deville. *Direct Flight to Allah*. Trans. of *Les têtes de Stéphanie* by J. Maxwell Brownjohn. London: Collins.
————. *The Enchanters*. Trans. of *Les enchanteurs* by Helen Eustis. New York: Putnam.
————. Émile Ajar. *Madame Rosa*. Trans. of *La Vie devant soi* by Ralph Manheim. New York: Berkley Books.

1977. *Your Ticket Is No Longer Valid.* Trans. of *Au-delà de cette limite votre ticket n'est plus valable* by Sophie Wilkins. New York: George Braziller.

1978. *Europa.* Trans. of *Europa* by Barbara Bray and Romain Gary. Garden City, NY: Doubleday.

1983. *King Solomon* with "The Life and Death of Emile Ajar." Trans. of *L'Angoisse du roi Salomon* by Barbara Wright. New York: Harper & Row.

———. "Life and Death of Emile Ajar." See *King Solomon.*

PREFACES, STORIES, AND ARTICLES (SELECTED)

1935. Romain Kacew. "L'Orage," 10. *Gringoire*: February 15.

———. Romain Kacew. "Une Petite femme," 13. *Gringoire*: May 24.

1945. "Tout va bien sur le Kilimandjaro," 22. *Cadran* 12 (May).

———. "Citoyen pigeon," 30–31. *Cadran* 18 (August).

1946. "Sergent Gnama." *Bulletin de l'Association des Français Libres* (January).

1957. "Le moment de la vérité: Entretien avec Romain Gary," 3–7. Interview with François Bondy. *Preuves* (March).

———. "Je rencontre un barracuda," 11–13; "L'Évasion du professeur Ostrach," 14–15. *Preuves* (March).

1959. "The Colonials," 86. *Holiday* (April).

1960. "Party of One: What's Happening to the Human Race," 13. *Holiday* (January).

———. "Trois histoires pour rire d'un diplomate." *Les Œuvres Libres* 166 (March).

———. "The Man Who Stayed Lonely to Save France." Pamphlet. New York: Ambassade de France, 1960. Rpt. from *Life* 40: 23 (December 8, 1958): 144–58.

1961. "The Anger That Turned Generals into Desperados," 26–27. *Life*: May 5.

———. "L'ONU n'existe pas," 4. *Le Nouveau Candide*: December 21–27.

1962. "Avant-propos," xiii–xv. James Jones. *Mourir ou crever*. Paris: Stock, 1962.

1965. "Romain Gary s'attaque au Nouveau Roman," 1, 8, 14. *Le Figaro littéraire*: September 23–29.

———. "Assassins," 8. *Le Figaro littéraire*: September 30-October 6.

1967. "Entretien avec Romain Gary," 3. Interview with K. A. Jelenski. *Livres de France* (March).

———. "Lettre à ma voisine de table." *Le Figaro*: April 24.

———. "Le mort saisit le vif," 38–40. Interview with Marguerite Kagan. *Droit et liberté: Revue mensuelle du Mouvement contre le Racisme, l'Antisémitisme et pour la Paix* 262 (May).

1968. "Gaulliste inconditionnel," 6. *Le Monde*: June 23–24.

———. "Je suis un irrégulier," 1, 14. Interview with Louis Monier and Arlette Merchez. *Les Nouvelles littéraires*: October 31.

1969. "To mon Général: Farewell, with Love and Anger," 24–29. *Life* 66: 18 (May 9).

———. "Romain Gary," 139–41. In *Cent écrivains répondent au 'questionnaire' Marcel Proust*. Pref. Léonce Peillard. Paris: Éditions Albin Michel, 1969.

1970. "Romain Gary: Lettre aux Juifs de France," 8–9. *Le Figaro littéraire*: March 9–15.

———. "L'Europe-patrie." *France-Soir*. March 26.

———. "Le grand couteau," 4. *France-Soir*: April 3.

———. "Romain Gary avec 'Chien blanc': 'J'ai fait sans le vouloir, dans ce livre où tout est authentique, une anatomie de la haine,' " 4. Interview with Paule Neuvéglise. *France- Soir*: August 28.

―――. "Les Français Libres." *La Revue de la France Libre.* Special issue (October 1970).

―――. "A la recherche du 'je' gaullien," 8–10. *Le Figaro littéraire*: October 26-November 1.

―――. "Speaking the Unspeakable." *New York Times*: November 7.

―――. "Ode to the Man Who Was France," 42–44d. *Life* 69: 21 (November 20).

1971. "Faux romantisme et avenir," 23. *Le Monde*: December 11.

1972. "Lettre ouverte à Jean Chauvel." *Le Figaro*: December 9.

1974. "Carnet d'un électeur," 1, 4. *Le Figaro*: April 16.

1975. "Mœurs: Voie libre pour la société de provocation," 2. *Le Figaro*: December 27–28.

1976. "Introduction: How Many Warnings Do We Need, How Much Beauty Gone?" 11–24. *Vanishing Species.* New York: Time-Life Books.

1977. "Last Post for the Playboys of the Western World." Interview with Alec Hamilton. *Guardian*: June 29.

―――. "André Malraux," 11–17. *Exposition André Malraux.* Paris: Chancellerie de l'Ordre de la Libération.

1978. Preface, 9–15. *Ciel de sable.* By Claude Raoul-Duval. Paris: Éditions France-Empire.

PAPERS AND ARCHIVES

Diego Gary (private). Includes manuscript *Le vin des morts* and final chapter of *Gros-Câlin.*

Éditions Calmann-Lévy. Publishers' archives. 4 vols. Paris.

Éditions Gallimard. Press clippings. 21 vols. Paris.

Harper and Row Papers. Columbia University, New York.

Herbert Mitgang Papers. New York Public Library, New York.

John Huston Papers. Academy of Motion Picture Arts & Sciences, Margaret Herrick Library, Beverly Hills, Calif.

Joseph Barnes Papers. Columbia University, New York.

Max Lincoln Schuster Papers. Columbia University, New York.

Mercure de France. Press clippings. 7 vols. Paris.

RADIO AND TELEVISION APPEARANCES (SELECTED)

Romain Gary

1970. "Invité du dimanche." November 15. TF1.

1973. *La vie entre les lignes.* Dir. Patrice Galbeau. Radio-France.

1975. "La mémoire courte: Romain Gary." *Un jour futur.* January 18.

―――. *Radioscopie.* Dir. Jacques Chancel. June 10. Radio-France.

―――. "La sexualité racontée par les hommes." *Apostrophes.* June 13.

―――. "L'impuissance masculine." *Aujourd'hui Madame.* October 16.

―――. "De Gaulle, première." Prod. Daniel Costelle. November 9. TF1.

1977. "Clair de femme." *Pleine page.* February 25.

————. "Des auteurs face à leurs lectrices." *Aujourd'hui Madame.* April 4.
————. Interviews musician Peter Townsend. *Questions sans visage.* April 9.
————. "L'homme objet." *Aujourd'hui Madame.* September 19.
1978. "Clair de femme." *Aujourd'hui Magazine.* February 27.
————. *Propos et confidences.* Dir. Jean Faucher. Radio-Canada.
————. "Romain Gary évoque André Malraux." *Chroniques de France* 149.
1979. Press conference: Jean Seberg and the FBI. *Journal télévisé.* September 10.
    Antenne 2.
1981. "Bonjour, bonsoir la nuit." Pres. Philippe Labro. July 4. TF1.
1985. *Romain Gary.* Dir. Variety Moszynski. Pres. Jacques Marchais.
1989. *Ex-Libris.* Pres. Patrick Poivre d'Arvor. November 22.
1993. *Une vie, une œuvre: Romain Gary, l'insaisi.* Dir. Nancy Huston. France-Culture.
1995. *Répliques: Hommage à Romain Gary.* Pres. Alain Finkielkraut. France-Culture.
    June.
1998. *Un siècle d'écrivains: Romain Gary.* Dir. Olivier Mille and André Asseo. July 22.
    France 3.

Paul Pavlowitch

1981. "Romain Gary et Émile Ajar." *Apostrophes.* July 3.
1986. "*La peau de l'ours.* Ajar et après." *Contre Enquête.* May 14. TF1.
————. "*La peau de l'ours.*" *Plateau.* June 12. Midi 2.

FILMS WRITTEN AND DIRECTED

1967. *Les Oiseaux vont mourir au Pérou.* With Jean Seberg, Danielle Darrieux. Universal Studios.
1971. *Kill.* With Jean Seberg, James Mason. Cocinor.

SCREENPLAYS

1962. *The Longest Day.* Prod. Darryl Zanuck. Cowritten with Cornelius Ryan, James Jones, et al. Twentieth Century Fox.

FILM AND THEATER ADAPTATIONS OF GARY NOVELS

1958. *The Roots of Heaven.* Dir. John Huston. Prod. Darryl Zanuck. With Trevor Howard, Errol Flynn, Juliette Greco, Orson Welles. Twentieth Century Fox.
1959. *The Man Who Understood Women.* Adaptation of *The Colors of the Day.* Dir. Nunnally Johnson. With Henry Fonda, Leslie Caron. Twentieth Century Fox.
1961. *Lady L.* Dir. George Cukor. With Tony Curtis, Gina Lollabrigida. MGM. Unfinished.
1962. *First Love.* Broadway theatrical adaptation of *La promesse de l'aube,* by Samuel Taylor.

1965. *Lady L.* Dir. Peter Ustinov. Screenplay Ustinov. With Sophia Loren, Paul Newman, David Niven. MGM.

1970. *La promesse de l'aube.* Dir. Jules Dassin. With Melina Mercouri, Assaf Dayan. MGM.

1971. *The Ski Bum.* Dir. Bruce D. Clark. With Zalman King, Charlotte Rampling.

1977. *Madame Rosa.* Dir. Moshe Mizrahi. Screenplay Mizrahi. With Simone Signoret, Claude Dauphin.

1979. *Womanlight.* Adaptation of *Clair de femme.* Dir. Constantin Costa-Gavras. With Yves Montand, Romy Schneider.

———. *Gros-Câlin.* Dir. Jean-Pierre Rawson. Screenplay Age and Scarpelli. With Jean Carmet.

1981. *Your Ticket Is No Longer Valid.* Dir. George Kaczender. Screenplay Ian McLellan Hunter, Leila Basen. With Richard Harris, Jeanne Moreau, George Peppard.

1982. *Trained to Kill.* Adaptation of *White Dog.* Dir. Samuel Fuller. With Kristy McNichol, Paul Winfield, Burl Ives.

1984. *Les cerfs-volants.* Television miniseries. Dir. Pierre Badel. With Jacques Penot, Anne Gauthier.

1994. *Genghis Cohn: Revenge Can Be Hilarious.* Dir. Elijah Moshinsky. Screenplay from *The Dance of Genghis Cohn*: Stanley Price. With Robert Lindsay, Diana Rigg, Antony Sher. PBS & BBC.

———. *The Impostors.* Adaptation of *The Guilty Head.* Dir. Frédéric Blum. With Gérard Jugnot, Viktor Lazlo.

The Talent Scout. Unproduced screenplay by Alex Tartaglia. N.d.

Other Works

Abastado, Claude. *Mythes et rituels de l'écriture.* Bruxelles: Éditions Complexe (Creusets), 1979.

Abdeljaouad, Firyel. *Les figures de l'autre dans l'œuvre de Romain Gary et Émile Ajar ou comment le vif saisit le mort.* Lille: Éditions de Septentrion, 2001.

Albalat, Antoine. *Comment on devient écrivain.* Paris: Armand Colin (Coll. L'Ancien et le Nouveau), 1925, 1992.

Albert, Pierre. *La presse française.* Paris: La Documentation française, 1998.

Amossy, Ruth. *Les idées reçues: Sémiologie du stéréotype.* Paris: Éditions Nathan, 1991.

———. "Stéréotypie et valeur mythique: Des aventures d'une métamorphose," 161–80. *Études littéraires* 17: 1 (April 1984).

Anglard, Véronique. *25 Prix Goncourt.* Alleur/Belgique: Marabout, Hachette, 1993.

Aron, Raymond. *Memoirs: Fifty Years of Political Reflection.* Trans. George Holoch. New York: Holmes & Meier, 1990.

Assouline, Pierre. *Gaston Gallimard: A Half Century of French Publishing.* Trans. Harold J. Salemson. New York: Harcourt Brace Jovanovich, 1988.

———. *Simenon.* Paris: Julliard, 1992.

Atack, Margaret. *Literature and the French Resistance: Cultural Politics and Narrative Forms, 1940–50.* Manchester: Manchester University Press, 1989.

Audi, Paul. Préface, 11–35; Postface, 127–52. Romain Gary, *Ode à l'homme qui fut la France suivi de Malraux, conquérant de l'impossible.* Paris: Calmann-Lévy, 1997.

Barthes, Roland. "Myth Today," 109–59. *Mythologies.* Trans. Annette Lavers. New York: Hill & Wang, 1981.

Bayard, Pierre. *Il était deux fois Romain Gary*. Paris: PUF (Coll. Le Texte Rêve), 1990.

Bellanger, Claude, ed. *Histoire générale de la presse*. Vol. 4. Paris: PUF, 1976.

Belle-Isle, Francine. "Autobiographie et analyse: Là où le rêve prend corps," 371–80. *Études littéraires* 17: 2 (fall 1984).

Bellos, David. "Ce que Momo veut dire: La mémoire de la Shoah dans *La vie devant soi* de Romain Gary," 55–66. *Perspectives: Revue de l'Université Hébraïque de Jérusalem* 6 (1999).

Béranger, Nicole. *Un jour, nous épouserons Romain Gary*. Montréal: Les Intouchables, 2000.

Beyala, Calixthe. *Le petit prince de Belleville*. Paris: Albin Michel, 1992.

Blanch, Lesley. *Romain, un regard particulier*. Trans. Jean Lambert. Arles: Actes Sud, 1998.

Blanchot, Maurice. "The Essential Solitude," 63–78. *The Gaze of Orpheus and Other Literary Essays*. Ed. P. Adams Sitney. Trans. Lydia Davis. Barrytown, N.Y.: Station Hill Press, 1981.

Blot, Jean. "The Jewish Novel in France." *European Judaism* 5 (1970).

Boillat, Gabriel. *Un maître de 17 ans, Raymond Radiguet*. Neuchâtel: La Baconnière, 1973.

Boisen, Jørn. "La conception du temps chez Romain Gary," 51–70. *Revue Romane* (Copenhagen) 19: 1 (1994).

———. *Un picaro métaphysique: Romain Gary et l'art du roman*. Odense: Odense University Press, 1996.

Bona, Dominique. *Romain Gary*. Paris: Mercure de France, 1987.

Boncenne, Pierre. "Pierre-Jean Rémy s'explique," 28–48. *Lire* (September 1977).

Boncenne, Pierre, and Valérie Laille. "Dix métamorphoses du livre," 81–90. *Lire* (September 1985).

Bondy, François. "A Man and His Double," 42–43. *Encounter* 57: 4 (October 1981).

———. "On the Death of a Friend," 33. *Encounter* 57: 2 (August 1981).

Bonnefis, Philippe. Commentaires, 181–210. *Le Horla*. By Guy de Maupassant. Paris: Albin Michel (Livre de poche), 1984.

Bonnefoy, Claude, et al., eds. *Dictionnaire de littérature française contemporaine*. Paris: Jean-Pierre Delarge, 1977.

Bory, Jean-Louis. *French Village*. London: Dennis Dobson, 1948.

Boschetti, Anna. "Légitimité littéraire et stratégies éditoriales," 511–66. *Histoire de l'édition française*, vol 4. Ed. Henri-Jean Martin et al. Paris: Promodis, 1986.

Braester, Marlena. " 'Le sens propre du figuré': Questions sur la 'texture' linguistique de l'humour," 489–95. *From Sign to Text: A Semiotic View of Communication*. Ed. Yishai Tobin. Amsterdam: Benjamins, 1989.

Braud, Michel. *La Tentation du suicide dans les écrits autobiographiques, 1930–1970*. Paris: PUF (Perspectives critiques), 1992.

Braudy, Leo. *The Frenzy of Renown: Fame and Its History*. New York: Oxford University Press, 1986.

Brenner, Jacques. "Romain Gary," 190–93. *Mon histoire de la littérature française contemporaine*. Paris: Bernard Grasset, 1987.

Brodin, Pierre. *Présences*. Vol. 4. Paris: Éditions Debresse, 1957.

Caffier, Michel. *L'Académie Goncourt*. Paris: PUF, 1994.

Caillois, Roger. *Le mythe et l'homme*. Paris: Gallimard (Coll. Folio essais), 1938, 1972.

Caradec, François. *La farce et le sacré: Fêtes et farceurs, mythes et mystificateurs*. Paris: Casterman (Synthèses contemporaines), 1977.

Carrière, Jean. *L'épervier de Maheux*. Paris: Jean-Jacques Pauvert, 1972.

————. *Le prix d'un Goncourt*. Paris: Robert Laffont/Jean-Jacques Pauvert, 1987.

Catonné, Jean-Marie. "Écrivains faussaires," 117–22. *Quai Voltaire Revue Littéraire* 1: 4 (winter 1992).

————. *Romain Gary / Émile Ajar*. Paris: Éditions Belfond, 1990.

Céline, Louis-Ferdinand. *Conversations with Professor Y*. Trans. Stanford Luce. Hanover, N.H.: Brandeis University Press, 1986.

Cendrars, Blaise. "Publicité = poésie" [1928], 115–22. *Aujourd'hui: 1917–1929 suivi de Essais et réflexions, 1910–1916*. Paris: Éditions Denoël, 1987.

Chalais, François. *Garry*. Novel. Paris: Plon, 1983.

Charon, Jean-Marie. *La presse en France de 1945 à nos jours*. Paris: Éditions du Seuil, 1991.

Chellabi, Leïla. *L'Infini, côté cœur*. Paris: Éditions Mengès, 1984.

Chiaselotti, Lucien. *Dans les coulisses d'Apostrophes*. Paris: Presses de la Cité, 1989.

Clark, Priscilla Parkhurst. *Literary France: The Making of a Culture*. Berkeley: University of California Press, 1987.

Colonna, Vincent. *L'autofiction: Essai sur la fictionnalisation de soi en littérature*. 2 vols. Diss. EHESS, 1989.

Colquhoun, Robert. *The Philosopher in History, 1905–1955*. Vol. 1 of *Raymond Aron*. London: Sage Publications, 1986.

"Comment l'esprit du 18 juin 1940 pourrait-il se manifester aujourd'hui?" 19. *L'Appel* 66 (June 1980).

Contat, Michel. "L'auteur comme espace biographique," 39–46. *De la genèse du texte littéraire*. Ed. A. Grésillon. Aigre: Du Lérot, 1988.

————. "La question de l'auteur au regard des manuscrits," 7–34. *L'auteur et le manscrit*. Ed. Michel Contat. Paris: PUF (Perspectives critiques), 1991.

Courtois, Stéphane, et al., eds. *The Black Book of Communism: Crimes, Terror, Repression*. Trans. Jonathan Murphy and Mark Kramer. Cambridge, Mass.: Harvard University Press, 1999.

Crémieux-Brilhac, Jean-Louis. *La France Libre: De l'appel du 18 juin à la Libération*. Paris: Éditions Gallimard, 1996.

Damisch, Hubert. "Alphabet des masques." *Nouvelle Revue de la Psychanalyse* 21 (spring 1980).

Davis, Garry. *The World Is My Country*. New York: Putnam, 1961.

Day, Leroy T. "Gary-Ajar and the Rhetoric of Non-Communication," 75–83. *French Review* 60: 1 (October 1991).

Debord, Guy. *Commentaires sur la société du spectacle*. Paris: Éditions Gérard Lebovici, 1988.

Debray, Régis. "André Malraux ou L'impératif du mensonge," 109–46. *Éloges*. Paris: Éditions Gallimard, 1986.

Deguy, Michel. *Le Comité: Confessions d'un lecteur de grande maison*. Seyssel: Éditions Champ Vallon, 1988.

Desanti, Dominique. "Masquer son nom," 91–98. *Corps écrit* 8 (1983).

Descaves, Pierre. *Mes Goncourt*. Paris: Calmann-Lévy, 1949.

Descles, Jean-Pierre. "Les référentiels temporels pour le temps linguistique," 9–36. *Modèles linguistiques* 16: 2, 32 (1995).

Divoire, Fernand. *Stratégie littéraire*. Paris: Éditions Baudinière, 1928.

Doubrovsky, Serge. "Autobiographie/vérité/psychanalyse," 61–79. *Autobiographiques: De Corneille à Sartre*. Paris: PUF (Perspectives), 1988.

Dragonetti, Roger. *Le mirage des sources: L'art du faux dans le roman médiéval*. Paris: Éditions du Seuil, 1987.

Drumont, Édouard. *Testament d'un Antisémite.* Paris: E. Dentu, 1891.

Dubois, Jacques. *L'institution de la littérature.* Brussels: Éditions Labor (Coll. Dossiers Média), 1986.

Dulière, André. *Une amitié littéraire: Correspondance d'Émile Henriot avec un jeune journaliste (1950–1961).* Lausanne: Éditions André Delcourt, 1989.

———. *Émile Henriot: Sa vie, son œuvre.* Paris: Éditions Universitaires, 1963.

Dutourd, Jean. *The Best Butter.* Trans. Robin Chancellor. New York: Greenwood Press, 1969.

Dyer, Richard. *Heavenly Bodies: Film Stars and Society.* New York: Macmillan, 1987.

———. *Stars.* London: British Film Institute, 1979.

Eakin, Paul John. *Fictions in Autobiography: Studies in the Art of Self-Invention.* Princeton, N.J.: Princeton University Press, 1985.

Espey, David. "Imperialism and the Image of the White Hunter," 12–19. *Research Studies* 46 (1978).

Ezine, Jean-Louis. *L'écrivain sur la sellette.* Paris: Éditions du Seuil, 1981.

Faessel, Sonia. "Simenon, Gary: Deux lectures du mythe de Tahiti," 379–95. *Travaux de littérature* 10 (1977).

Fedler, Fred. *Media Hoaxes.* Ames: Iowa State University Press, 1989.

Feuerlicht, Ignace. "Portrait of the Artist as a Young Swindler," 92–107. *Thomas Mann.* New York: Twayne, 1968.

Foucault, Michel. "What Is an Author?" 141–60. *Textual Strategies.* Ed. Josué V. Harari. Ithaca, N.Y.: Cornell University Press, 1979.

Fouché, Pascal. "L'Édition littéraire, 1914–1950," 211–68. *Histoire de l'édition française,* vol. 4. Ed. Henri-Jean Martin et al. Paris: Promodis, 1986.

Fuentes, Carlos. *Diana, the Goddess Who Hunts Alone.* Novel. Trans. Alfred J. MacAdam. New York: Farrar, Straus & Giroux, 1995.

Furlan, Francis. *Casanova et sa fortune littéraire.* Bordeaux: Éditions Ducros, 1971.

Gaède, Édouard. *L'écrivain et la société: Dossier d'une enquête.* 2 vols. Nice: Université de Nice, 1972.

Gaillard, Pol, ed. *Les critiques de notre temps et Malraux.* Paris: Garnier Frères, 1970.

Ganne, Gilbert. *Messieurs les Best-Sellers.* Paris: Librairie Académique Perrin, 1966.

Garliński, Józef. *Poland in the Second World War.* New York: Hippocrene Books, 1985.

Gasquet, Dominique de. "Auteur caché/auteur révélé: Le rôle du pseudonyme chez Romain Gary, Marguerite Duras et Marguerite Yourcenar," 61–76. *Elseneur* 11. Special issue: *De l'auteur au sujet de l'écriture* (December 1996).

Gauguin, Paul. *Lettres de Paul Gauguin à Daniel de Monfreid.* Pref. Victor Segalen. Paris: G. Falaize, 1918, 1950.

Gaulle, Charles de. *Mémoires de guerre.* 3 vols. Paris: Librairie Plon, 1989.

Geng, J. M. *L'illustre inconnu: Une tératologie de la notoriété ou Portrait du perceur par lui-même.* Paris: Union Générale d'Édition (Coll. 10/18), 1978.

Gide, André. *The Counterfeiters.* Trans. Dorothy Bussy. New York: Penguin, 1966.

Glicksberg, Charles I. *The Literature of Commitment.* Cranbury, N.J.: Associated University Presses, 1976.

Gouillou, André. *Le book-business ou l'édition française contre la lecture populaire.* Paris: Tema Éditions, 1975.

Gourfinkel, Nina. "Note sur 'Le Dibouk,'" 67–76. *Le Dibouk: Légende dramatique en trois actes.* By Chalom Anski. Paris: L'Arche, 1957.

Gracq, Julien. *La littérature à l'estomac.* Paris: Librairie José Corti, 1950.

Grasset, Bernard. *La chose littéraire.* Paris: Éditions Gallimard, 1929.

Gray, Frederic. "Romain Gary and the End of an Old Dream," 137–40. *Proceedings: Pacific Northwest Conference on Foreign Languages.* Ed. Walter C. Kraft. Corvallis: Oregon State University Press, 1973.

Grenier, Jean. *Carnets: 1944–1971.* Paris: Seghers, 1991.

Gronewald, Claudia. *Die Weltsicht Romain Garys im Spiegel seines Romanwerkes.* Münster: Nodus Publikationen, 1997.

Guide des prix littéraires. 4th ed. Paris: Cercle de la Librairie, 1960.

Guillaumin, Jean. "Entre Romain Gary et Émile Ajar ou La mort par l'écriture," 105–19, 128–31. *Souffrance, plaisir et pensée.* J. Caïn et al. Premières Rencontres psychanalytiques d'Aix-en-Provence, 1982. Paris: Société d'Éditions Les Belles Lettres, 1983.

Harris, Geoffrey T. "André Malraux: Une esthétique du mensonge," 251–60. *Cahiers de l'Association Internationale des Études françaises* 33 (May 1981).

Heath, Stephen. "Friday Night Books: The 500th Program of *Apostrophes* Is Broadcast on Antenne 2," 1054–60. *A New History of French Literature.* Ed. Denis Hollier. Cambridge, Mass.: Harvard University Press, 1989.

Heinich, Nathalie. *Être écrivain: Rapport de l'étude réalisée pour le Centre National des Lettres.* Paris: Association Adresse, 1990.

Horn, Pierre. "Romain Gary: Lone Rider," 53–64. *Modern Jewish Writers of France.* Lewiston, Maine: Edwin Mellen Press, 1997.

Huston, Nancy. "Romain Gary: A Foreign Body in French Literature," 281–304. *Exile and Creativity: Signposts, Travelers, Outsiders, Backward Glances.* Ed. Susan R. Suleiman. Durham, N.C.: Duke University Press, 1998.

———. "Romain Gary: Last Judgment Questionnaire," 28–34. *Brick* 47 (winter 1993).

———. *Tombeau de Romain Gary.* Arles: Actes Sud, 1995.

Institut Charles de Gaulle. *De Gaulle et les médias.* Paris: Librairie Plon, 1994.

———. *De Gaulle et Malraux.* Paris: Librairie Plon, 1987.

Ionesco, Eugène. *The Killer. The Killer and Other Plays.* Trans. Donald Watson. New York: Grove Press, 1960.

Jeandillou, Jean-François. "Émile Ajar," 431–47. *Les supercheries littéraires: La vie et l'œuvre des auteurs supposés.* Paris: Usher, 1989.

———. *Esthétique de la mystification littéraire: Tactique et stratégie littéraires.* Paris: Éditions de Minuit, 1994.

Jollin, Sophie. "From the Renaudot Prize to the Puterbaugh Conference: The Reception of J. M. G. Le Clézio," 735–40. *World Literature Today* 71: 4 (fall 1997).

Jouvenel, Renaud de. *L'Internationale des traîtres.* Paris: Bibliothèque Française, 1948.

Kauffmann, Judith. "La danse de Romain Gary ou Gengis Cohn et la valse-hora des mythes de l'Occident," 71–94. *Études littéraires* 17: 1 (April 1984).

Kelly, Michael. "The View of Collaboration During the 'Après-Guerre,'" 239–51. *Collaboration in France: Politics and Culture During the Nazi Occupation, 1940–1944.* Ed. Gerhard Hirschfeld and Patrick Marsh. New York: St. Martin's Press, 1989.

Kessel, Joseph. "Romain Gary," 42–44. *Des hommes.* Paris: Éditions Gallimard, 1972.

Knowlson, James. *Damned to Fame: The Life of Samuel Beckett.* New York: Simon & Schuster, 1996.

Krefeld, Thomas. "Substandard als Mittel literarischer Stilbildung: Der Roman *La Vie devant soi* von Émile Ajar," 244–67. *Sprachlicher Substandard.* Vol 3. Ed. Günter Holtus, Edgar Radtke. Tübingen: Niemeyer Verlag, 1990.

Kris, Ernst, and Otto Kurz. *Legend, Myth, and Magic in the Image of the Artist.* Trans.

Alastair Laing. Pref. E. H. Gombrich. New Haven, Conn.: Yale University Press, 1979.

Lacassin, Francis. "Préface: Une apologie de l'infra-littérature," 1183–95. *Le mystérieux Docteur Cornélius*. By Gustave Le Rouge. Paris: Robert Laffont (Coll. Bouquins), 1986.

Lacouture, Jean. *Malraux: Une vie dans le siècle (1901–1976)*. Paris: Éditions du Seuil, 1976.

Lalande, Bernard. "Ajar, pour une lecture de *La vie devant soi*," 37–40, 57–59. *Le Français dans le monde* 158 (1981).

Lalo, Charles. *Les grandes évasions esthétiques*. Paris: Librairie Philosophique J. Vrin, 1947.

Lamont, Rosette C. "*La Vie devant soi*," 952–53. *French Review* 50, 6 (May 1977).

Larat, Fabrice. *Romain Gary: Un itinéraire européen*. Chêne-Bourg: Éditions Médecine et Hygiène, 1999.

Laugaa, Maurice. "Autobiographies d'un pseudonyme," 111–35. *Textuel* 22, *Images de l'écrivain* (winter 1989).

———. *La pensée du pseudonyme*. Paris: PUF (Coll. Écriture), 1986.

Laughlin, James. "Afterword to *The Life Before Us*, by Romain Gary," 18–22. *French-American Review* 62: 1 (spring 1991).

Leclerc, Gérard. *Le sceau de l'œuvre*. Paris: Éditions du Seuil (Coll. Poétique), 1998.

Leclercq, Pierre-Robert. *Avez-vous vu Daradada? Essai sur le métier de romancier*. Paris: Pierre Horay Éditeur, 1977.

Lederer, William, and Eugene Burdick. *The Ugly American*. New York: Norton, 1958.

Lehrmann, Charles C. *The Jewish Element in French Literature*. Trans. George Klin. Rutherford, N.J.: Fairleigh Dickinson University Press, 1971.

Lejeune, Philippe. *On Autobiography*. Trans. Katherine Leary. Minneapolis: University of Minnesota Press, 1988.

Lepape, Pierre. "Télévision et littérature," 2273–75. *Dictionnaire des littératures de langue française*. Vol. 3. Ed. Jean-Pierre de Beaumarchais et al. Paris: Bordas, 1984.

LeSage, Laurent, and André Yon. *Dictionnaire des critiques littéraires: Guide de la critique française au XXe siècle*. University Park: Pennsylvania State University Press, 1969.

Lorian, Alexandre. "Les Raisonnements déraisonnables d'Émile Ajar," 120–45. *Hebrew University Studies in Literature and the Arts* (spring 1987).

Lustig, Bette H. "Émile Ajar Demystified," 203–12. *French Review* 57: 2 (December 1983).

Malraux, André. *Anti-Memoirs*. Trans. Terence Kilmartin. New York: Holt, Rinehart & Winston, 1968.

———. *The Conquerors*. Trans. Stephen Becker. Chicago: University of Chicago Press, 1992.

———. *Felled Oaks: Conversations with de Gaulle*. Trans. Irene Clephane. New York: Holt, Rinehart & Winston, 1971.

———. "Laclos," 377–89. *Tableau de la littérature française: De Corneille à Chénier*. Allain et al. Paris: Éditions Gallimard, 1939.

———. *Man's Fate*. Trans. Haakon M. Chevalier. New York: Modern Library, 1934.

———. *Oraisons funèbres*. Paris: Éditions Gallimard, 1971.

———. *The Royal Way*. Trans. Stuart Gilbert. New York: Vintage Books, 1961.

———. *The Voices of Silence*. Trans. Stuart Gilbert. Princeton, N.J.: Princeton University Press, 1978.

Mann, Thomas. *Confessions of Felix Krull, Confidence Man.* Trans. Denver Lindley. New York: Vintage Books, 1969.

Mauriac, François. *Nouveaux mémoires intérieurs. Œuvres autotobiographiques.* Paris: Éditions Gallimard (Bibliothèque de la Pléiade), 1990.

May, Karl Friedrich. *Winnetou.* New York: Seabury Press, 1977.

McKee, Jane. "The Symbolic Imagination of Romain Gary," 60–71. *Maynooth Review* 6: 2 (May 1982).

Mehlman, Jeffrey. "On the Holocaust Comedies of 'Emile Ajar,' " 219–34. *Auschwitz and After: Race, Culture, and "the Jewish Question" in France.* Ed. Lawrence D. Kritzman. New York: Routledge, 1994.

Mendès-France, Pierre. *S'engager: 1922–1943. Œuvres complètes.* Vol. 1. Paris: Éditions Gallimard, 1984.

Michaux, Henri. "Voix," 34–38. *Épreuves, exorcismes: 1940–1944.* Paris: Éditions Gallimard (Poésie), 1946, 1973.

Mille, Pierre. *L'écrivain.* Paris: Hachette, 1925.

Moreau, J. A. "Le langage devant soi," 1197–99. *Critique* 30: 342 (1975).

Morin, Edgar. *La rumeur d'Orléans.* Paris: Éditions du Seuil, 1982.

Morris, Alan. *Patrick Modiano.* Washington, D.C.: Berg, 1996.

Mortimer, Edward. *The Rise of the French Communist Party: 1920–1947.* London: Faber & Faber, 1984.

Nachin, Claude. "Crypte et création littéraire: L'œuvre de Romain Gary," 61–76. *Le deuil d'amour.* Paris: Éditions Universitaires (Emergences), 1989.

Nadeau, Maurice. *Le roman français depuis la guerre.* Paris: Éditions Gallimard (Coll. Idées), 1963.

Nøjgaard, Morten. *En kvælerslange som kæledyr, Om dobbeltmennesket Gary-Ajar* (A python as a pet: The double Gary-Ajar). Copenhagen: Museum Tusculanums Forlag, 1985.

Öostman, Anne-Charlotte. *L'utopie et l'ironie: Étude sur* Gros Câlin *et sa place dans l'œuvre de Romain Gary.* Stockholm: Almqvist & Wiksell, 1994.

Out-Breut, Michèle. "Romain Gary, le mangeur d'étoiles, 21–28. *Rapports: Het Franse Bœk* 2 (1986).

Parinet, Élisabeth, and Valérie Tesnière. "Une entreprise: La maison d'édition." *Histoire de l'édition française.* Vol. 4. Ed. Henri-Jean Martin et al. Paris: Promodis, 1986.

Pavlowitch, Paul. *L'homme que l'on croyait.* Paris: Librairie Arthème-Fayard, 1981.

———. *La peau de l'ours.* Paris: Mazarine, 1986.

———. *Victor.* Paris: Fayard, 2000.

Pawlowski, Adam. *Séries temporelles en linguistique: Avec application à l'attribution des textes, Romain Gary et Émile Ajar.* Paris: Honoré Champion, 1998.

Payot, Marianne. "Comment ils se protègent pour écrire," 47–48. *Lire* (October 1992).

Pfefferkorn, Eli. "The Art of Survival: Romain Gary's *The Dance of Cohn,*" 76–87. *Modern Language Studies* 10: 3 (fall 1980).

Picard, Roger. *Artifices et mystifications littéraires.* Montréal: Éditions Variétés, 1945.

Pingaud, Bernard. "L'écrivain en quête d'auteur," 299–312. *Comme un chemin en automne.* Vol. 2 of *Inventaire.* Paris: Éditions Gallimard, 1979.

———. "Être écrivain," 273–98. *Comme un chemin en automne.*

———. "La non-fonction de l'écrivain," 74–79. *L'Arc* 70 (1977).

Pivot, Bernard. *Les critiques littéraires.* Paris: Flammarion (Coll. Le Procès des Juges), 1968.

Pleasance, Antony. "Variations on the American Cliché: Aymé, Gary, Obaldia,"

32–37. *Proceedings: Pacific Northwest Conference on Foreign Languages.* Ed. Walter C. Kraft. Corvallis: Oregon State University, 1971.

Pline. *Portraits de l'écrivain d'aujourd'hui.* Paris: Julliard, 1986.

Poier-Bernhard, Astrid. *Romain Gary, das Brennende Ich.* Tübingen: Niemeyer, 1996.

———. *Romain Gary im Spiegel der Literaturkritik.* New York: Peter Lang, 1999.

Poirot-Delpech, Bertrand. "Ajar, Alias Gary," 173–78. *Feuilletons, 1972–1982.* Paris: Éditions Gallimard, 1982.

Ponchardier, Dominique. *La mort du Condor.* Paris: Éditions Gallimard, 1976.

Ponton, Rémy. "Programme esthétique et accumulation de capital symbolique: L'exemple du Parnasse," 202–20. *Revue française de Sociologie* 14 (1973).

Pratiques. Special issue: *L'écrivain aujourd'hui: Images de l'écrivain dans les institutions.* 26 (Mar 1980).

———. Special issue: *La littérature et ses institutions* 31 (December 1981).

Proust, Marcel. *Against Sainte-Beuve and Other Essays.* Trans. John Sturrock. New York: Penguin, 1994.

Puech, Jean-Benoît. "Du vivant de l'auteur," 279–300. *Poétique* 63 (September 1985).

Queneau, Raymond. *The Flight of Icarus.* Trans. Barbara Wright. New York: New Directions, 1973.

———. *We Always Treat Women Too Well.* Trans. Barbara Wright. New York: New Directions, 1981.

Radiguet, Raymond. *The Devil in the Flesh.* Trans. A. M. Sheridan Smith. New York: M. Boyars, 1986.

Raimond, Michel. "Le roman et la littérature industrielle," 106–14. *La crise du roman: Des lendemains du Naturalisme aux années vingt.* Paris: Librairie José Corti, 1966.

Rambures, Jean-Louis de. *Comment travaillent les écrivains.* Paris: Flammarion, 1978.

Rank, Otto. *Don Juan et le double.* Trans. S. Lautman. Paris: Éditions Payot, 1973.

Réage, Pauline. *The Story of O.* New York: Ballantine Books, 1992.

Rebatet, Lucien. *Décombres.* Paris: Éditions Denoël, 1942.

Rémy, Pierre-Jean. *Midi ou l'attentat.* Paris: R. Julliard, 1963.

Richards, David. *Played Out: The Jean Seberg Story.* New York: Random House, 1981.

Robichon, Jacques. *Le défi des Goncourt.* Paris: Éditions Denoël, 1975.

Rollin, André. *Ils écrivent: Où? quand? comment?* Paris: Éditions Mazarine, 1986.

Romain Gary. Special issue of *Livres de France* 18: 3. Paris: Librairie Hachette, 1967.

Rosello, Mireille. "Cheating on Stereotypes: Emile Ajar, Calixthe Beyala, and Didier van Cauwelaert," 128–49. *Declining the Stereotype: Ethnicity and Representation in French Cultures.* Hanover, N.H.: University Press of New England, 1998.

Rosenmary, Amy Dayan. *Des cerfs-volants jaunes en formes d'étoiles.* Paris: Temps Modernes, 1993.

Rosse, Dominique. *Romain Gary et la modernité.* Ottawa: Presses Universitaires d'Ottawa, 1995.

Rousseau, Jean-Jacques. *Confessions. The Collected Writings of Rousseau.* Vol. 5. Ed. and trans. Christopher Kelly. Hanover, N.H.: University Press of New England, 1995.

Rousso, Henry. "La Seconde Guerre mondiale dans la mémoire des droites," 549–619. *Cultures.* Vol. 2 of *Histoire des Droites en France.* Ed. Jean-François Sirinelli. Paris: Éditions Gallimard, 1992.

————. *Le syndrome de Vichy: De 1944 à nos jours*. Paris: Éditions du Seuil (Coll. Points Histoire), 1990.

Roux, Dominique de. *Entretiens avec Gombrowicz*. Paris: Éditions Pierre Belfond, 1968.

Saint-Exupéry, Antoine de. *The Little Prince*. Trans. Richard Howard. San Diego: Harcourt, 2000.

Saint-Lorges. *Le prix Goncourt*. Paris: Éditions du Rocher, 1993.

Sapiro, Gisèle. *La guerre des écrivains, 1940–1953*. Paris: Librairie Arthème Fayard, 1999.

Sartre, Jean-Paul. "La Nationalisation de la littérature," 193–211. *Les Temps modernes* 1: 2 (November 1, 1945).

Schwarz-Bart, André. *The Last of the Just*. Trans. Stephen Becker. Woodstock, N.Y.: Overlook Press, 2001.

Sciascia, Leonard. "Le Visage sur le masque (Post-Scriptum)," 40–44. Trans. Jean-Noël Schifano. *Nouvelle Revue française* 356 (September 1, 1982).

Seinfelt, Mark. *Final Drafts: Suicides of World-Famous Authors*. Amherst, N.Y.: Prometheus Books, 1999.

Sheringham, Michael. *French Autobiography: Devices and Desires, Rousseau to Pérec*. Oxford: Clarendon Press, 1993.

Simon, General Jean. "Romain Gary, Commmandeur de la Légion d'Honneur, Compagnon de la Libération," 45–46. *Espoir* 34 (March 1981).

Soucy, Robert. *French Fascism: The Second Wave, 1933–1939*. New Haven, Conn.: Yale University Press, 1995.

Spire, Antoine, and Jean-Pierre Viala. *La bataille du livre*. Paris: Éditions Sociales, 1976.

Spivey, Ted. *The Journey Beyond Tragedy*. Orlando: University Press of Florida, 1980.

Starobinski, Jean. *Portrait de l'artiste en saltimbanque*. Paris: Éditions d'Art Albert Skira, 1970.

Steegmuller, Francis. *Cocteau: A Biography*. Boston: Little, Brown, 1970.

Stendhal. *Memoirs of Egotism*. Trans. Hannah and Matthew Josephson. New York: McGraw- Hill Paperbacks, 1975.

Styron, William. *Darkness Visible: A Memoir of Madness*. New York: Random House, 1990.

Sungolowsky, Joseph. *La Judéïté dans l'œuvre de Romain Gary*. Québec: Presses de l'Université de Laval, 1993.

————. "La Judéïté dans l'œuvre de Romain Gary: De l'ambiguïté à la transparence symbolique," 111–27. *Études littéraires* 26: 1 (summer 1993).

Svevo, Italo. *Confessions of Zeno*. Trans. Beryl de Zoete. New York: Vintage International, 1989.

Thérien, Michel, Murielle de Serres, and Julie Jean, eds. La Vie devant soi. *Romain Gary/Émile Ajar*. Laval: Éditions Beauchemin (Coll. Littératures et Cultures), 1996.

Thogmartin, Clyde. *The National Daily Press of France*. Birmingham, Ala: Summa Publications, 1998.

Tison-Braun, Micheline. "*Les voix du silence* interprété par Romain Gary," 133–36. *Revue des Lettres Modernes* 1219–28 (1995).

Todd, Christopher. *A Century of French Best-Sellers, 1890–1990*. Lewiston, Maine: Edwin Mellen Press, 1994.

Todorov, Tzvétan. "Labor of Love," 375–83. Trans. Jim Tucker. *Partisan Review* 64: 3 (1997).

————. "Le siècle de Romain Gary," 233–46. *Mémoire du mal, tentation du bien: Enquête sur le siècle.* Paris: Robert Laffont, 2001.

Tolstoy, Leo. *The Kreutzer Sonata and Other Stories.* Trans. Louise Maude et al. New York: Oxford University Press, 1997.

Tournier, Michel. "Ajar ou la vie derrière soi," 329–44. *Le vol du vampire: Notes de lecture.* Paris: Mercure de France, 1981.

Viala, Alain. "L'auteur et son manuscrit dans l'histoire de la production littéraire," 95–117. *L'auteur et le manuscrit.* Ed. Michel Contat. Paris: PUF (Perspectives critiques), 1991.

————. *La naissance de l'écrivain.* Paris: Éditions de Minuit, 1985.

Vian, Boris. *I Shall Spit on Your Graves.* Trans. Milton Rosenthal. Los Angeles: Tam Tam Books, 1998.

Von Chamisso, Adalbert. *Peter Schlemihl.* Intro. Pierre Péju. Trans. Hippolyte and Adalbert von Chamisso. Paris: José Corti, 1989.

————. *The Wonderful History of Peter Schlemihl.* London: Rodale Press, 1954.

Wardi, Charlotte. *Le génocide dans la fiction romanesque.* Paris: PUF, 1986.

————. "Le génocide des Juifs dans la fiction romanesque française (1945–1970): Une expression originale; *La danse de Gengis Cohn* de Romain Gary," 215–25. *Digraphe* 25 (spring 1981).

West-Sooby, J. N. "Romain Gary et le goût du paradoxe: L'exemple de *Clair de femme* et de *La Vie devant soi*," 307–13. *Studi Francesi* 36: 107 (May-August 1992).

Woodmansee, Martha and Peter Jaszi, eds. *The Construction of Authorship: Textual Appropriation in Law and Literature.* Durham, N.C.: Duke University Press, 1994.

Wurmser, André. *De Gaulle et les siens.* Paris: Éditions Raisons d'être, 1947.

Yogev, Michael. "The Fantastic in Holocaust Literature: Writing and Unwriting the Unbearable," 32–49. *Journal of the Fantastic in the Arts* 5:2, 18 (1993).

Index

Acknowledgments

Romain Gary: The Man Who Sold His Shadow has taken shape with the help of many institutions, colleagues, and friends. I would like to thank the librarians and staff at Emory University; the École Normale Supérieure of St.-Cloud, France; the University of Oklahoma; Texas A&M University; and the Rare Book and Manuscript Library of Butler Library at Columbia University. Invaluable assistance in Paris was cordially provided by Mme Vuillemin for the archives at Éditions Gallimard. I would also like to thank the staff at Mercure de France; Olivier Nora and my esteemed friend Anne Maupas-Lycoudis, both formerly with Calmann-Lévy; and Mme Barbier-Bouvet and the helpful research technicians at France's Institut National de l'Audiovisuel (INA). Jean-Marie Catonné's kind response to a letter helped me early in my research, as did meetings with Maurice Laugaa and Jean-François Jeandillou. Finally, though to speak of cheerful assistance would be a grave injustice to its staff's professional reputation, I am grateful for access to the tremendous resources of the Bibliothèque Nationale de France in its former rue de Richelieu incarnation.

Generous grants from the Department of French and Italian at Emory University; the Office of the Vice President for Research, the College of Arts and Sciences, and the Department of Modern Languages, Linguistics, and Literatures at the University of Oklahoma; the Department of Modern and Classical Languages and Dean Woodrow Jones, Jr., of the College of Liberal Arts at Texas A&M University were instrumental in funding the research and publication of this book.

I have been very fortunate to count among my professors and colleagues a number of people who embody what is to be admired in this vocation. I would like to thank, in a vague chronological order, for their intellectual standards, ethics, mentoring, and friendship: Malina Stefanovska, Alain Viala, Roland Racevskis, Michael Winston, Alain-Philippe Durand, Nathalie Vincent-Munnia, Ora Avni, Luis Cortest, and Joe Golsan. Mark Bauerlein deserves special mention for his careful reading of the manuscript. And I would be remiss if I did not also mention Bruce and Martine Klein and Bob Lee and Emily Smith-Lee (though I have rarely encountered them in the library).

Finally, and most importantly: my parents, who instilled in me the love of the life of the mind; Eric Halpern, Erica Ginsburg, and Carol Ehrlich, whose expertise, patience, and commitment to excellence steered me through the final stages of this project; and Josué V. Harari, to whom this book is dedicated.